THE GROUP WORKERS' HANDBOOK

THE GROUP WORKERS' HANDBOOK

VARIETIES OF GROUP EXPERIENCE

Edited by

ROBERT K. CONYNE, Ph.D.

*Associate Vice Provost for
Student Life and Programs*

and

*Professor of Counselor Education
University of Cincinnati*

CHARLES C THOMAS • PUBLISHER
Springfield • Illinois • U.S.A.

Published and Distributed Throughout the World by
CHARLES C THOMAS • PUBLISHER
2600 South First Street
Springfield, Illinois 62717

© *1985 by* CHARLES C THOMAS • PUBLISHER

ISBN 0-398-05049-x

Library of Congress Catalog Card Number: 84-8696

With THOMAS BOOKS *careful attention is given to all details of manufacturing and design. It is the Publisher's desire to present books that are satisfactory as to their physical qualities and artistic possibilities and appropriate for their particular use.* THOMAS BOOKS *will be true to those laws of quality that assure a good name and good will.*

Printed in the United States of America
Q-R-3

Library of Congress Cataloging in Publication Data
Main entry under title:

The Group workers' handbook.

  Bibliography: p.
  1. Group counseling. 2. Problem solving, Group.
3. Group psychotherapy. I. Conyne, Robert K.
BF637.C6G77   1985   302.3   84-8696
ISBN 0-398-05049-X

I dedicate this book to the diverse "small group" of wonderful women in my life: My Mother; my wife and colleague, Lynn; my four-month old daughter, Suzanne; my 14 year-old dog, Luv; and to my secretary, Mary. Each, in her own way, helped make this book possible.

CONTRIBUTORS

JEROLD D. BOZARTH, Ph.D., University of Georgia, Athens, Georgia.

CARY CHERNISS, Ph.D., Graduate School of Applied and Professional Psychology, Rutgers — The State University, Piscataway, New Jersey.

EDWARD W. CHRISTENSEN, Ed.D., Division of Continuing Education, State University of New York at Albany.

R. JAMES CLACK, Ph.D., Associate Director of Counseling, Learning, and Career Services, The University of Texas at Austin.

ROBERT K. CONYNE, Ph.D., Professor of Counselor Education, Associate Vice Provost of Student Life and Programs, University of Cincinnati, Cincinnati, Ohio.

DAVID J. DRUM, Ph.D., Director, Counseling-Psychological Services Center, University of Texas, Austin, Texas.

ALLAN DYE, Ph.D., Associate Professor of Education, Purdue University, West Lafayette, Indiana.

CHARLES D. GARVIN, Ph.D., School of Social Work, University of Michigan, Ann Arbor, Michigan.

GEORGE M. GAZDA, Ed.D., Research Professor of Education and Coordinator of Counseling Psychology Program, University of Georgia and Clinical Professor, Department of Psychiatry, Medical College of Georgia, Athens, Georgia.

WM. FAWCETT HILL, Ph.D., California State Polytechnic University — Pomono.

RONALD LIPPITT, Ph.D., Professor Emeritus, University of Michigan, President, International Consultants Foundation; and also President of Organizational Renewal, Inc.

vii

RICHARD E. PEARSON, Ph.D., Syracuse University, Syracuse, New York.

LYNN S. RAPIN, Ph.D., Consulting Psychologist, Cincinnati, Ohio.

GLENN D. SHEAN, Ph.D., College of William and Mary, Williamsburg, Virginia.

PHYLLIS R. SILVERMAN, Ph.D., Associate Professor, Massachusetts General Hospital Institute of Health Professions, Boston, Massachusetts.

JAMES P. TROTZER, Ph.D., Psychologist, Private Practice, Exeter, New Hampshire and Executive Director, Renew Counseling Center, Portsmouth, New Hampshire.

PREFACE

CONTEMPORARY group work is an impressively varied intervention. It includes the traditional forms of group counseling and psychotherapy but also groups designed for specific skill training, for organization development, and for community change, along with several other varieties.

Although I had for some time considered it to be so, I readily became aware of the varieties of group work experience during my early tenure as Editor of the *Journal for Specialists in Group Work,* the official scholarly publication of the Association for Specialists in Group Work. Let me extract a short section from an editorial I wrote for a special issue of the *Journal* ("Group Work and Organizational Development," guest edited by Peter Maynard), as it is particularly relevant to this *Handbook:*

> "On Expanding Horizons"
> Group work is a robust technology for human improvement. The group medium provides a basic structure that can be modified and applied in a variety of ways, for different purposes, with an ever-expanding list of populations, and in a number of settings. Consider some examples. The group work umbrella covers the familiar forms of group counseling, guidance, and psychotherapy. But it also can include experiences in training and development, task accomplishment, family work, and teaching. It can be used to correct, to enhance, and to prevent. Group work is used in business and industry, education, families, clinics, and agencies. The technology is used with and without leaders, and with a range of population sizes and types.
> Despite all of this richness, I am struck by the realization that most of our training programs and scholarly journals maintain

an emphasis on the "traditional" forms of group work and how group counseling can be used to assist in the remediation of client psychological concerns, for instance. While I do not at all question the importance of learning about or investigating such fundamental group work forms, I believe that short shrift is given to the less traditional ones. An unintended side effect results which keeps the lid on group work innovation (Conyne, 1982, p.2).

But not only training programs and scholarly journals tend to ignore the varieties of group experience. So do most of the major texts in the group helping field. These texts, and we are blessed with some truly fine ones, are usually geared "vertically" within a particular group work modality, such as in group counseling, group psychotherapy, or in techniques for counseling groups. Generally missing from our major texts is attention given to the range of group experiences available today; in that sense, reality is being ignored. Thus, I strongly felt that a book needed to be written that attempted to fill this gap by presenting a "horizontal" view of group work, its horizon, if you will.

I soon discovered that it is easier to talk about this group work variety than it is to adequately conceptualize and organize it. Any organizational model would be rife with holes and overlap due to both differences — and commonalities — existing in the group work field. The "Group Work Grid," which I created to organize this *Handbook*, is an imperfect but somewhat courageous attempt to conceptualize the robust nature of contemporary group work. The "Group Work Grid" (see Figure 1) is comprised of two major dimensions: (a) the *purpose* of the group work intervention, whether that be generally for correction or for enhancement; and (b) the *level* of the group work intervention, whether that be located at individual, interpersonal, organizational, or community points. In turn, both the corrective and enhancement purposes are sub-divided by the general emphasis given by the group to the accomplishment of *personal* or of *task* goals.

Although the categories and cells of the grid suggest that conceptual neatness can be found when group work is differentiated, reality belies that suggestion. Thus, dotted lines are used inside the Grid to indicate the permeability and fluidity that exists in group work. The single dotted lines, appearing between personal and task

Intervention Purpose Emphases

Intervention Level Emphases		Correction		Enhancement	
		Personal	**Task**	**Personal**	**Task**
Individual	Type	Personality Change	Rehabilitation	Personal Growth	Skill Development
	Eg.	Psychotherapy	Remedial Social Skills	Personal Development	Human Relations Skills Training
Interpersonal	Type	Interpersonal Problem Solving	Resocialization	Interpersonal Growth	Learning
	Eg.	Counseling	Social Control	T-groups	Systematic Group Discussion
Organization	Type	Employee Change	Organization Change	Management Development	Organization Development
	Eg.	Employee Assistance	Social Climate	Team Development	Quality Circles
Community-Population	Type	Secondary/Tertiary Prevention	Community Change	Health Promotion/Primary Prevention	Community Development
	Eg.	Mutual Help	Action	Life Transition	Futuring

Figure 1. Group Work Grid

emphases, suggest the presence of fluidity and overlap. For instance, a "task-oriented" group includes personal emphases, and vice-versa. The double dotted lines, dividing corrective and enhancement purposes and separating the four intervention levels, imply relatively greater differentiation, but with permeability still being present. For example, "enhancement" groups at the individual level can include "corrective" purposes aimed at an interpersonal level. Despite these realities, the Grid can enable us to better understand the sometimes bewildering group work field by organizing and consolidating it in a way that holds conceptual meaning.

The interaction of Grid components yields 16 different group types that are presented as representing the varieties of group work experience. These types range from personality change groups, illustrated by psychotherapy groups, to community development groups, exemplified by community futuring groups.

A *Handbook* chapter is presented that describes 15 of these group work types. To provide some consistency throughout the chapters, authors were asked to generally cover the following important areas, which they did in different ways:

- Intervention level
- Intervention purpose
- Supportive theory
- Main intervention change techniques used
- Primary intervention target populations
- Primary group leader functions
- Primary group leader training
- Evidence of intervention effectiveness
- Illustrative intervention case example
- Application possibilities

The authors are all well known and respected theorists and/or practitioners of the group work type about which they are writing. We think the groups covered in this *Handbook* well represent the robust variety of group work types:

Psychotherapy, social skills, personal development, human relations skill training, counseling, social control, laboratory, content discussion, employee assistance, social climate, quality circles, mutual help, action, life transition, and community futuring.

The *Handbook* chapters addressing each of the above group types are sectioned by intervention level, and I have written an introduction to each of the four sections. *Section I* includes groups aimed generally at the *individual* level: George Gazda and Jerold Bozarth write about group psychotherapy, Glenn Shean about remedial social skills groups, David Drum about personal development groups, and James Clack about human relations skill training.

Section II includes groups focused generally at the *interpersonal* level. James Trotzer writes about counseling groups, Charles Garvin about social control groups, Allan Dye about laboratory groups, and Wm. Fawcett Hill about groups for systematic content discussion.

Section III includes groups targeting generally the *organizational* level. Cary Cherniss writes about employee assistance groups, I consider social climate groups, and Lynn Rapin writes about quality circles. A planned Chapter on management development groups is not included.

Section IV includes groups aimed broadly at the *community* level. Phyllis Silverman describes mutual help groups, E.W. Christensen writes about community change groups, Richard Pearson about primary prevention groups, and Ronald Lippitt considers community futuring groups.

Producing an edited book, as this one, that is designed around a conceptual model, offers special challenges and satisfactions. Among them are achieving a certain level of conceptual and organizational integrity while providing a breadth of coverage that may extend the thinking about group work uses. Disappointments occur, also, the most notable of which, in this case, is the failure to be able to include the planned chapter on management development. This omission was due to production problems, and is not a sign that group work in management development is unimportant. To the contrary, group-based management development approaches, such as managerial team building, can greatly improve the performance of not only the managers involved but, also, of their organization.

However, I hope that the main purposes of this book — to broaden horizons and to help consolidate practical understandings about group work — have been met. Of the two purposes, I anticipate that consolidation may be a bit less well achieved due to the limitations of existing models (including the "Grid") to validly and reliably differentiate the wide variety existing in group work. If so, I'll be relatively content to settle for expanded horizons.

Group work courses, such as those in group dynamics and in group counseling, are beginning to address the expansion of group work that is currently underway. This *Handbook*, then, is presently suitable as a supplementary text in introductory group work courses and it is appropriate as a main text in most advanced group courses that already address a comprehensive view of group work, or that would like to do so. Finally, the *Handbook* should be especially germane to group work practitioners who are interested in the varieties of group experiences available for use today.

Robert K. Conyne

Cincinnati, Ohio

and

St. Joseph Island, Ontario

REFERENCE

Conyne, R.: On Expanding Horizons. *Journal for Specialists in Group Work*, 1982, 7, 2.

CONTENTS

THE GROUP WORKERS' HANDBOOK

SECTION I
INDIVIDUAL LEVEL OF INTERVENTION

THE group experiences written about in this section of the *Handbook* are aimed generally at the individual level of intervention. That is, these groups all attempt to produce some kind of positive movement within the group members by focusing on individual member phenomena. These phenomena vary according to the group's purpose, the developmental functioning of its members, its task or personal emphasis, and other factors.

The four chapters addressing this intervention level illustrate some of the important variations and commonalities found. The chapter by Gazda and Bozarth on personality change groups (group psychotherapy) and that by Drum on personal development groups illustrate an emphasis on the *personal* issues of individual members. In the case of psychotherapy groups, this emphasis is operationalized by attempting to remediate the broadly experienced intrapersonal deficits of individuals, such as excessive anxiety or a generalized sense of worthlessness. These individual members are in a general problem state. By contrast, the individuals of a personal development group are generally not experiencing extensive deficiencies but they need assistance in better handling a common intrapersonal life issue, such as jealousy, intimacy, or shyness, or in increasing their self awareness in some meaningful area. These individuals are in a general developmental state.

Shean's chapter on remedial social skills groups and Clack's on skill development groups (human relations skill training groups) share the skills training *task* approach to individual group work. Their divergence is illustrated by their general purpose for use; that

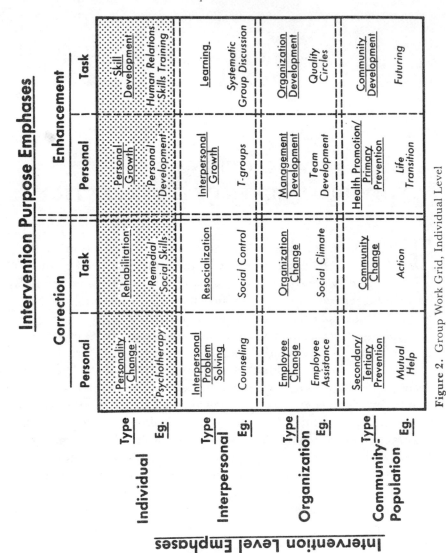

Figure 2. Group Work Grid, Individual Level

is, correction or enhancement. Individuals in the remedial social skills group lack the present ability to adequately execute specific, basic social task skills, such as starting a conversation. Conversely, individuals in the human relations skill training group can adequately perform most necessary social task skills but they learn how to perform them and other social skills at a more proficient level. Thus, these group members may advance the skill of starting a conversation to that of starting an affectively—or a cognitively—oriented conversation.

As you will note in all four sections of the *Handbook*, clean cleavages between group types do not always hold. Thus, for instance, remedial purposes are sometimes accomplished in personal development groups, with enhancement goals being occasionally met in psychotherapy groups. Reality is mirrored in such instances but, we intend, in a more clearly defined reflection. Broad differentiation and general tendencies are more easily demonstrated.

CHAPTER 1

PERSONALITY CHANGE
Personality Change Groups

GEORGE M. GAZDA

JEROLD D. BOZARTH

T HIS chapter examines the use of groups that seek to correct individual psychological function. The psychotherapy group as the primary example of personality change groups is emphasized. Several other types of groups that are directed toward personality change are identified.

Unfortunately, there are not unequivocal homogeneous categorizations that define groups which are directed toward personality change. Psychotherapy groups and other groups that focus on personality change are akin to Bergin's (1963) statement that psychotherapy is a heterogeneous rather than homogeneous phenomenon. There has been an absence of a definitive formulation of group psychotherapy (Slavson, 1964, p. 36). As Slavson notes: "The human personality is a combination of biologically inherent features and psychic potentials shaped by the influence of the physical, economic, and human environment" (p. 37). Shapiro (1978) offers the following definition of group psychotherapy:

> Group psychotherapy consists of processes occurring in formally organized, protected groups, conducted by a trained leader. The group is designed to produce rapid amelioration in attitudes and behavior of individual members and leaders. Such changes occur as a function of specified and controlled interactions (p. 7).

7

Personality change is defined on the basis of multiple personality theories. These theories include holistic, trait-type, psychodynamic and biological orientations (Stagner, 1965). The variation in dimensions of personality, intervening variables and constructs may not be agreed upon by the various personality theorists; however, there is the implication that "...personality is an event in nature, an observable phenomenon upon which competent observers can agree" (Stagner, 1965, p. 277).

Personality change will thus refer to a theoretical conceptualization about human "...inner organization and its resistance to modification" (Stagner, 1965, p. 278). The explication, interventions, and functions of the group intended to implement personality change may vary according to the underlying assumption of the personality theory being applied.

It is necessary to delimit the theoretical speculations for the purpose of this chapter. The purpose of this chapter is to identify operational frameworks that will serve as a guideline for *groups seeking to correct individual psychological dynsfunctions via personality change.*

There are fundamentally three major theoretical approaches which have different underlying assumptions: Psychoanalytic, Humanistic, and Behavioral. The Psychoanalytic approach operates on the basic assumption that the human being is continually in conflict between his/her dual nature as a biological animal and a social being (Arlow, 1979). The therapeutic objective is for the person to control his/her basic, biological hedonistic impulses in a way which adjusts to social demands.

The humanistic approach operates on the fundamental assumption that human beings tend to move in a direction of growthful change when certain conditions exist (Meador and Rogers, 1979). This assumption is expressed in various ways. Gestaltists indicate that humans are born with the innate capacity to cope with life (Simkin, 1979). Reality therapists assume a basic psychological need to identify (Glasser and Zunin, 1979). Jungian therapists refer to individuation (Kaufman, 1979); and Individual psychologists refer to social interest (Mosak, 1979). Although the role of humanistic therapists may vary according to other tenets of the various therapies, the underlying assumption dictates therapeutic actions different from those who operate on the basic premises of psychoanalytic or behavioral therapies.

The behavioral approach operates on the premise that people become what they are through environmental/genetical interaction. Problems are learned (Chambless and Goldstein, 1979). The assumption of the behavioral approaches does not lend itself to the central conceptualization for personality change groups predicated upon personality theory, i.e., Stagner's notion of the "...nature of this inner organization of its resistance to modification" (p. 278). Even the more prevalent neo-behavioral group approaches, such as Multimodal therapy, assess individuals by dissecting interactive modalities (Lazarus, 1981).

Behaviorism has given little attention to a theory of personality (Goldstein, 1973). Rather, the underlying characteristic of behavior therapy is the use of principles and precedents of the scientific method (Thoresen and Coates, 1978, p. 5). Although behavioral approaches in groups may seek to remediate personality disorders, the goal is to remediate the inappropriate behavior. The concept of remediation of personality is not consistent with the behaviorist paradigm. According to Spotnitz (1971), however, "Some investigators report that personality *is* dealt with in behavioral therapy. The crucial issue is whether the therapist does so sufficiently to prevent some part of the personality from becoming inhibited and repressed" (p. 94).

This chapter delimits examination of personality change groups to those that operate on either the underlying assumptions of psychoanalytic or humanistic approaches. Personality change for our purpose, therefore, refers broadly to one of two possibilities, depending upon whether the fundamental assumptions of psychoanalytic or humanistic theory underlie the group therapist's stance.

The purpose for the psychoanalytic group therapist is to bring about significant alteration in the personality that has developed distressing behavior in response to stressful conflict (Motto, 1973). The humanistic purpose may be stated as that of encouraging change of self-concept (or, promoting self-authenticity, etc.), by allowing participants the opportunity for their inner health process to function.

The need for parsimony in this chapter dictates that we present only one theoretical position within the humanistic paradigm. We have chosen the Person-Centered Approach (PCA) for several reasons. First, the PCA is more explicit than most other humanistic theories about personality changes via self-concept change. Second, the PCA offers examples of a variety of personality change groups that are not psychotherapy groups. Also, more than any other therapy, Carl Rogers's client centered approach (now PCA) was the forerunner of the humanistic approach. Farson (1975) eloquently points this out:

> Actualizing human potentialities for creativity and growth, re-garding the person in the here and now, emphasizing the cen-trality of the self, and placing significance on experience as well since as behavior were the fundamental building blocks of hu-manistic psychology and Rogers supplied them (p. xxxvi).

SUPPORTIVE THEORIES

A representative, basic assumption of humanistic theory for groups is not apt to satisfy proponents of many specific humanistic theories. Rogers's (1959) definition of self-actualization does, how-ever, include the tenets of inner health, self-responsibility and indivi-duality of the client. Rogers defines self-actualization in relation to the self-structure:

> Following the development of the self-structure, the general ten-dency toward actualization expresses itself also in the actualiza-tion of that experience of the organism which is symbolized in the self (p. 196).

Gaylin (1974) more specifically refers to personality change as fol-lows:

> Personality change for individuals is identified by them becom-ing less defensive, more open to experience, more fully function-ing, and becoming increasingly psychologically healthy (p. 349).

The basic assumption of psychoanalytic theory is that the human being is continually in conflict between his/her dual nature as a biological animal and a social being. The aim of psychotherapy groups is to "...change the personality structure more or less per-manently..." (Slavson, 1964, p. 107). Slavson's (1964) definition of psychotherapy is also applicable, i.e., "...the process by which a patient is rendered accessible to the total educative influences of his world" (p. 38). He identifies the tasks to accomplish in psychoanalytic group therapy as: "(1) to free the libido from overcathected foci; (2) to strengthen the ego; (3) to correct the superego; and (4) to improve the self-image" (p. 39).

INTERVENTION LEVEL

The level of intervention in the person centered approach to personality change groups is determined by each participant within the context of interaction with group therapists (referred to as facilitators) and other group members. The level of intervention using the psychoanalytic assumption is ultimately to encourage and assist participants to: a) examine the basic life patterns imposed upon their current life situations, and b) live current situations without the transference of past earlier disruptive patterns of interaction.

INTERVENTION PURPOSE

The purpose of the PCA is to permit the participant to move in the most appropriate direction with the most appropriate degree of self change he/she is capable of at the time. The purpose is defined by each participant.

The intervention purpose of group psychotherapy from the psychoanalytic base is operationally different from the PCA. The intent of the therapist is "to try to bring about some change and/or disappearance of the symptom in as early and direct manner as possible" (Motto, 1973, p.1). It is the task of the therapist to uncover underlying feelings that instigate reactions.

CHANGE TECHNIQUES USED

Techniques used within the person centered assumption are idiosyncratic to the facilitators, participants, and their interactions. Facilitators, in interaction with the participants, permit the techniques to emerge. These techniques might be determined by either participants or facilitators. The intent of the group encounter is to meet without premeditated structure or predetermined techniques that might be used.

The therapist who uses psychoanalytic concepts decides upon techniques that will correct the intrapsychic triad of the id, ego, and superego. The therapist may use any of the following techniques:

   a. Free associative communication. (Topics considered by the therapist as leading to intrapsychic change are encouraged.)
   b. Analyze resistances to communications.
   c. Assist the group participant to increase insight.
   d. Explore and interpret transferences and resistances.
   e. Pursue unconscious sources and determinants.

TARGET POPULATIONS

Anyone who believes that he/she might benefit from altering his/her self-concept or changing his/her personality is considered acceptable for PCA therapy according to PCA assumptions. This guideline would allow for inclusion of hospitalized mental patients, university students, outpatients, or any group that has members who seek to change themselves. Each group participant decides in consort with the group facilitator whether he/she should enter a particular group.

The target populations predicated on psychoanalytic assumptions include groups of individuals who seek treatment for pervasive problems. These include psychiatric problems and long term pervasive behavioral problems such as alcoholism and drug abuse. Groups formed from any target population pre-suppose planned selection. Included are guiding principles for determining the capacity for minimal primary relations, identifying the degree of sexual disturbances, minimal ego strengths, and minimal super ego development (Slavson, 1964, p. 178).

LEADER FUNCTIONS

The PCA facilitators' functions are primarily attending to their own transparency, concentrating their attention on group members, and attempting to understand other members' perceptions of the world. Other major characteristics of the group facilitator have been identified for person-centered large community groups (Bozarth, 1981):

a. Willingness to participate as a member of the group.
b. Willingness to attempt to understand and to accept each member of the group. (Hopefully, many of the participants will perceive this in the facilitator if it does in fact exist.)
c. Willingness to share his/her struggles when such struggles exist.
d. Willingness of the facilitator to give up institution "position power" for the opportunity to have personal influence, interaction with other members, and group membership.
e. "Confidence" that group members will move in positive and healthy directions (pp. 118-119).

Slavson (1964) describes four generic functions of the group therapist in psychoanalysis. These are the directional, stimulative, extensional, and interpretative functions:

a. The therapist directs sessions away from unfruitful discussion, and helps the group to concentrate on the common unconscious elements, or move to less disruptive material.
b. The stimulative function is often employed through questions, retracing previous background material, or encouraging recall of previous ideas or topics. This stimulative role is assumed when the group has reached an impasse.
c. The extensional function is employed to help the group extend communications beyond a psychological block. This can be done through questioning, introduction of new elaboration of the topic, or associating it with another significant event or emotion.
d. The interpretative function consists of the therapist's efforts to induce insight.

The psychoanalytic group therapist functions as guide, controller, and overall seer of the group.

LEADER TRAINING

The following statement on primary group training provides a thorough overview of one of the major professional organization's stipulations concerning group leader training.

The American Group Psychotherapy Association (AGPA) has developed certification criteria for group psychotherapists. These criteria are outlined in *Guidelines for the Training of Group Psychotherapists* (AGPA, 1978). The Association guidelines address primarily the technical aspects of group psychotherapy training and leave to the local training committee selection criteria concerning personal qualities. The AGPA training criteria will be used to represent training criteria for group psychotherapists.

Professional Prerequisites

Inasmuch as clinical professionals may enter training programs from diverse backgrounds, graduate level courses in normal growth and development, personality theory and psychodynamics, psychopathology, and clinical diagnosis are considered necessary for admission by the American Group Psychotherapy Association.

Training programs are required to have seminars in the theory and technique of group psychotherapy (90 hours), clinical group experience (120 hours), continuous conference in groups (45 hours), participation as a patient in group psychotherapy (120 hours), completion of direct treatment of patients in individual, group, or family (1200 hours).

Although these training guidelines are accepted by PCA group facilitators, they are usually not considered the most important aspects of training. The training emphasis is not upon "possession of a certain degree, didactic knowledge about the group process, or 'group certification' " (Bozarth, 1981, p. 119). The more important aspect of facilitator training from the perspective of the PCA is the development of facilitator attitudes that foster the self-directive forces of participants. There is more emphasis upon the experiential readiness than upon knowledge of group process or participation in any particular set of courses or practica. The training prescriptions are less important than for facilitators to be "in touch with themselves, empathic, and receptive to others" (Bozarth, 1981, p. 120).

INTERVENTION EFFECTIVENESS

In their review of group psychotherapy research, Bednar and Kaul (1978) reached some preliminary conclusions regarding the effectiveness of group psychotherapy. "Accumulated evidence indicates that group treatments have been more effective than no treatment, than placebo or nonspecific treatments, at least under some circumstances" (p. 792). Bednar and Kaul concluded that group treatments "work," but this conclusion must be qualified inasmuch as the data "have been gathered under a variety of conditions, from a wide range of individuals, and in many different ways" (p. 792).

Bednar and Kaul report that the follow-up literature is encouraging insofar as some of the treatment effects persist over time. However, evidence regarding the comparative effectiveness of group treatment is unclear; they perceived it as encouraging that group psychotherapy treatments compare favorably to other forms of group treatment. Nevertheless, they caution that: "Causal statements about the curative forces operating in the group context, the circumstances under which they may be brought to bear, or the form in which they may be expressed cannot be supported on the basis of the available literature" (Bednar and Kaul, 1978, p. 793).

In a review of group psychotherapy outcome literature by Gazda and Peters (1975), the following general conclusions were reached:

(1) group therapy produces good results when it is used to supplement other treatment methods; (2) group therapy seems to have less effectiveness with psychotic clients; conversely, it seems to be more effective with nonpsychotic clients; and (3) individual therapy appears to be more effective with grossly psychotic clients and less effective with non-psychotic clients (p. 44).

Others (Bednar and Lawlis, 1971; Meltzoff and Kornreich, 1970; Parloff and Dies, 1977; Stotsky and Zolik, 1965) have found group psychotherapy with schizophrenics and other psychotics to be of questionable effectiveness.

Parloff and Dies (1977) found that, among other difficulties in the group psychotherapy research, it is frequently considered an entity that it is not. Their recommendations for improving group psychotherapy research include as a highest priority explicit definitions and descriptions of specialized forms and techniques of group psychotherapy with treatment manuals of various group therapy approaches for specified classes of patients (p. 315).

Research on group psychotherapy and on other groups involving personality change also need to consider the basic assumptions applied by the group facilitators.

CASE EXAMPLES
PCA[1]

Wood (1982) describes a PCA community encounter group which deals with a troubled individual who exhibited psychotic behavior.

This example is one from a personality change group other than a psychotherapy group, i.e., a PCA community group. The PCA community group usually consists of 50 to 100 persons (but may include members from 20 to 2000) who have come together for the experience of the community. There is little emphasis on theme or pre-determined structure. The example involves a community group of 100 participants and six group facilitators.

Wood (1982) reports an episode synthesized from hundreds of hours of interaction in a community group. The episode reports group interaction which begins with a concern about Galin who another member reports as "screaming and acting aggressive this afternoon." With Galin as the center of concern, the group members express various other concerns, e.g., feelings of inadequacy as a therapist, the best way to treat Galin (as a sick person, someone in an altered state), concern about why someone doesn't do something for Galin, the acceptance of personal fears, and numerous other themes. Themes about Galin included: "We should treat Galin like a person." "I think he should be left to do as he pleases." "We should go to him, support him." "Take him away. Get him out of here." "Call a psychiatrist."

---

[1]This case example is taken from Wood, J.K. Person-Centered Group Therapy. In G.M. Gazda (Ed.) *Basic approaches to group psychotherapy and group counseling* (3rd ed.) Springfield, Ill.: Charles C Thomas, 1982. Reproduced by permission of Charles C Thomas, Publisher.

Wood then describes Galin's arrival at the meeting:

> (At the morning meeting Galin appears clean shaven, for the first time in several days. His hair is shampooed and combed neatly and he is wearing a clean suit. He speaks without a hint of peculiarity, completely in the "consensual reality." He has spent several hours last night (as in previous nights) in a discussion with Frederick, Mario, and Sally with whom he has formed close friendships).
> GALIN (in a strong voice): I have learned a lot about myself here. I had to do it. But I really need to go home *now*. I need to rest, to get away from this noise, from these people, from the "energy" here. At home I can be quiet in my garden with my own music, my own personal things around me. Me and Saturna. You know I have a cat? In my own home I can reflect on what has happened to me here. I've asked Frederick and Mario to drive me home. (Most of an hour is spent in tear-filled farewells) (pp. 266-270).

Wood's (1982) comments about this group interaction clarify the "effect" of the group from his perspective:

> This one total group had faced the disruption of its community in a new way, making the best possible decisions. Each person was part of the deliberations. No one, least of all Galin, was kept apart from the discussions. Galin made his own decisions. No one decided for him. Yet, each person contributed to the eventual "answer." Moment by moment the course was "decided." In *this* process, in healing itself, even transcending itself, the community was completely "successful." For a different time, location, and another group of individuals, no doubt, the outcome would be different. However, if the people spoke honestly, remaining open to surprise, this group concluded, the best decision could not be avoided (pp. 270-271).

Psychoanalytic[2]

A case example from the perspective of the analytic approach is presented by Pines, Hearst, and Behr (1982). Excerpts are included from an "Emotionally Deprived Mothers" group reported in a presentation by Hearst in 1980 to the VII International Congress on Group Psychotherapy. Segments of this case example, where the group therapist is termed a "conductor," are presented here:

> Five mothers meet with their conductor weekly for 1 ½ hour sessions. The group is in its second year of treatment. Two weeks prior to this session, the conductor drew the group's attention to the imminent summer break. The patients had been given the year's time-table at the beginning of the treatment year.

The case presentation demonstrates Wendy's absence of 5 minutes as one which makes the group take up the pain of the imminent break. The authors then describe the excerpts from the session with the following analyses of particular segments:

> In response to feelings of abandonment displaced on Wendy from the conductor's and the group's break, the group retreats with Sylvia to the fantasy life with the good mother.
>
> The anguish of the nonsustaining environment is verbalized. Wendy resonates to the group's agony of abandonment. From her own past, she relives the burden of mothering her young siblings with inadequate means at her disposal.
>
> Physical intervention and support are used to help Wendy "hold" the physically experienced (cold and hunger) emptiness. Help is needed and given by the conductor (pp. 166-172).

Pines et al. summarize the group's analytic approach represented by the above interaction in the following way:

> Group-analytic treatment takes place in a face-to-face stranger group of eight or so members who meet regularly, usually once or twice a week, with their conductor for the purpose of psychotherapeutic treatment. Placed in such a group, the individual reestablishes his or her typical conflicts and behavior patterns endowing the conductor, the group members, and the group as such with properties of seminal persons in his or her past and present life. He or she uses them as personifications of his or her

---

[2]This case example is taken from Pines, M., Hearst, L.E., and Behr, H.L. Group analysis (Group Analytic Psychotherapy). In G.M. Gazda (Ed.), *Basic approaches to group psychotherapy and group counseling* (3rd ed.). Springfield, Ill.: Charles C Thomas, 1982. Reproduced by permission of Charles C Thomas, Publisher.

inner object constellations, that is, as transference objects. In the analytic group, the individual is conceived of as a nodal point in an interrelated network, influencing and influenced by the interpersonal processes that form the dynamic field, the matrix (p. 172).

EMPLOYMENT—WORK SETTING

The work settings for personality change groups, especially group psychotherapy, may involve any institutional setting that includes the goal of personality change. Psychotherapy groups that operate on the premise of either the psychoanalytic or humanistic assumptions most often exist in medical hospitals and clinics, hospitals for the emotionally disturbed, private and public mental health clinics, and in settings developed by private practitioners. Many of the groups in medical settings will often have as their premise the psychoanalytic assumption. Groups that exist for personality change predicated upon the humanistic assumption are more often the type of personal change groups found in educational settings or special workshop settings (e.g., the large community group or Person Centered Approach encounter groups).

SUMMARY

This chapter reviewed the use of groups that seek to correct individual psychological function. The psychotherapy group was the primary group intervention considered.

The absence of a homogeneous approach to personality change groups necessitated the consideration of two basic assumptions to personality change. One assumption, which is characteristic of humanistic personality theories, was considered. The Person-Centered Approach was used as our example of the application of humanistic theories for several reasons. The other assumption considered was that from psychoanalytic theory.

The framework for group therapy with personality change groups was reviewed in relation to both theoretical assumptions.

The other major theoretical assumption mentioned was behaviorism, but it was not considered because of the lack of theoretical conceptualization about human "...inner organization and its resistance to modification" (Stagner, p. 278).

Wood's (1982) summary of PCA group therapy captures the essence of group psychotherapy from the humanistic perspective:

> Person-centered group therapy earned its reputation and developed its effectiveness by turning attention to and following the lead of the *person*. In the person's inner world was found the capacity for self-healing, growing into completeness, and the means for reliably guiding one's life. One's own direct experiencing, one's alive insight, is a capable authority to which one may return to uncover a closer approximation to truth. With an open heart, experience may be checked, corrected, moved forward under the influence of the formative tendency of life (p. 271).

Pines et al. (1982) summarize the analytical psychotherapy group in a way which captures the essence of that approach:

> Individual disturbances are seen as disturbances in communication, originally in the network of the primary group, the family. The analytic group creates a framework and a unit of observation within which the individual's disturbed communications can emerge and be taken into the field of observation. The therapeutic process within this framework is identical with the ever-widening and deepening process of communication.
>
> The analytic group has its group-specific dynamics, which are distinct from the sum of the individuals that form the group. Thus we speak of a "group-as-a-whole." Within this group, all mechanisms known from psychoanalysis are present and are translated in group dynamic terms. For example, displacement can be expressed in the attack on a group member instead of the conductor, splitting in subgrouping, polarization and so on...(p. 172).

The application of the two perspectives to personality change depicts considerable differences on many variables. However, the major difference is probably that the psychoanalytically oriented group therapist assumes that he/she can best identify the appropriate directions that will lead the participants to more adequate personality change. The humanistic approach, as represented by the PCA, presumes the client to be his/her own best expert—from beginning to end. The practitioner who is interested in personality change groups must operate on either the assumption that the participants are in conflict with their dual animalistic and social conflicts, or on the assumption that the person will move toward growthful change when conditions are created which will allow such change to take place.

The underlying assumption of the therapist will determine the actual modes of operation. The goals of the participants will determine the need for a personality change group.

REFERENCES

American Group Psychotherapy Association: *Guidelines for the Training of Group Psychotherapists: A Model Suggested by the American Group Psychotherapy Association, Inc.* New York: Author, 1978.

Arlow, A.: Psychoanalysis. In R. Corsini (Ed.), *Current Psychotherapies.* Itasca, Ill.: F.E. Peacock, 1979.

Bednar, R., and Kaul, T.: Experiential group research. In S.L. Garfield and A.E. Bergin (Eds.) *Handbook of Psychotherapy and Behavior Change: An Empirical Analysis* (2nd ed.) New York: Wiley, 1978.

Bednar, R., and Lawlis, S.: Empirical research in group psychotherapy. In A.E. Bergin and S.L. Garfield (Eds.), *Handbook of Psychotherapy and Behavior Change: An Empirical Analysis.* New York: Wiley, 1971.

Bergin, A.: The effects of psychotherapy: Negative results revisited. *Journal of Counseling Psychology,* 1963, *10*, 244-255.

Bozarth, J.: The person centered approach in the large community group. In G.M. Gazda (Ed.), *Innovations to Group Psychotherapy* (2nd ed.). Springfield, Ill.: Charles C Thomas, 1981.

Chambless, P., and Goldstein, A.: Behavioral therapy. In R. Corsini (Ed.), *Current Psychotherapies* (2nd ed.). Itasca, Ill.: F.E. Peacock, 1979.

Farson, R.: Carl Rogers, quiet revolutionary. In R.T. Evans (Ed.), *Carl Rogers. The Man and his Ideas.* New York: E.P. Dutton, 1975.

Gaylin, N.: On creativeness and the psychology of well-being. In D.A. Wexler and L.N. Rice (Eds.), *Innovations in Client-Centered Therapy.* New York: Wiley, 1974.

Gazda, G., and Peters, R.: An analysis of research in group psychotherapy, group counseling and human relations training. In G.M. Gazda (Ed.), *Basic Approaches to Group Psychotherapy and Group Counseling* (2nd ed.). Springfield, Ill.: Charles C Thomas, 1975.

Glasser, W., and Zunin, L.: Reality therapy. In R. Corsini (Ed.), *Current Psychotherapies*. Itasca, Ill.: F.E. Peacock, 1979.

Goldstein, A.: Behavior therapy. In R. Corsini (Ed.), *Current Psychotherapies*. Itasca, Ill.: F.E. Peacock, 1973.

Kaufman, Y.: Analytic psychotherapy. In R. Corsini (Ed.), *Current Psychotherapies*. Itasca, Ill.: F.E. Peacock, 1979.

Lazarus, A.: The Practice of Multi-Modal Therapy. New York: McGraw-Hill, 1981.

Meador, B., and Rogers, C.: Client centered therapy. In R. Corsini (Ed.) *Current Psychotherapies* (2nd ed.). Itasca, Ill.: F.E. Peacock, 1979.

Meltzoff, J., and Kornreich, M.: *Research in Psychotherapy.* New York: Atherton Press, 1970.

Mosak, H.: Adlerian Psychology. In R. Corsini (Ed.), *Current Psychotherapies* (2nd ed.). Itasca, Ill.: F.E. Peacock, 1979.

Motto, R.: Psychotherapy. In R.M. Mitchell and C.D. Johnson (Eds.), *Therapeutic Techniques: Working Models for the Helping Profession.* Fullerton, Cal.: California Personnel and Guidance Association, 1973.

Parloff, M., and Dies, R.: Group psychotherapy outcome research. *International Journal of Group Psychotherapy.* 1977, *27*, 281-319.

Pines, M., Hearst, L., and Behr, H.: Group analysis (Group Analytic Psychotherapy). In G.M. Gazda (Ed.), *Basic Approaches to Group Psychotherapy and Group Counseling* (3rd ed.). Springfield, Ill.: Charles C Thomas, 1982.

Rogers, C.: A theory of therapy, personality, and interpersonal relationships, as developed in the client-centered framework. In S. Koch (Ed.), *Psychology: A Study of Science* (Vol. 3). *Formulations of the Person and the Social Context.* New York: McGraw-Hill, 1959.

Shapiro, J.: *Methods of Group Psychotherapy and Encounter.* Itasca, Ill.: F.E. Peacock, 1978.

Simkin, J.: Gestalt therapy. In R. Corsini (Ed.), *Current Psychotherapies.* Itasca, Ill.: F.E. Peacock, 1979.

Slavson, S.: *A Textbook in Analytic Group Psychotherapy.* New York: International Universities Press, 1964.

Spotnitz, H.: Comparison of different types of group psychotherapy. In H.I. Kaplin & B.J. Sadock (Eds.), *Comprehensive Group Psychotherapy.* Baltimore: William & Wilkins, 1971.

Stagner, A.: Theories of personality. In B.B. Wolman (Ed.), *Handbook of Clinical Psychology.* New York: McGraw Hill, 1965.

Stotsky, B., and Zolik, E.: Group psychotherapy with psychotics: 1921-1963 — A review. *International Journal of Group Psychotherapy,* 1965, *15*, 321-344.

Thoresen, C., and Coates, T.: What does it mean to be a behavior therapist? *The Counseling Psychologist,* 1978, *7*, 3-21.

Wood, J.: Person centered group therapy. In G.M. Gazda (Ed.), *Basic Approaches to Group Psychotherapy and Group Counseling* (3rd ed.), Springfield, Ill.: Charles C Thomas, 1982.

CHAPTER 2

REHABILITATION
Social Skills Groups

GLENN D. SHEAN

INTERVENTION LEVEL

REHABILITATION groups are based on a psychoeducational approach that attempts to remedy specific interpersonal skills deficits. These deficits are assumed to be the basis of many "problems in living" associated with developmental issues as well as psychiatric "illness." This approach to change has been referred to variously as Structured Learning Therapy (Goldstein, 1973) and/or Social Skills Training (Bellack, Hersen, Himmelhoch, 1981). Derivative intervention strategies focus on changing maladaptive patterns of thinking, feeling, and expression as evidenced through action. Treatment places primary emphasis on the directed training and practice of new interpersonal skills in the context of a graded series of supportive interpersonal environments. Intervention strategies attempt to directly change cognition and behavior.

INTERVENTION PURPOSE

Social skills groups are based on the assumption that many psychological difficulties are the result of inadequate or deviant social-learning histories. Such deviant personal histories, perhaps in conjunction with biological factors, are assumed to result in inadequate or inappropriate patterns of thinking, feeling and behavior.

The purpose of skills training is to identify and prioritize those inadequate or inappropriate action patterns that interfere with the client's psychological and social adjustment, and to create structured learning opportunities in which more adequate or appropriate patterns of interpersonal behavior can be understood, practiced, learned, applied, and generalized to everyday life. Social skills training focuses on bringing about specific changes in thought and action that in turn *may* lead to improvements in psychological constructs or traits such as self-esteem, depression, heterosexual-social anxiety, self-control and reality contact. These improvements are conditional on the newly acquired skills being associated with significant environmental change.

SUPPORTIVE THEORY

Social skills groups focus on the training of appropriate social and instrumental role behaviors. Skills groups use a psychoeducational approach based on a rationale derived from studies of human learning and the principles of reinforcement. As well, these groups are adapted from the extensive literature on the social psychology of interpersonal behavior (Mehrabian, 1972).

The clinical work of Salter (1949), Wolpe (1969), and Lazarus (1971) on assertiveness training and Goldstein (1973) on Structured Learning Therapy have contributed to current methods of skills training. Strategies for changing cognitive factors that maintain maladaptive behaviors, as described by Ellis (1973), Beck (1976) and others, have also been incorporated into the techniques of social skills training.

The basic techniques of skill training include instruction, modeling, discussion, behavior rehearsal/role-playing, coaching, performance feedback (including videotape playback), relaxation training, operant shaping, social reinforcement, and graded-steps of practice in the natural environment. These techniques are derived from the impressive body of research literature and from theoretical concepts broadly described as cognitive-behavioral theory. A comprehensive review of the rationale for and research findings on the effects of social skills training for long-term psychiatric patients has been published by Hersen and Bellack (1976).

MAIN INTERVENTION TECHNIQUES USED

In a prototypical skills training session (see Liberman, King, De Risi and McCann, 1975 for more complete description), participants are presented with a conceptual model containing learning steps or key elements of a skill, such as identifying and responding appropriately to the feelings being expressed by someone else. The skill and components are described and discussed and the trainers may role-play or model (positive and/or negative examples) the skill. Participants then are asked to act out the interpersonal situation with the trainer or another participant. Participants' performance is reviewed (videotaping may be used as an aid), correct behaviors are recognized and reinforced, and instructions are provided for further improvement. The cycle is repeated until each group member's performance reaches criterion. Feedback typically focuses on both *content related behaviors,* such as expressions of appreciation, compliance, or anger, and on *non-content related behaviors*, such as eye contact, voice intonation, posture, response latency, facial responsiveness and hand gestures. Instruction, modeling, role-playing (behavioral rehearsal), coaching, prompting, feedback, reinforcement and homework assignments are the educational strategies used to teach social skills and, presumably, to increase the potential for community adjustment.

Homework assignments are used to extend the effects of training beyond the immediate training session. Assignments may be performed alone, by participants in pairs, or the trainer may accompany participants. Trower, Bryant and Argyle (1978) and Goldstein, Sprafkin and Gershaw (1976) have designed programs to improve participants' awareness of and influence over their own internal states by training observational skills such as getting information about the situation and others' feelings, recognizing emotions, gathering information, concentrating on a task, decision making, problem solving, timing responses, and generating the cause of other's behavior.

Criteria are an important concern for selecting skills to be covered in a limited number of training sessions. The usual procedure is based on self-reports by participants about situations that have been mishandled or that have elicited anxiety. This practice, as has been pointed out by Wallace, Nelson and Liberman (1980), maximizes the relevance of training but may overlook social inadequacies of which patients are unaware. A second approach emerges from *a priori* decisions made by the trainers. These decisions acknowledge data produced from instruments such as the Skills Survey, developed by Goldstein, Martens and Hubben (1973), and the Behavioral Assertiveness Tests (BAT), developed by Hersen and Bellack (1977).

METHODS OF SOCIAL SKILLS TRAINING

The number and variety of topics that can be addressed, and of approaches to learning in a skills group, are limited only by the creativity, imagination and resources of the facilitators. Each session, however, should be highly focused on a specific goal or set of goals. Typically, however, a variety of learning techniques are applied in all skill training groups. Six general categories of skills training techniques or approaches are described in the following paragraphs.

Modeling

Modeling refers to the social learning process which occurs when facilitators demonstrate a situation relevant to the skill being discussed. The facilitators attempt to perform the skill accurately and naturally, giving the participant good example(s) to imitate. It is often useful for the facilitators to practice modeling situations prior to the group meeting. Such practice assures the selection of good examples and smooth and comfortable performances.

Goldstein, *et al.* (1976) have listed three stages that are involved when learning takes place by modeling. First, the facilitators should be aware of the group members' attention. Attention to what is being modeled is necessary if any learning is going to occur. The facilitators should make their modeling demonstration as specific to the steps to be learned as possible so the group members will learn only the desired behaviors. Irrelevant comments and interactions could cause the participants' attention to wander, or undesirable behaviors could be unintentionally presented.

The second phase in the modeling process relates to the goal of getting the group member to remember the behaviors that have been modeled. Remembering modeled behaviors is aided by having the trainees participate in the role-plays.

The third phase is associated with the goal of getting the group members to actually perform the desired pattern of behavior. The probability that a person will repeat the expected behavior usually depends on factors such as interest, motivation, social support, and reward expectation. Lively, interesting groups with meaningful topics, appropriate social reinforcement, and opportunities for success enhance future motivation and reward expectations.

Role Playing

Role-playing is another important technique that has been found to be effective in skills groups. Role-playing is learning by doing, an activity which is the foundation of skill acquisition. Understanding can only assist such learning; it cannot replace practice.

Role-playing could be defined as having a person step into a role or situation which requires use of the skill being studied. Role-playing in skills groups involves getting the group members to participate in and experience behaviors that are new or need improvement. The member learns the skill well enough to try it outside of the group by practicing repeatedly until the skill can be performed easily and correctly.

Role playing consists of at least two participants, with the facilitators often acting as "directors." The facilitators should provide as much information as possible concerning the individual roles as well as the overall scene. This information aids the actors and nonparticipating members in understanding the roles they are to assume or observe.

Learning Techniques

Two areas exist in which modeling and role-playing are not effective. First, in some instances, learning steps are based on the incorrect assumption that the member understands a concept or is able to make a particular distinction that the member cannot practice. Second, there are certain skills which involve little observable behavior. Practicing such a skill is not easy or natural using a technique like role-playing.

Learning techniques were developed (Shean, Carrol, Arledge, and Trevor, 1981) when it was recognized that many activities other than role-playing and modeling could meet the needs of these certain areas. The term, "learning technique," is used as a general category within which a wide variety of exercises, planned discussions, games, and other activities are used to compensate for the limitations described above. No general theme or structure runs through the different techniques. They can be as different as a scavenger hunt (for practicing the skill of "Following Instructions") and charades (for learning "Identifying and Labeling Emotions"), or deep breathing exercises (for improving "Relaxation"). What unifies these activities and justifies labeling them with one title, learning techniques, is a common purpose. Each technique is created or adapted to clarify a particular learning point, or to facilitate practice of a skill.

Learning techniques are generally used after the initial introduction of a skill or learning point, and any subsequent discussion. For example, assume that one learning point of a particular skill instructs the member to "decide if the other person is interested in what you are saying." If the member has difficulty identifying those body signals which indicate interest, he or she will not be able to adequately handle this learning point. Role-playing is not a particularly good agency for teaching such decision-making behaviors. Frequently, when role-playing is the only practice technique used, cognitive skills such as those underlying this learning point are not really tested and deficits are ignored or go undetected.

A variety of techniques can be used to focus on this type of deficit. They allow the member to improve his/her vocabulary, or "emotion word," and to be sensitive to the body language of other people. Once the member has some basis for judging "if the other person is interested," role-playing can proceed with the practice of this new component of the skill becoming extremely beneficial.

Homework

The facilitator's first concern when teaching a skill is that the member correctly carry out the required steps. When these steps are mastered, a situation can be created where the skill can be practiced as a unit. This occurrence is a major function of role-playing, after several successful performances in group, the member can then begin to integrate the skill into the normal behavior repertoire. Integration requires that he/she be able to see when it is appropriate or inappropriate to try the skill. An explanation of when to implement the skill is of limited value. An understanding of the "right time" grows through experience. Participants will increasingly come to recognize a wider variety of situations in which the skills can be appropriately used.

Training techniques and role-playing can be used in group meetings to add to the vitality of the skills. Still, the facilitator can only teach good examples of the way to perform each skill. Too rigid an adherence to the suggested sequence and contents of a skill may eventually lead to a limited ability to apply the skill in daily situations. With proper encouragement and, again, through experience members can learn to adapt a skill to their particular needs.

Homework can serve the joint goal of stimulus and response generalization in two ways: a) by guiding or coaching members in their initial attempts to apply the skill, and b) by buffering some of the anger or sense of defeat when an attempt is unsuccessful. Homework is not a haphazard assignment. The groundwork for each task must be carefully laid when it is given. Generally, a skill should not be assigned as homework unless it has been practiced in and mastered within the group. This condition allows the facilitators to prepare members for possible difficulties and to work with them in adapting the skill to the situation.

Feedback

Positive feedback about appropriate aspects of the client's performance is an important aspect of social skills training. Critical comments are avoided, particularly in light of the probable learning histories of most group participants. The focus is on recognition of, and personally appropriate praise for, small steps taken toward a broader goal.

Prompting

Instructions and modeling should be given before a client practices a skill. Facilitators may coach or prompt a client during a role-play interaction when appropriate, for example, if eye contact is not maintained during an interaction, or if the client fails to acknowledge a clearly expressed feeling statement.

PRIMARY INTERVENTION TARGET POPULATIONS

Social skills training has been employed with a wide range of populations, including alcoholics, teenagers, college students, depressed clients, prison inmates, delinquents, and long-term schizophrenics (Timnick, 1982). This chapter will focus on the application of social skills training to hospitalizing psychiatric patients. It should be emphasized, however, that the same basic approach, strategies and procedures can apply across populations with only the level of focus and skills trained changing.

Social competence has been found to be a better indicator than psychiatric diagnosis in discriminating people who are hospitalized from those who are not (Zigler and Phillips, 1961). Over 80 percent of psychiatric patients surveyed report difficulties in dealing with a variety of interpersonal situations (Goldsmith and McFall, 1975). A survey of social situations reported to be difficult for male psychiatric patients (Goldsmith and McFall, 1975) identified two complex clusters of skill deficits labeled "situational" and "interpersonal." Situational problem contexts include dating, making friends, having job interviews, interacting with authorities, and interacting with people viewed as more intelligent or attractive, or who appeared in some way different. Interpersonal contexts include initiating and terminating interactions, making personal disclosures, handling conversational silence, responding to rejection and being assertive.

PRIMARY GROUP LEADER FUNCTIONS

Facilitation of a structured group requires more detailed preparation than is demanded by groups whose content is determined by the group members. It is important to understand that a skills group has a clearly specified goal which is achieved by combining several relevant social skills. Social skills, as defined in this text, are "chunked" into a sequence of specific patterns of behavior referred to as steps.

Guidelines for Teaching Social Skills

The actual skills group progresses as follows. First, steps are studied individually to assure that they are clearly understood. As additional steps are mastered, they are put together into a sequence which is also rehearsed. In this fashion, an entire sequence of steps eventually comes to comprise a single skill. When this basic sequence can be performed with ease, variations on the skill and applications of it to new situations can be studied.

The various training methods are designed to clarify the subject matter and to encourage practice and performance of the skills. The speed with which a skill is mastered is irrelevant, within practical limits. Depending on the group members, a one-hour session might concentrate on a single learning point or on an entire skill. Success can be measured only by change as defined by the group member's ability to correctly perform the skill.

Groups should develop a hierarchy of goals. Initially each skill should be studied separately, so that the learning of a single skill becomes a goal for a certain time. Finally, the clarification and mastery of one or several steps become the short-term goals of a group meeting.

Goals and purposes can be made constantly available to the group members. Using a public, shared medium, such as posters, allows the group to be brought closer together. Members become better able to help each other, and memory becomes a less important factor in accurate performance of skill. When someone forgets a learning point, he/she can refer to the information displayed before the group. Later, after much practice, this will no longer be necessary.

However, cognitive understanding is no replacement for learning by doing. Knowing a skill means being able to do it, with ease and in a variety of situations. Many groups are oriented to talking about

things, about problems, solutions, ways of doing. The talking undertaken in a skills group is usually a prelude to practice. The majority of time in group must be spent trying the skills, correcting
mistakes, improving the flow. As the skill is mastered within the
group, time is designated out of group for further practice. Until the
skill has become "second nature," that is, until it has been integrated
into the typical behavioral pattern of the individual, it has not been
practiced enough.

Establishing a Learning Environment

If a group is to run effectively, it must provide an atmosphere
conducive to learning. An important job of the facilitator is to establish a climate in the group where learning is encouraged.

Perhaps because it seems so simplistic, people tend to ignore the
idea that group meetings ought to be interesting. Motivation of
group members, particularly in the early stages of a group, will be
determined largely by how interesting the activities and exercises of
a group are perceived by the members.

Facilitator Attitude

The group facilitator plays several roles in the group. He or she is
the teacher, a model, and a fellow group member. The way facilitators act can greatly influence the perceptions and behaviors of group
members. Facilitators are responsible for adopting behaviors and attitudes consonant with their various roles and consistent with themselves.

Facilitators must convey four attitudes in their group sessions in
order to conduct successful skills groups: respect, patience, enthusiasm and encouragement. In addition to the above attitudes the facilitator must learn to relinquish control in order to foster participant's ability to act as mature, responsible persons.

Problem Behaviors

Many so-called problem behaviors can be understood as the result of skills deficits. It is logical then to consider these behaviors as

opportunities for skill training and use the situation to discuss and role-play more acceptable alternative ways of interacting.

Co-Facilitation

The skills program has been designed for leadership by two people. Clearly, one person can handle the duties of facilitation. However, a team can be more flexible and more effective.

Structured group activities are different from those of a discussion group. In skills groups, the participants are often doing things and moving around. At times, the groups can split for a time into two smaller groups in order to work separately on a problem.

When the group is working as a single unit, one facilitator can guide the discussion or activity while the other models proper group membership behavior. Such modeling is important and effective. If problems arise, one facilitator can intervene while the other keeps the group's activities going or enlists the rest of the group to control the disruptive behavior. If one leader becomes involved in a conflict with a group member, the other is there to mediate.

Two people are very helpful in keeping up each other's enthusiasm and perspective on problems. And when people work as a team to plan the group, to lead it, and to evaluate its effectiveness, the process can be rewarding and even enjoyable.

Primary Group Leader Training

One of the most important advantages of social skills groups is that effective group facilitators need not hold professional degrees or have taken extensive training in insight oriented group techniques. Rather, the essential characteristics of an effective group leader are: enthusiasm, genuineness, average intelligence, sensitivity, and caring for others. Given the above, the theoretical concepts and intervention strategies can be taught to all levels of staff in four two-hour group training sessions (Shean, *et al.*, 1981). The most effective preparation is on-the-job training, as a co-facilitator with someone who is interested, experienced, and who accepts as useful the rationale of lower training groups.

Facilitators must be trained in understanding the principles of learning and in applying the group facilitator techniques described in earlier sections of this chapter. Role playing and co-facilitation are the best training techniques. An effective incentive program for staff who undertake and do a good job of leading such groups is also relevant to the long-term enthusiasm and performance of group leaders.

EVIDENCE OF INTERVENTION EFFECTIVENESS

Social skills training with individual clients and with groups has been evaluated in terms of its effect on a wide variety of dependent measures, including internal emotional states and specific topographic behaviors. A second series of studies has attempted to determine the key components of skills training procedures. Finally, a third group of studies has focused on the behavioral results of skills training, these include individual case descriptions, single subject designs and group comparisons. This section will summarize and cite representative studies. For more complete reviews see Bellack, Hersen and Turner (1976) and Wallace *et al.* (1980).

Dependent Measures

Internal States

Few studies exist of the effects of skills training on the internal states of patients. Results from a number of studies indicate that skills training combined with densensitization does reduce levels of self-reported anxiety and discomfort in social situations (Argyle, Trower, and Bryant, 1974; Falloon, Lindley, McDonald and Marks, 1977; Goldsmith and McFall, 1975).

Topographical Behaviors

Studies have assessed the effects of skills training on behaviors such as smiles, gestures, praise and eye contact. Most often patients are asked to role-play standardized situations, such as those found in the BAT-R (Eisler, Hersen, Miller and Blanchard, 1975). Performances are videotaped and later observed for the occurence of variables such as eye contact, response durations, smiles, appreciation and speech duration, latency and intonation. The results of these studies (Bellack, *et al.*, 1976; Field and Test, 1975; Hersen, Eisler and Miller, 1973; Shepherd, 1977) indicate that patients who have participated in skills training evidence significant increases in targeted topographical response categories in training related test role-play situations. These results have not as yet been demonstrated in everyday interactions outside of the hospital.

Outcome — Increased Skills

A number of studies have used confederates in contrived situations to test for the generalization of previously trained skills. The findings of these studies indicate that clients are able to utilize social skills in training similar test situations after training; however, skills do not appear to generalize significantly to situations that differ from the training situations (Goldsmith and McFall, 1975; Liberman, Lillie and Falloon, 1978). Thus, research evidence suggests that social skills training may be far more specific and limited in its effects than expected.

Key Components of Skills Training

The relative effects of the component techniques of skills training have been evaluated by Hersen, *et al.* (1973) and Goldstein, *et al.* (1973). These studies, though limited in scope of techniques evaluated, suggest that modeling and instructions are among the most effective component skills training techniques.

Results of Skills Training

Single Subject Studies

Studies using this design attempt to demonstrate the effectiveness of skills training of single subjects by associating change in dependent measures of social skills with systematic variations in training interventions. Frederiksen, Jenkins, Foy, and Eisler (1976) separately trained two verbally abusive patients to increase rates of looking, to make appropriate requests, and to decrease their rates of hostile and irrelevant comments and of inappropriate requests. Results of an extended ward observation period indicated that behaviors changed only as training was applied, and that training did generalize to interactions with confederates in test situations. Generalization of appropriate requests to novel situations, as opposed to trained situations, decreases significantly in this study even if the confederate had been the trainer. Similar results were reported by Bellack, Hersen and Turner (1976), who found that skills such as "appropriate" requests did not generalize to novel situations as well as they did to topographic behaviors, such as eye contact.

Questions about the generalization of skills to novel social contexts and the duration of skills gains remain unanswered. There is evidence that more complex skills may not generalize significantly beyond training and evaluation sessions. Matson and Stephens (1978), for example, found that skills gains in nurses' ratings of cooperativeness, appropriateness of verbal statements, and appropriateness of requests for attention, "rapidly deteriorated to baseline levels" (p. 74), following monitoring during a 12-week follow-up.

Group Studies

These studies have compared the effects of a variety of different training methods (skills training, relaxation, discussion) on different outcome measures. Trends in the findings of these studies will be described here (see Wallace, *et al.*, 1980 for a more detailed discussion).

Most studies using patient self-reporters of discomfort in interpersonal situations report improvement as a result of skills training (Argyle, Trower and Bryant, 1976; Finch and Wallace, 1977). Topographical behaviors have also been observed to improve as a result of skills training (Field and Test, 1975), with improvement noted to persist as long as 24 months (Monti, Fink and Norman, 1979). When measures of gains in topographical aspects of social skills are evaluated in situations dissimilar to the format of training, however, results are not so encouraging (Jaffe and Carlson, 1976).

Evidence for the effectiveness of social skills training remains problematic. Several methodological shortcomings (Wallace, *et al.*, 1980) make it difficult to draw general conclusions from existing evidence. First, diagnosis and severity of impairment is rarely specified, thus it is difficult to compare findings across studies. Medication, levels of skills training, and characteristics of comparison group participants are rarely given. Finally, there is no uniformity to the duration, frequency, content or techniques used in studies of the effects of skills training. Thus, the term, "social skills training," does not refer to an adequately uniform set of interventions to allow for comparison across studies.

In summary, there is evidence that skills training is effective in improving patient's self reports of discomfort in social situations and in improving specific behaviors, such as eye contact. Skills training has also been demonstrated to be effective in increasing the frequency of more complex behaviors when tested in situations that are similar to the training sessions. Serious questions remain about the degree to which these gains are generalized outside the training situation and how long they last after training stops. Further, progress in our understanding of the effective component skills training must await broader and more uniform definitions of social skills, and greater connection between these definitions and intervention strategies.

Several researchers have presented conceptual definitions of social skills that could serve as a basis for enhanced understanding and effectiveness of skills training. Hoephner and O'Sullivan (1968), for example, have identified six cognitive factors independent of verbal comprehension that load on social intelligence: correct recognition of gestures and posture as expressions of thoughts and feelings; resolving contradictory information received from two modes of expression; comprehending a sequence of social events; and predicting the consequences of a social situation. Such an expanded definition of social skills should assist in the design of more effective intervention strategies.

Wallace (1978) and Wallace, Nelson and Lukoff (1978) and his colleagues have also developed a broadened model of socially skilled behavior. They define socially skilled behavior as the end of a chain of cognitions and behaviors that begins with accurate reception of relevent interpersonal stimuli, moves to flexible processing of these stimuli to generate and evaluate possible response options, and ends with appropriate sending of the chosen option. These researchers, along with several others working independently (Siegel and Spivack, 1973; Trower, *et al.*, 1978), have developed integrated skills assessment and training programs based on expanded definitions of social skills. Use of these programs, in addition to better descriptions of populations characteristics by independent groups of researchers, should do much to clear up existing questions about the effects and limits of skills training.

CASE EXAMPLE

Eisler, Hersen and Miller (1974) have provided a detailed case description of the applications of skills training to several psychiatric inpatients. Interventions are individualized but represent training strategies similar to those that would also be applied in a group context in which participants share a common skills deficit such as poor anger control. In one case example, a 28 year-old painter was admitted to the hospital after firing a shotgun into the ceiling of his home. His background included a history of angry acting out often following a consistent failure to express anger in social situations. Assessment was conducted by asking the patient to role play situations related to current experiences in which he was unable to express anger. These situations included receiving criticism from a co-worker, disagreeing with his wife, and refusing requests by his son. The client's reactions in the role plays, with an assistant playing the complementary role (that of co-worker, wife or son), were videotaped and observed through a one-way mirror. Assessment of his reactions by the authors revealed deficits in four topographic components of assertiveness: eye contact, loudness of voice, speech duration and behavioral requests (he did not ask his partners to change their behavior).

Twelve situations unrelated to the client's specific problem areas, but requiring assertive behavior, were employed during training sessions. Each situation was role played five times over training sessions. Instructions during each role play were offered to the client, as appropriate, through a miniature radio receiver. Instructions were related to only one of the four problem behavior areas at any one time. During initial scenes the client was coached to look at this partner when speaking and during the second to increase the loudness of his voice. During the fourth series he was coached to speak for longer intervals and during the last to ask his partner for behavior change. Feedback about positive aspects of performance was given after each role play. Intervention was thus applied to only one behavior at a time allowing for a multiple-baseline analysis. Each response category was found to increase after specific instructions and coaching was given. The authors report that effects generalized to role plays of the specific situations that were problematic for the client as measured by ratings of videotapes of his performance. There was no report of ratings of the use of trained social skills at home or at work, however.

APPLICATION POSSIBILITIES

Social skills groups are an enjoyable, practical educational approach to helping any group of people who experience difficulties in achieving satisfactory and acceptable interactions with others. The straight-forward, concrete goals and learning steps associated with these groups make them acceptable to a wide range of individuals who may reject or fail to benefit from more abstract exploratory groups. Skills groups should be viewed as one approach to the application of cognitive-behavior learning principles. As such, possibilities for application are virtually limitless.

REFERENCES

Argyle, M., Trower, P., and Bryant, B.: Explorations in the treatment of personality disorders and neuroses by social skills training. *British Journal of Medical Psychology, 47*:63-77, 1974.

Argyle, M., Trower, P. and Bryant, B.: Desensitization and social skills training for socially inadequate and socially phobic patients. *Psychological Medicine, 4:*435-443, 1976.

Beck, A.: *Cognitive Therapy and the Emotional Disorders.* New York: International Universities Press, 1976.

Bellack, A.A., Hersen, M., and Turner, S.M.: Generalization effects of social skills training with chronic schizophrenics: An experimental analysis. *Behavior Research and Therapy, 14*:391-398, 1976.

Bellack, A.S., Hersen, M., and Himmelhoch, G.: Social skills training for depression, a treatment manual. *Journal of Selected Abstract Service Catalog of Selected*

*Documents, 11:*36, 1981.

Eisler, R.M., Hersen, M., and Miller, P.M.: Shaping components of assertive behavior with instructions and feedback. *American Journal of Psychiatry, 131*:1344-1347, 1974.

Eisler, R.M., Hersen, M., Miller, P.M., and Blanchard, E.B.: Situational determinants of assertive behaviors. *Journal of Consulting and Clinical Psychology, 43*:330-340, 1975.

Ellis, A.: *Humanistic Psychotherapy.* New York: McGraw-Hill, 1973.

Falloon, I.R.H., Lindley, P., McDonald, R. and Marks, I.M.: Social skills training of out-patient groups: A controlled study of rehearsal. *British Journal of Psychiatry, 131*:599-609, 1977.

Field, G.D., and Test, M.A.: Group assertive training for severely disturbed patients. *Journal of Behavior Therapy and Experimental Psychiatry, 6*:129-134, 1975.

Finch, B.E., and Wallace, C.J.: Successful interpersonal skills training with schizophrenic inpatients. *Journal of Consulting and Clinical Psychology, 45*:885-890, 1977.

Frederickson, L.W., Jenkins, J.O., Foy, D.W., and Eisler, R.M.: Social skills training to modify abusive verbal outbursts in adults. *Journal of Applied Behavioral Analysis, 9*:117-127, 1976.

Goldsmith, J.B. and McFall, R.M.: Development and evaluation of an interpersonal skills training program for psychiatric inpatients. *Journal of Abnormal Psychology, 84*:57-58, 1975.

Goldstein, A.P., Martens, J., and Hubben, J.: The use of modeling to increase independent behavior. *Behavior Research and Therapy, 11*:31-42, 1973.

Goldstein, A.P., Sprafkin, R.P., and Gershaw, N.J.: *Skill training for Community Living: Applied Structured Learning Therapy.* New York: Pergammon Press, 1976.

Hersen, M. and Bellack, A.S.: A multiple baseline analysis of social skills training in chronic schizophrenics. *Journal of Applied Behavioral Analysis, 9*:239-245, 1976.

Hersen, M., and Bellack, A.S.: Assessment of social skills. In Ciminero, A.R., Calhoun, K.S., and Adams, H.E., eds., *Handbook of Behavioral Assessment.* New York: Wiley, 509-554, 1977.

Hersen, M., Eisler, R.M., and Miller, P.M.: Effects of practice, and modeling on components of assertive behavior. *Behavior Research and Therapy, 11*:4-16, 1973.

Hoephner, R., and O'Sullivan, M.: Social intelligence and I.Q. *Educational and Psychological Measurement, 28*:339-344, 1968.

Jaffe, P.F., and Carlson, P.M.: Relative efficacy of modeling and instructions in eliciting social behavior from chronic psychiatric patients. *Journal of Consulting and Clinical Psychology, 44*:200-207, 1976.

Lazarus, A.A.: *Behavior Therapy and Beyond.* New York: McGraw-Hill, 1971.

Liberman, R.P., King, L.W., DeRisi, W.J., and McCann, M.: *Personal Effectiveness.* Champaign, IL: Research Press, 1975.

Liberman, R.P., Lillie, F., and Falloon, I.R.H.: Social Skills Training for Schizophrenic Patients and their families. Unpublished manuscript, Clinical

Research Center, Box A, Camarillo, CA, 1978.

Matson, J.L., and Stephens, R.M.: Increasing appropriate behavior of explosive chronic psychiatric patients with a social-skills training package. *Behavior Modification, 2*:61-77, 1978.

Mehrabian, A.: *Nonverbal Communication.* Chicago: Aldine-Atherton, 1972.

Monti, P.M., Fink, E., and Norman, W.: Effects of social skills training groups and social skills bibliotherapy with psychiatric patients. *Journal of Consulting and Clinical Psychology, 47*(1):189-191, 1979.

Salter, A.: *Conditioned Reflex Therapy.* New York: Creative Age Press, 1949.

Shean, G.D., Carrol, P., Arledge, S., and Trevor, M.: *Social Skills Training Manual.* Clearinghouse for Structured Group Programs. Counseling Center, University of Rhode Island, 1981.

Shepherd, G. Social skills training: The generalization problem. *Behavior Therapy, 8*:1108-1119, 1977.

Siegel, J.M. and Spivack, G. *Problem-Solving Therapy: A New Program for Chronic Schizophrenic Patients.* Research and Evaluation Report No. 23. Philadelphia: Hahnemann Medical College and Hospital, 1973.

Timnick, L. Social skills training. *Psychology Today,* August, 43-49, 1982.

Trower, P., Bryant, B. and Argyle, M. *Social Skills and Mental Health.* Pittsburgh: University of Pittsburgh Press, 1978.

Wallace, C.J. The Assessment of Interpersonal Problem Solving Skills with Chronic Schizophrenics. Presented at the Annual Meeting of the American Psychological Association, New York: September, 1978.

Wallace, C.J., Nelson, C., and Lukoff, D. Cognitive Skills Training. Presented at the Annual Meeting of the Association for the Advancement of Behavior Therapy, Chicago, IL., November, 1978.

Wallace, C.J., Nelson, C.J., and Liberman, R.P. A review and critique of social skills training with schizophrenic patients. *Schizophrenia Bulletin, 6*(1):42-63. 1980.

Wolpe, J. *The Practice of Behavior Therapy.* New York: Pergammon Press, 1969.

Zigler, E. and Phillips, L. Social competence and outcome in psychiatric disorder. *Journal of Abnormal and Social Psychology, 63*:264-272, 1961.

CHAPTER 3

PERSONAL GROWTH
Personal Development Groups

DAVID J. DRUM

PERSONAL development groups focus on helping people achieve integrity and intentionality. Integrity is the ability to lead an unimpaired existence by adhering to a personal code of behavior satisfying to oneself, while accommodating to the legitimate needs of others. Intentionality means making clear, self-aware choices at important life crossroads, in light of knowledge about early life choices which have become self-defeating, enslaving, ritualistic, alienating, and frustrating.

An individual's style of relating, being, feeling, and perceiving is formed as a result of life experiences that place subtle but direct pressures on the individual to make adaptions. Although these accommodations help to preserve the self from disintegration, they can also form the basis for a growing sense of self-dissatisfaction.

Devised for precisely these kinds of problems, personal development groups provide a productive growth atmosphere safe for self-disclosure, give participants a chance to examine their self-defeating beliefs and behaviors, and help them develop self-satisfying, intentional life styles.

These groups divide sharply into two distinct types: *self-awareness* and *life-theme* (See Table III-1). A participant joining a self-awareness group can expect to discuss any issue that concerns a group member: the degree to which they would like to be self- or other-directed, interpersonally close or detached, to express or

42

Table III-I

PERSONAL DEVELOPMENT GROUPS

Issues	*Self-Awareness Groups*	*Life-Theme Groups*
Intervention Purpose	open to any issue or group of issues that individual group members are concerned about	restricted to a single issue that group members have agreed to address
Group Goals	understanding changes that individual group members may wish to pursue	effecting the specific change that the group is designed to accomplish
Depth of Change	concerned with exploring *what* problems group members are experiencing and *why* they have those problems	often require that group members gain insight into *how* they acquired the problem
Leader Involvement	individual treatment in the group setting or group treatment designed for individuals	group treatment designed for individuals
Group Structure	structure devised *in vivo*	highly pre-planned and structured to achieve a specific change
Curative Factors Emphasized	universality, altruism imitative behavior, group cohesion, interpersonal learning, corrective emotional experience, catharsis	imparting information, instillation of hope, development of socializing techniques, group cohesion, interpersonal learning, corrective emotional experience, catharsis

withhold feelings and thoughts, to act controlled or show feelings of vulnerability. Participants of life-theme groups, on the other hand, share a common problem, such as isolating shyness, raging jealousy, or excessive self-criticism, and join the group with the expectation that the focus will be on that specific issue. Since this major difference in participant expectation affects leader functions, change techniques, and intervention level and purpose, the differences between self-awareness and life-theme groups will be clearly identified throughout this discussion.

The remainder of this chapter discusses the nature of personal development groups, including basic theory, leadership issues, curative forces, and an illustrative example.

INTERVENTION LEVEL AND PURPOSE

Of the four levels of intervention — individual, interpersonal, organization, and community — personal development groups focus on the individual, zeroing in on either maladaptive behaviors, strengths, fears, aspirations, or the underlying dynamic that imprisons the person in some self-defeating life pattern.

The purpose of personal development groups is to invigorate people who feel stalled and frustrated. By offering a respectful and trustful atmosphere in which participants can freely examine, openly share, affirm, or disavow elements of their lives, these groups help members become more self-enlightened and intentional about their future pursuits. Sometimes this can be achieved without unearthing buried psychological dynamics. At other times, these dynamics must be identified and resolved. This need to attend to entrenched personality variables creates some overlap between personal development groups and psychotherapy groups. However, two essential differences exist. Personal development groups are more highly structured interventions than psychotherapy groups and, in the case of life-theme groups, have a single goal, such as overcoming jealousy or managing emotions.

GROUP THEORY

Just as in individual counseling and therapy, it is essential that the leaders of personal development groups operate from a theoretical framework that gives coherence and direction to the change process. As Corey notes, "leading a group without an explicit theoretical rationale is somewhat like attempting to fly a plane without a map and without instruments" (1981, p. 117).

As Cohen and Smith point out, different theoretical "camps" prescribe different group leadership procedures (1976). These range from those specifying rules or guidelines that the leader should adopt, to those which are more general and offer the leader more leeway in deciding how to structure the group.

Necessary elements to the creation of change in groups are: (1) an understanding of the individual; (2) the specific change sought; and, (3) a theory that accounts for how people change in the group context. Furthermore, the group change process requires that the group leader build a healthy group by setting appropriate norms, minimizing attrition, building cohesion, and encouraging disclosure and trust. To foster change, the leader must focus on building and orchestrating self-awareness, insight, and new behavior among participants.

CHANGE TECHNIQUES

The selection and use of specific change techniques are based on a number of factors:

1. Leader's Theoretical Framework

The specific change technique selected by the group leader must be consistent with the leader's model of group change and theoretical beliefs. Not all change techniques are compatible with a given theory. In some cases, use of techniques inappropriate to the leader's theoretical framework may undermine progress toward change.

2. Depth and Purpose of Change

Yalom outlines four levels at which the change or insight process can occur in groups (1975, p. 42). Group members may: (1) "gain a more objective perspective on their interpersonal behavior;" (2) "gain some understanding into what they are doing to and with other people;" (3) "learn why they do what they do to and with other people;" and, (4) "understand how they got to be the way they are."

Most personal development groups help participants gain insight at the "what" level, giving perspective on behavior and its effects on others. Other groups focus on the "why" of behavior. Traditionally, personal development groups have not attempted to intervene at the "how" or "history" level, usually reserved for psychotherapy groups. However, in the past five years, with the advent of life-theme groups, the demarcation between personal development groups and psychotherapy groups has blurred. Many leaders of life-theme groups believe members must gain insight into how problems were acquired in order to make meaningful changes.

Change techniques vary according to the level of intrapsychic resolution the leader seeks. For example, once the leader moves beyond the question of *what* a person is doing and attempts to establish the *why* and *how* of behavior, different forms of resistance are encountered, greater skill, patience, and timing is needed to build associations, and reality-testing becomes more challenging. Consolidating the gains of group members becomes more complex. All of these require the leader to adjust theory, technique, pace, and group structure.

3. Group Goals

To increase the self-awareness of group members, personal development group leaders usually choose techniques that build intra-group trust and disclosure, that handle resistance, and that encourage adoption of more functional and congruent behaviors. In contrast, psychotherapy group leaders rely more on techniques which help members understand the genesis of deeply-rooted personality disturbances.

Life-theme groups exist to achieve a specific, delimited goal common to all group members. Thus, the change effort is more highly concentrated and structured than in self-awareness groups, where needs, desires, and problems often differ dramatically among group members. The singular focus of life-theme groups allows the leader to anticipate group needs with precision, to prepare a format for diagnosing and resolving the problem, to become expert on specific problems, and to structure the change effort for maximum efficiency.

4. Time Constraints

Time is a factor influencing the leader's choice of change techniques. Personal development groups are usually composed of intact, relatively healthy people who are not deeply distressed. Motivation for change is generally not as high in these groups as in psychotherapy groups, which are composed of members whose problems cause more life disruption. Lower motivation often translates into reduced participant energy and time commitment, because the change they seek is truly optional. The leader must take this into account when choosing change techniques, using predominately those that make self-discovery as enjoyable and efficient as possible.

5. Leader Involvement

Personal development groups use two styles of leader involvement. The first, labelled by Shapiro as "intrapersonal orientation," is defined as *individual treatment occurring in a group setting* (1978). In such a setting, the leader is the change agent, focusing attention on one or two members of the group, while the other members observe or help clarify points, and occasionally role play, demonstrate resistance, or otherwise help influence change. The second treatment style is *group treatment designed for individuals*. Here, the change effort focuses on all participants simultaneously. The leader plans and conducts the exercises, activities, information dissemination and processing so that everyone is included and engaged.

Self-awareness groups are usually characterized as individual treatment in the group setting, while life-theme groups are normally group treatments designed for individuals. This difference influences which change techniques the leader uses and which curative factors are emphasized. Individual treatment in a group context requires leader behavior quite different from that needed in whole-group interactions.

6. Amount of Structure

In group counseling, structure refers to "intervention in a group's process that involves a set of specific instructions for participants to follow" (Kurtz, 1975, p. 168), and "the degree to which behavioral demands are implicit or explicit" (Bednar and Kaul, 1978, p. 770). Marks and Davis have identified three types of group structure — social, technical, and pacing (1975).

Social structure of a group refers to the leader's expectations of: (1) explicit and implicit norms, such as privacy, confidentiality, and disclosure; (2) interaction patterns in and out of group; and, (3) preparation of group members for treatment. Most personal development group leaders use pre-group screening to ensure that the needs of participants match the group's goals, methods, and style.

Compared to self-awareness groups, life-theme groups provide a higher degree of preplanned in-session social structure. The rationale is based on the shared purpose and the group's time-limited format. Through the use of social structure, life-theme group leaders attempt to limit negative interpersonal group processes. Through structured activities, interaction patterns can be prearranged to avoid undesired dynamics, such as silent power, non-productive self-disclosure, recognition-seeking, or domination of the group by one member.

Technical structure refers to the methods leaders use to amplify and clarify self-discovery and problem resolution, and consists of the exercises and activities that support and create change. Well in advance, leaders of life-theme groups plan the specific technical structure to be used, as well as the sequence in which it will be used, to foster change. Self-awareness group leaders, on the other hand, are unable to predict the types of issues that will be encountered, so they operate *in vivo*.

Pacing structure is important to personal development groups. The change process must be paced in a manner that allows for discovery, for working through resistance, for consolidating gains, and for appropriate termination. If the leader creates a slow pace, the chances of boredom and attrition increase. On the other hand, a rapid, jarring pace will result in resistance, threat, and dissatisfaction. Factors influencing a group's pace include: (1) the leader's theoretical framework; (2) commonality of purpose; (3) clarity, type, and acceptability to the members of the group's social structure; (4) adequate and proper use of technical structure; and, (5) the curative factors the leader considers essential.

7. Curative Factors

In his review of the research on curative factors in group psycho-therapy, Yalom lists ten factors he considers essential to positive change in a group context (1975, p. 3). These are: (1) imparting of information; (2) instillation of hope; (3) universality; (4) altruism; (5) corrective recapitulation of the primary family group; (6) development of socializing techniques; (7) imitative behavior; (8) interpersonal learning; (9) group cohesion; and, (10) catharsis. Many of these curative factors also operate in personal development groups.

Imparting information is stressed in both life-theme and self-awareness group sessions. However, life-theme group leaders are usually more explicit and direct in providing information about the problem at hand, and structure the group so that important information is transmitted, understood, integrated, and acted upon. Since self-awareness groups often focus on a variety of member problems simultaneously, the leader cannot readily preplan the use of information, but remains alert to occasions when specific information would promote group movement.

Instillation of hope, the feeling that one can overcome problems and have a better life, is important to participants of both types of personal development groups. Hope that improvement will be attained is sparked as fellow members experience change. In life-theme groups, hope is further supported by the existence of a plan for accomplishing a specific goal.

Universality, the knowledge that one is not alone or unique in his or her suffering, is a more important curative factor in self-awareness groups than in life-theme groups. Life-theme groups, because of their narrower focus, generate less of a sense of universality, and more of a feeling of commonality. Members in these groups find that the issue at hand is a problem for everyone in the group, and perhaps for many others, but that not everyone is troubled by this problem.

Altruism unfolds in almost every successful personal development group through participant feedback and sharing of feelings. However, altruism is a stronger curative force in self-awareness groups, where it emerges spontaneously as members feel engaged by the disclosures or struggles of others, than in life-theme groups,

where the roles of participants are more structured by specific assigned activities.

Corrective recapitulation of the primary family group is less
central to change in either type of personal development group than
it is in psychotherapy groups, where members usually have strong
feelings of dissatisfaction and disappointment with the primary family. While to some extent life-theme groups focus on autonomy, competition, and emotional-control issues originating from family
instruction, for the most part problems introduced in personal development groups stem from multiple sources.

Development of socializing techniques is either a goal or a by-
product of most group experiences, regardless of category. Increasing use of behavior rehearsal, role-playing, and between-session
assignments suggests that personal development group leaders are
giving more importance to this curative factor today than they did in
the past. For a few life-theme groups, such as one for overcoming
shyness, development of socializing techniques serves as a central
curative factor.

Imitative behavior is more likely to occur in members of self-
awareness groups than in life-theme groups. The more unstructured
atmosphere of self-awareness groups, the diversity of problems, and
the greater flexibility in relationships, increases the likelihood that
members will imitate other members or the group leader. Life-theme
groups—with their greater leader control, higher orchestration of
member roles, and less mystery about how change is created—create
fewer opportunities for imitative behaviors.

Interpersonal learning, the blending of self-awareness with self-
understanding, is a curative factor personal development group
leaders consider highly important. Yalom indicates that an important component of interpersonal learning is the "corrective emotional experience" (1975, p. 27). This comprises: "(1) a strong
expression of emotion which is interpersonally directed and which
represents risk taking; (2) a group supportive enough to permit this
risk taking; (3) reality-testing which allows the (member) to examine
the incident with the aid of consensual validation from others; (4) a
recognition of the inappropriateness of certain interpersonal feelings
and behavior or...of certain avoided interpersonal behaviors; and,
(5) the ultimate facilitation of the individual's ability to interact with

others more deeply and honestly."

"Corrective emotional experience" is essential to the change process in personal development groups. Self-awareness groups allow such experiences to unfold naturally as the group develops, leaving it up to the participant to decide if or when to take the risks necessary for interpersonal learning. In life-theme groups, specific exercises, activities, or between-session assignments are often used to create a context for the corrective emotional experience or to encourage the emergence of certain interpersonal dynamics.

Group cohesion is another important curative force in personal development groups. Both self-awareness and life-theme group leaders work to ensure the emergence of a sense of cohesiveness, the counterpart to the client-therapist relationship in individual counseling. The opportunity for participants to bond with the leader or with other members is far greater in a cohesive group than it is in a group which fails to attain a satisfactory level of cohesion.

Catharsis is essential if the leader of a personal development group expects interpersonal learning and group cohesiveness to develop to its fullest. In life-theme groups, the urge to express emotion is heightened by carefully-planned and well-timed intervention techniques. In self-awareness groups, the leader needs to take advantage of "the moment" to encourage the participant to express rather than withhold emotion.

In summary, many of the same curative factors operate in both personal development and psychotherapy groups, but the emphasis on specific factors varies. In particular, personal development groups place less emphasis on recapitulation of the primary family group, while seeking insight into the "what" and the "why" behavior levels. Of the two types of personal development groups, only life-theme groups normally focus on the question of "how" participants developed their problem.

TARGET POPULATION

The target population for personal development groups is anyone who has a "need to know" more about themselves, their problems, or the life-styles they have acquired. These groups serve functioning individuals who are psychologically intact, can reality-test adequately, and are willing to take the risks of giving and receiving personal feedback. For the more structured life-theme groups, the target population is restricted to those individuals for whom the group purpose is relevant.

LEADER FUNCTIONS

To ensure that the conditions for change exist in a group, leaders must accomplish a number of tasks.

1. Pre-Group Planning and Preparation

Certain issues must be resolved prior to the actual formation of a personal development group. If a group is to have more than one leader, group planning (and session management) should be a joint venture, focusing on the following questions:

Should the treatment process be designed as group treatment of individuals, or as individual treatment in a group context? Group composition, techniques used, curative factors emphasized, and other key change variables are affected by the treatment style selected. Since both treatment styles successfully promote personal development, style choice is a matter of leader preference.

To what extent does the leader want to facilitate change? The responsibility the leader is willing to assume for change varies from taking minimal responsibility (set the time, place, and basic ground rules), to exercising responsibility for creating the context for change as well as the strategy or process for creating the change. During the past few years, there has been a trend among personal development group leaders to accept more responsibility for facilitating change. Supporting this trend is the greater availability of change techniques, more information about how strategies for change can be structured, and increasing leader experience with change techniques.

Should the group be open or closed? Should it accept new members at any time during its operation, or should it begin and end with the same members? Closed groups have the advantage of progressing through predictable phases, allowing the leader to plan intervention strategies accordingly. For example, Shapiro outlines four-phases of group development: preparation, learning the ground rules, therapeutic intervention, and termination (1978). Gazda, on the other hand, lists exploration, transition, action, and termination (1978). While their labels differ, the underlying descriptions of member needs, and the tasks associated with each group development phase, are similar. In open groups, the progression through phases is less predictable and certain, especially if a substantial turnover in membership occurs.

What is the ideal group size? Group size is an important consideration. If a leader employs the "individual treatment in group" approach, group size must be limited to the number of participants the leader can attend to in the allotted time. However, if the leader chooses a "group treatment" style, the number of participants can be increased depending on the change strategy and techniques employed. Some highly structured life-theme groups using a group treatment format can accommodate 20 or more participants.

Should the group be open-ended or time-limited? Since many people participating in self-awareness and life-theme groups are not experiencing deep discomfort or despair, they seem to prefer time-limited sessions. The added pressure on the leader of life-theme groups to accomplish specific goals within a certain number of hours requires greater reliance on structure and technique to make the best use of in-session and between-session time.

Which curative factors should be emphasized to create change? An important element of pre-group planning is identifying the curative factors the leader wishes to have operative during the change process. The specific curative factors emphasized are related to the leader's basic theory of personality change, and to the type of change the leader seeks to accomplish.

Should the treatment procedure be structured or largely unstructured? A key leader function is to determine whether the group's purpose will be better served with a highly-, moderately-, or minimally-structured format. In general, personal development groups tend to be more structured if the group's members share a common problem, or if the amount of change expected by participants requires a highly efficient use of time.

2. Formation of the Group

Once the basic issues of treatment style, group format, leader responsibility, curative factors, and structure are resolved, the challenge to the leader centers on formation of the actual group. The group leader must attract a pool of applicants for the proposed intervention within the ethical boundary of informed consent. Corey offers some advice about what an announcement about a group might include (1981, p. 24). He suggests: information about the type of group, the program, times and place of meetings, procedures for joining, a statement about what the members can expect from the leader, the leader's qualifications and background, the targeted population, and the fees (if any) being charged.

Selection of actual group members from the larger applicant pool is the next important leader task. Member selection has a dual focus. First, both the leader and the prospective group member must determine whether the intervention is appropriate to that individual's needs. Second, the group leader must assess the readiness of the prospective member to handle the interactions and peer feedback that will inevitably occur in group sessions.

Another key leader function is preparing members for what the group will actually be like. Many prospective members have questions about format, confidentiality, norms, expectations, and some have anticipatory anxiety about how they will be received by the leader and by other group members. Inevitably, failure to prepare members adequately for the group experience results in confusion, hesitancy, and negative interpersonal processes in early sessions. Studies of group leadership stress the value of actively and completely preparing group members for the work they are about to undertake (Corey, 1981; Eagan, 1976; and Yalom, 1970, 1975). Such preparation can be accomplished either through pre-group individual interviews, or by meeting with all participants in a pre-group session to answer questions, establish norms, and set goals.

3. Early Group Leader Functions

During the first few sessions, the leader has an important role in several activities. These are: (1) open each group session in such a way that members become immediately focused and engaged by the task at hand; (2) build the cohesion and trust essential to self-inquiry and disclosure; (3) help resolve the role dilemmas that participants typically grapple with in the first few sessions, such as being controlled or vulnerable, or being supportive or challenging, and point out the naturalness of such struggles; (4) encourage members to explore themselves by demonstrating appropriate interaction patterns, such as feedback and confrontation, and attributes, such as respect and openness; (5) help the group work with initial disclosures of fears, vulnerabilities, and beliefs; (6) establish a safe and productive growth environment; and (7) reinforce perceptions of the leader's skill and control.

4. The Working-Through Phase

The previously-described leader functions will, to a large extent, ensure a smooth progression to this most important phase of discovery and rebuilding, in which the process of changing perceptions, behaviors, thoughts, and feelings occurs.

Since healthy change demands an accurate, appropriate, and efficient self-inquiry procedure, the leader must either employ or help group members develop a discovery process. While participants are expected to share dissatisfactions, fears, and hopes, these disclosures are usually not sufficiently enlightening to stimulate corrective action. In order to gain more information, perspective, or context about the motivation or energy fueling the desire to change, the leader must use specific techniques designed to encourage participant self-inquiry.

While this additional inquiry is necessary to build a strategy for change in and of itself it is insufficient to create the amount of change desired. But as higher quality information is unearthed, and associative deficits are revealed, the group leader can demonstrate how inadequately or inappropriately developed cause-and-effect linkages can be replaced with more functional, accurate beliefs. Association-building has a central place in every personal development group, although its style and focus will depend on the theoretical preference of the group leader.

A certain amount of resistance, conflict, defensiveness, and acting-out will occur in the working-through phase. A primary function of the group leader is to manage such predictable hindrances to the change process, so that participants can overcome their self-inflicted interferences, and develop their natural abilities to handle these interferences.

The final working-through activity involves monitoring and maintaining the progress of participants. Most personal development groups are offered weekly and last long enough for members to not only identify desired changes, but also to try out such changes. The leader's role is to help members reality-test the changes they contemplate to trouble-shoot the problems they may encounter, and to encourage modification as needed.

5. The Ending Phase

The ending phase of personal development groups includes: (1) consolidation of gains; (2) review of progress; (3) commitment to new plans; and, (4) suggestions for further assistance. Most personal development group members will not want to require further assistance. However, one of the leader's last functions should be making appropriate referrals for those who do, and encouraging a commitment to ongoing change for those who do not.

LEADER TRAINING

Many studies have sought to identify the ideal temperament or personal characteristics associated with effective group leadership. Rogers (1961, 1970), Yalom (1970, 1975), and Corey (1981) are among others who subscribe to the importance of the change agent's personal attributes in promoting growth. For example, Corey identified 12 personal attributes he believes are closely related to good leadership (1981, p. 86). These are: presence, personal power, courage, willingness to confront oneself, self-awareness, sincerity, authenticity, sense of identity, belief in group process, enthusiasm, inventiveness and creativity, and stamina.

As well as possessing certain personal attributes, leaders of life-theme and self-awareness groups should have expertise in the following six areas.

First, knowledge of personality development and structure is of critical importance to the group leader. In order to develop the skills needed to help people modify or affirm their belief systems, leaders must have an informed perspective on how individuals form self-concepts, values, and other enduring qualities.

Second, the leader should understand the curative factors that operate in groups, how they promote change, and which are important to specific types of groups.

Third, the group leader should understand how the various elements of a psychotherapeutic change system harmonize and interact to support change in a group context. The leader must be able to pace the elements in a change system so that the methods used to promote change do not trigger negative interpersonal group dynamics.

Fourth, the group leader should be aware of the importance of structure in encouraging growth in group members, and be able to determine the amount of structure necessary to ensure effective group functioning. In particular, the leader needs to understand and be skillful in using structure to promote intrapersonal learning, to support group cohesion, to impart information, to stablilize group dynamics, to handle resistance, and to encourage catharsis.

Fifth, the leader should be conversant with the change technologies that can be applied to amplify, clarify, inform, or demonstrate points of interest to group members. New techniques, activities, information, exercises, and other leader-initiated change strategies are constantly being developed. The effective group leader skilled in the use of such methods can select the most appropriate method for the challenge at hand.

Sixth, the personal development group leader must understand small group dynamics. Without an understanding of how people function in groups, the leader is unlikely to be able to properly form a group, support its movement through the phases of group development, and end it effectively.   .

A LIFE-THEME GROUP IN ACTION

Part of a session from a life-theme group entitled, "Perfectionism:

The Double-Edged Sword," illustrates the foregoing discussion. This group was developed and co-led by Barnett and McNamara (1983), with the author of this chapter serving as a design consultant.

The group format was constructed to accommodate 14 pre-selected participants in eight two-hour sessions. A comprehensive manual was prepared, detailing the group's purpose and format, session-by-session goals and objectives, session outlines, lecturettes, exercises, and worksheets.

The group's purpose was to help participants eliminate perfectionistic behavior and to learn to strive in more functional and satisfying ways. To achieve this purpose, Barnett and McNamara identified a number of specific content and process goals (1983, p. 5).

The group's content goals included: (1) define perfectionism and distinguish it from healthy motivation and striving; (2) show how perfectionism actually fails to lead to the desired consequences; (3) show how internal conflicts produce perfectionistic tendencies; (4) show how negative thoughts, beliefs, or feelings about oneself serve to maintain perfectionism; (5) describe how the sequence of thoughts, feelings, and behaviors create a perpetual cycle of perfectionistic striving; (6) outline key attitudinal and cognitive guidelines for overcoming habitual perfectionistic tendencies; and, (7) establish an internal locus of control and change.

The group's process goals included: (1) establish a sense of group cohesion; (2) equalize the rate of participation of group members; (3) establish an atmosphere of openness and safety for self-disclosure; and, (4) provide experiences to enable clients to derive high levels of personal meaning from the group.

One of the group's session outlines will show how these goals were implemented.

Session 1

OBJECTIVE: Define perfectionism and distinguish it from healthy motivation and striving: (1) to help alert participants to the illusion that perfection is attainable; (2) to clearly define perfectionism and distinguish it from healthy striving; and, (3) to help each participant identify personal patterns of striving for perfection.

Introduction (10-15 minutes): Leaders introduce themselves. Briefly state how they got interested in perfectionism. Offer brief overview of the group: "We plan to look at these areas:" (1) what is perfectionism?; (2) what role(s) does it play in each of our lives?; (3) what are the advantages and disadvantages of perfectionism?; (4) how did we learn to be perfectionistic?; and, (5) what strategies can we explore that will change our dealings with perfectionism so life is more convenient, satisfying, and less self-defeating?

Offer quick look at today's session: (1) get acquainted with each other; (2) begin to explore what perfectionism means; and, (3) get a sense of what people want or need from the group.

Parallel Lines exercise (10 minutes): (goal) This exercise is designed to act as an icebreaker to promote group involvement and to begin development of group cohesion. It also provides an initial look at some aspects of perfectionism.

Ground rules (5 minutes): (1) come on time; (2) come every week and stay until the end of the session; (3) call and tell one of the leaders if you can't make it; (4) drop out policy: contact one of the leaders and arrange for a brief meeting with one or both to discuss why you have decided to leave; (5) confidentiality policy; (6) video-taping policy - consent form; (7) offer feedback if we are not meeting your needs; please do this as we go along rather than wait until the end; and, (8) have fun!

Whys and Whats exercise (30 minutes): (goal) This exercise is designed to help group members gain clarity on their goals for the group and begin to understand how they are perfectionistic. It also aims to begin to build alliances between members.

Continuum exercise (20-30 minutes): (goal) This exercise is designed to promote group involvement and to act as an icebreaker activity; it also gives each person an opportunity to assess his or her own perfectionism.

Lecturette (15 minutes): What is perfectionism?

Homework (5 minutes): Now that we have presented our definition of perfectionism, we would like to have you consider what perfectionism means to you. The meaning is probably somewhat different for each of you. Before the next session, we would like you to think over what you heard and experienced today and try and come up with a brief personal definition of perfectionism that you can share with the group.

This outline of Session 1 illustrates that the leaders' efforts centered on: (1) accomplishing the content goal of defining perfectionism and distinguishing it from healthy motivation and striving; (2) accomplishing the process goals of establishing a sense of group cohesion; (3) equalizing the rate of participation of group members; and, (4) establishing an atmosphere of openness and safety for self-disclosure through the use of specially-created exercises and lecturettes. Each of the other seven session outlines of "Perfectionism: The Double-Edged Sword" served to accomplish similar content and process goals.

Certain curative factors were relied upon in all of the group's eight sessions: *instillation of hope, imparting of information, interpersonal learning, group cohesion,* and *catharsis.* Other curative factors — *altruism, development of socializing techniques,* and to a lesser extent, *corrective recapitulation of the primary family group* — were operative in many, but not all, sessions. The emergence of these curative factors was carefully orchestrated by the leaders through the effective use of social, technical, and pacing structure.

EVIDENCE OF EFFECTIVENESS

Evidence of the effectiveness of personal development groups to promote change comes from several sources: studies using experimental designs, researcher-designed measures or questionnaires, expert ratings of behavior segments, and structured and unstructured self-reports. Evaluation data from each shows that personal development groups, whether self-awareness or life-theme, produce change in the desired or predicted direction. The magnitude of the change, however, varies considerably across types of groups within this category.

Studies employing appropriate experimental design have shown significant results in a substantial majority of cases (Gazda, 1978; Lieberman, Yalom, and Miles, 1973). Gazda, in his review of over 300 studies on the outcomes of group counseling, states: "a significant majority of published studies in recent years has reported at least one statistically significant result consistent with predictions"

(1978, p. 255). Despite this favorable appraisal of the results obtained through group counseling approaches, Gazda believes that more research on groups must be conducted.

Because a group's participants often seek outcomes that are at variance with one another, researchers have turned increasingly toward the use of researcher-designed questionnaires in order to individualize the evaluation process and to identify specific participant accomplishments. For instance, structured self-report measures, such as the Goal Attainment Scaling Model of Paritsky and Magoon (1982), and expert ratings of behavior segments (Eisler, Miller, and Blanchard, 1973; Eisler, Hersen, Miller, and Blanchard, 1975) are being used to better determine outcomes.

EMPLOYMENT

Since personal development group leaders are typically broadly-trained professional counselors or psychologists, very few make their livings by offering these groups exclusively. Nevertheless, personal development groups are offered in a wide variety of settings — in educational institutions as well as industry, in private practices as well as for-profit and non-profit agencies.

SUMMARY

Personal development groups offer a powerful tool in the group worker's arsenal of change techniques. Life-theme and self-awareness groups represent different degrees of specificity for helping people achieve change, and their formats cover the range of group member needs for structure and depth of inquiry. Life-theme groups, in particular, are likely to continue their current rapid growth in sophistication and popularity. Predicted to be one of the therapies of choice in the future, life-theme groups are most attractive because they use both the leader's and the member's time to extremely good advantage.

REFERENCES

Barnett, D.C. and McNamara, K.: Perfectionism: The double edged sword. Structured group manual. Austin, Counseling-Psychological Services Center, The University of Texas at Austin, 1983.

Bednar, R.L. and Kaul, T.J.: Experimental group research: Current Perspectives. *Handbook of Psychotherapy and Behavior Change: An Empirical Analysis* (2nd ed.). New York: Wiley, 1978.

Cohen, A.M. and Smith, R.D.: *The Critical Incident in Growth Groups.* La Jolla: University Associates Publishers, 1976.

Corey, G.: *Theory and Practice of Group Counseling.* Monterey: Brooks/Cole, 1981.

Eagan, G.: *Interpersonal Living: A Skills/Contract Approach to Human Relations Training in Groups.* Monterey:Brooks/Cole, 1976.

Eisler, R., Hersen, J., Miller, P., and Blanchard, E.: Situational determinants of assertive behavior. *Journal of Consulting and Clinical Psychology, 43:*330-340, 1975.

Eisler, R., Miller, P., and Hersen, J.: Components of assertive behavior. *Journal of Clinical Psychology, 29:*295-299, 1973.

Gazda, G.M.: *Group Counseling: A Developmental Approach* (2nd ed.) Boston: Allyn and Bacon, 1978.

Kurtz, R.R. Structured experiences in groups: A theoretical and research discussion. *The 1975 Annual Handbook for Group Facilitators.* La Jolla: University Associates Publishers, 167-171, 1975.

Lieberman, M.S., Yalom, I.D., and Miles, M.B.: *Encounter Groups: First Facts.* New York: Basic Books, 1973.

Marks, S.E. and Davis, W.L.: Use of structures in experiential learning. Paper presented at the meeting of the *Third Annual Conference of Group.* Philadelphia, 1975.

Paritzky, R.S. and Magoon, T.M.: Goal attainment scaling model for assessing group counselors. *Personnel and Guidance Journal, 6:*381-384, 1982.

Rogers, C.: *On Becoming a Person.* Boston: Houghton Mifflin, 1961.

Rogers, C.: *Carl Rogers on Encounter Groups.* New York: Harper and Row, 1970.

Shapiro, J.S. *Methods of Group Psychotherapy and Encounter: A Tradition of Innovation.* Itasca: Peacock, 1978.

Yalom, I.D.: *The Theory and Practice of Group Psychotherapy.* New York: Basic Books, 1970.

Yalom, I.D.: *The Theory and Practice of Group Psychotherapy.* (2nd ed.). New York: Basic Books, 1975.

CHAPTER 4

SKILL DEVELOPMENT
Human Relations Skills Training Groups

R. JAMES CLACK

HUMAN relations skill training (HRST) groups train individuals in the skills that establish and maintain effective interpersonal relationships. Human relations skills include listening, speaking, and non-verbal behaviors that prevent misunderstanding, promote understanding and problem solving, and generate good will.

HRST groups are learning laboratories focusing on acquiring and improving participants' ability to communicate effectively in dyadic and small group settings. In this context, *learning laboratory* means a situation in which a trainer develops and presents a curriculum of activities such as instruction, demonstration, simulation, role-playing, skill practice, and corrective feedback to promote the learning of a specific set of skills. Learning laboratory also implies the experiential nature of the HRST group. Skills are taught in an environment where trial of new behavior and corrective feedback are prominent features. Group interaction therefore, becomes a major force for learning.

The goal of HRSTG's is to promote effective communication. This requires that participants develop an awareness of the need for, and values of, human relations training and also that they acquire behavioral skills to implement these values. Even well-intentioned individuals who value human relationships may flounder in their efforts to establish and maintain relationships if they do not have

63

behavioral skills. Some individuals operating as technicians in the use of the behavioral skills of human relations, lack awareness of, and commitment to, appropriate goals and values. This diminishes their efforts to establish effective human relationships.

INTERVENTION LEVEL

The individual is the focus of HRST interventions. The goal of such training is for individual participants to learn, practice, and improve these skills so that they can proficiently apply them in "back home" settings and situations, e.g., work, home, community. The training focus is upon the growth and learning of the individual participant. However, attention also must be paid to the functions of the group as the medium and the support for individuals' learning. The group setting serves as a laboratory for this type of training in that: (a) a critical mass of individuals is available; (b) participants may practice the dyadic use of human relations skills and receive corrective feedback from a range of other individuals; (c) groups are available for participants to learn in, since a number of the human relations skills are focused upon small group membership and leadership activities; and (d) cohesion, team building, trust, collaboration, and other group dynamics generally develop as a by-product of individuals and groups helping other individuals work toward skill acquisition and refinement.

INTERVENTION PURPOSE

The purpose of human relations skill group training is for individual participants to learn and be able to competently use a consolidated series of skills. Selection of the exact nature of these skills varies, but major emphases are generally given to basic dyadic communication skills and small group membership and leadership skills.

In order for such skill training to be effective, participants must already possess, or begin to adopt, an attitudinal set supportive of human relations. In broad terms, successful participants must (1) value other human beings, (2) must believe that it is important to treat others with respect, and (3) must be convinced that treating others in such a humanistic manner will lead to both improved task accomplishment and increased good will. If participants have not been screened, so that only those holding such a value stance are included, then part of the training should focus on the development of such awarenesses.

MAIN INTERVENTION CHANGE TECHNIQUES USED

The major change methodologies used in this skills training intervention are adapted from micro-counseling (Ivey, 1971) training paradigms. The presentation and training of each skill follows a basic five-step outline.

First, the trainer introduces each skill with a lecture that generally does not exceed twenty minutes in length. In these "lecturettes," the following dimensions are covered: (a) a rationale for the use of this particular behavior; (b) a brief summary of any research that supports the use of a particular behavioral skill; (c) the common-sense reasons for why this skill is used and why it is effective; (d) a definition of the skill in behavioral terms (this is what one does in order to perform this skill effectively), and (e) comments on the appropriate use of the skill in terms of both time and purpose.

Second, the trainee receives a written summary of the content of the lecture. This summary is concise and generally does not exceed one type-written page. Thus, the trainee has available a set of ready references describing the behavioral skills being learned.

Third, the trainer demonstrates the use of the skill under discussion, showing how the skill's absence or its ineffective use influences an interaction. This is followed by a demonstration of the effective use of the skill, either "live," by role-play or simulation, or by media presentation, such as film, video tape replay, or audio tape replay. In any case, the trainee sees and hears the actual behavior to be learned.

Fourth, the trainees then practice the use of the particular skill in role-playing situations. Then, immediately upon completion of practice, each trainee receives critical performance feedback from the trainer and/or other trainees. This feedback pinpoints those skill elements each trainee performed effectively, as well as those aspects either performed ineffectively or omitted entirely. Trainees who ineffectively perform or omit some aspect of the skill are given individualized instruction and further effective performance demonstrations by the trainer.

Fifth, and finally, the trainees continue to practice using each of the behavioral skills, receiving constructive feedback until competency in the use of the skills is attained.

This training paradigm contains a wide range of proven learning strategies that enable trainees to change their behaviors. The training materials are presented through a variety of sensory modes, i.e., hearing, seeing, reading, and doing. This "hands on" learning, whereby trainees have the opportunity to try out and practice a skill, is reinforced with immediate performance feedback. Also, each trainee has the opportunity to practice the behavioral skill until mastery is attained.

It must be noted that human relations skills are taught in a cumulative fashion, beginning with the more elementary and moving to the complex. As each skill is learned, it becomes part of the trainee's repertoire of skills. In many respects, this training paradigm is similar to time-honored methods used to teach individuals to learn to play a musical instrument, to drive a car, or to play a sport.

In the fourth and fifth steps of the learning paradigm, positive group interaction is imperative to promote skill acquisition. A spirit of cooperation and collaboration among group members is needed. They promote each other's learning by serving as "helpful" interviewees or clients, by giving accurate and well-intentioned feedback, and by serving as a supportive learning community.

Often, a trainer may find that group members enter training with a bent toward being competitive, uncooperative, and nonhelpful. Such members may appear to want to develop human relations skills for themselves. But in their desire to be the best or the "star" of the group, their behavior may actually impede the learning of other group members. Such behavior includes: (1) being an antagonistic or difficult interviewee in practice situations; (2) giving inaccurate or excessively critical feedback; (3) being unwilling to give the time for others to do skill practice. A trainer may address such group membership problems in a variety of ways: by introducing an exercise, such as the X-Y: a Three Way Intergroup Competition (Pfeiffer and Jones, 1976); by giving corrective feedback; or by explaining the advantages of cooperation and collaboration for learning.

PRIMARY INTERVENTION TARGET POPULATION

The potential target populations for human relations skill training are as diverse as the number of people who live, work, or socialize with each other. The need for effective communicators who have respect for the dignity of others has been identified at all levels of business, industry, government, educational and social enterprises, service organizations, and the military. In sum, any individual or group of individuals are good candidates for human relations skill training.

PRIMARY LEADER FUNCTIONS

The primary functions of a leader of HRST programs include those of designer-organizer, teacher, demonstrator, model, feedback agent, evaluator, supporter, and theoretician.

Once a leader decides to present a human relations skill development workshop, seminar, or training program, the task of *designing* the exact nature of the training becomes the preeminent function. In some cases, the trainer may have nearly complete freedom in design; in others, the training must be designed so that it will meet the specialized needs of members of a specific trainee group. In either case, to design the training format the leader must: (1) select the skills to be taught; (2) select the media to be used; (3) design the specific training paradigm; (4) select and prepare co-trainers (if any are to be used); (5) schedule all training activities; and, (6) plan evaluation methodologies. Additionally, the leader may have responsibility for choosing the type and location of physical facilities to be used, seating arrangements, grouping and sub-grouping of trainees, the timing and menu for "coffee breaks," and a myriad of other details that contribute to the ultimate effectiveness of the training.

A second major function of the leader is *teaching*. It is necessary for a human relations trainer to operate from a sound base of knowledge and theory. Also, in the teaching role, the trainer must transmit expertise in a manner, and use language, that is readily understood by trainees. Effective trainers present lectures and lead discussions using clear, concise language, replete with examples and analogies that are part of the trainees' frame of reference.

Third, the trainer must be an effective *demonstrator* of human relations skills. The trainer demonstrates the effective use of each skill introduced in the training paradigm. It is imperative that the trainer have such skills, to be able to teach them to others.

Fourth, the trainer is a *model* of effective human relations skills during both formal and informal contacts with trainees. As a model, the trainer demonstrates effective communication and problem-solving skills and exhibits concern and respect for the trainees. Such modeling serves as a potent reinforcer of the training.

A fifth function of the trainer is to provide skill performance *feedback* to trainees. The high quality feedback that a leader must give should be accurate and specific. It should pinpoint exactly what is effective or ineffective and, in the latter case, what needs to be done to correct performance. Further, effective feedback must be as immediate as is possible to be reinforcing or corrective.

A sixth function of the leader is to serve as a *support* agent for the trainees. For many training participants, the proper use of human relations skills is new and uncomfortable. Learning such skills is particularly difficult for: (1) those who are socially introverted; (2) those who typically take an authoritative stance in interpersonal relations; and, (3) those who already see themselves as human relations "experts," even though observing their behavior and the reactions of others suggests the contrary. Further, many trainees will be participating in a formal training situation for the first time in a long while. Such people often exhibit anxiety and a lack of confidence in their ability to learn new methods of interpersonal communication. Occasionally, trainees, particularly those "sent" by their company or organization, will be antagonistic and resistant to the training. Reassurance, clarification of the relevance of the training, and reducing the training experience threat should be provided these trainees.

Finally, a major function of the leader is to convert the theory, research, and techniques of such disciplines as psychology, management, and social work, into a language readily understandable by those unfamiliar with the technical terminology and jargon of business management and the social sciences. Successful group leaders and trainers de-mystify the learning process by speaking in understandable terms.

GROUP LEADER TRAINING

The training required for a skilled human relations trainer includes a knowledge-skills conglomerate comprising: (1) basic coun seling communication skills; (2) small group leadership and dynamics; (3) constructive feedback; (4) the design, implementation, and evaluation of a laboratory learning model; and, (5) the ability to relate effectively with individuals of diverse backgrounds.

The counseling skills mentioned above are commonly taught in "techniques" classes, or as pre-practicum laboratories in both clinical and counselor training. Carkhuff (1969), Ivey (1971), Danish and Hauer (1973), Gazda, Asbury, Balzer, Childers, Desselle, and Walters (1973), Egan (1970), Benjamin (1974), and Johnson (1972) are typical authors of models and training manuals in counseling, human relations, or interpersonal skills. All of the models contain certain basic skills in common, including: (a) paying attention to another person by posture, eye contact, and staying with a topic of conversation; (b) encouraging another person to talk by using general, open-ended questions or leading statements: (c) communicating understanding to another person by identifying and rephrasing the content of what they say and by noting any affective state that goes with the person's verbal statements; and, (d) clarifying another's communication by aiding them to be specific and concrete in what they say.

Knowledge and skills in small group leadership and dynamics appear to derive from two sources: a study of the theoretical formulations regarding small group dynamics; and, experience as a member and leader of small counseling, discussion, seminar, and similar groups. Yalom (1975), Solomon and Berzon (1972), Napier and

Gershenfeld (1981), Diedrich and Dye (1972), Rogers (1970), Johnson and Johnson (1975), Egan (1970), and Berg and Landreth (1979) exemplify authors who have addressed both the theoretical and technical aspects of small group work. A variety of programs ranging from formal academic training in counseling, clinical, and industrial-organizational psychology at colleges and universities, through nationally known training organizations and institutes, to weekend groups and seminars offered in local communities are available for basic training in small group dynamics and skills.

Training in giving and receiving feedback can be found in the sources mentioned above. In brief, the leader should be able to use feedback, which is defined as a message portraying how one's behavior is affecting others. The effective use of feedback requires that it be: (a) timed appropriately, so that the recipient is in as proper a frame of mind as is possible to receive the feedback; (b) specific, in that it tells recipients *precisely* their behavior and its effects; (c) based upon a pre-established set of performance criteria; and, (d) given for the purpose of improving trainee performance, not to simply evaluate, and certainly not as a punitive measure.

The ability to design, implement, and evaluate an experiential learning model is an essential requirement of the skilled human relations trainer. Reading and understanding the foundations of laboratory learning from such authors as Bradford, Gibb, and Benne (1964), and Benne, Bradford, Gibb and Lippitt (1975), as well as experience as a participant and co-leader of laboratory or experiential learning workshops, is necessary background for the human relations training leader.

However, the ability to communicate effectively — omitting jargon and relating with a variety of audiences in layman's terms — does not appear in the curriculum of any training program. Instead, this ability derives from a leader's experience and ability to profit from feedback received from trainees.

SUPPORTIVE THEORY

Conceptual support for human relations skill training groups comes primarily from three sources: (1) business management literature rooted in the social sciences; (2) laboratory training literature emanating from the National Training Laboratory movement; and, (3) counselor training literature, in this case from that of microcounseling (Ivey, 1971).

As a result of the 1924 Western Electric Company study of the effects of light intensity upon work production, a human relations school of thought developed in industrial and business management. Although no consistent relationship was found between changes in lighting and changes in work efficiency, behavioral scientists noted that workers participating in the study increased production because management paid attention to them, treated them with importance, and valued their opinions. A movement emphasizing people-oriented management sprang from this "Hawthorne Effect." Human relations training emerged from the research in workers' attitudes, morale, and managerial styles. With its focus upon managers learning the requisite skills and attitudes necessary to relate effectively with those they supervised, human relations training presaged organization development. It is the grandparent of such interventions as laboratory training, team-building, conflict management, job enrichment, participative management, and other interventions. All aim at increasing the active participation of employees in the organizational life of business and industries.

The laboratory method of training originated at a 1946 Workshop on Inter-Group Relations at the State Teachers College in New Britain, Connecticut. At this meeting the concept of the T-Group (training group) was discovered. Workshop participants met daily for formal presentations and structured discussions about the presentation's content. Feedback given to participants about their behavior stimulated informal and unplanned conversations during the unstructured evening hours. Leaders soon noted that these informal encounters led to more understanding and behavior change than did the formal program. It was apparent that the participants' experiences plus feedback from observations and analysis of the experiences, led to more learning about personal and group behavior than did lectures or seminars in which participants played a passive recipient role (Benne, Bradford, Gibb, and Lippitt, 1975).

The early history of T-groups was characterized by their being rather unstructured and generally having no pre-planned content.

The curriculum of the T-group became whatever members of the group desired. Such groups were usually titled intrapersonal or interpersonal growth groups (typical are those offered under the auspices of the National Training Laboratory [NTL] in the 1950's, '60's, and early '70's). As the group movement grew, the use of structured exercises, assessment, games, and simulations developed as techniques to stimulate and focus group members' attention. The human relations skill training group structured the entire experience into a curriculum focusing on acquiring individual and small group communication and leadership skills. This is an example of a hybrid T-group employing the principles of member participation, behavioral observation, and feedback as learning devices. However, in this hybrid, the unstructured nature of early groups was rejected in favor of a highly organized and focused format. The theory behind this approach is fairly common-sense: behavior is observed; feedback is given; new behavior is encouraged; and, resultant new behavior is tried, practiced, and learned.

The curriculum of the training described in this chapter is not original. It is a revision and adaptation of Ivey's (1971) pioneering work in developing, defining, and clarifying microcounseling—a method for training counselors in basic communication and helping skills. Briefly stated, microcounseling is a single skills approach to learning new behavior. A single skill is specified and defined, a written description presented, a demonstration shown, participants try out the new skill behavior, then receive feedback on their performance by observers, and, finally, continue to practice the skill and receive feedback until mastery is reached. A major aid in microcounseling training is the use of video taping and replay of group members' skill performance, with critique as part of the feedback process. The preferred format, when time and equipment are available, is the use of video (or audio) taping, although "live" observer feedback often serves this function.

The basic group leadership skills used in this human relations skill training format were developed by Clack and Conyne (1974). The skills are an adaptation of individual skills gleaned from Ivey's (1971) work, and from the group skills described by Johnson and Johnson (1975).

ILLUSTRATIVE INTERVENTION CASE EXAMPLE

The following describes a 40-hour human relations course presented over a two week period (four hours per day for ten days). The participant group was comprised of U.S. Air Force non-commissioned officers. Most of the 24 participants were volunteers (motivated by the fact that accumulating education credit is one route to more rapid promotion). A few of the participants attended the course at the command of their superior officers. For all practical purposes, volunteers and non-volunteers were indistinguishable in terms of their motivation and level of performance (the fact that two hours of undergraduate credit accompanies completion of the workshop appears to have no significant influence on participants' behavior).

The goals for the course were to improve participants' communication and problem-solving skills in both dyadic and small group settings. More specifically, objectives for improving of communication skills centered on each participant's ability to (1) perform higher quality listening, (2) identify both the content and underlying affective components of other participants' conversation, and, (3) accurately communicate that understanding to the group. Participants are expected to learn and use communication skills within a counseling/problem-solving frame of reference, i.e., (a) assisting others in identifying and clarifying concerns; (b) aiding others in specifying what they want to do about the concern; (c) helping others develop, explore and then choose a course of action; and, (d) devising a way to implement an action plan. The course format gives attention to the above objectives for both one-to-one (dyadic) relationships, and for small group situations. An overview of the training is presented in the following day-to-day description.

Day 1. In the first four-hour block, the leader introduced the group to the human relations skills training course by discussing goals, expected changes in participants' communication behavior, the learning format, and administrative procedures (including course registration and grading procedures). Also, the two major goals for the group, improved human relations communications skills and improved interpersonal problem-solving skills (in both dyadic and small group settings) are explained and clarified.

The leader continues the introduction by explaining the micro-counseling paradigm to be applied to all skills training. The leader notes that each skill will be clearly defined, a rationale for its use will be explained, a demonstration of the skill will be presented, a written behavioral description of the skill will be handed out, participants will then practice each skill, and, finally, feedback regarding participant skill performance will be given. The introduction takes approximately 60 minutes.

The leader then initiates a 30-minute period of getting acquainted. In this particular training model, participants are asked to pair off and interview each other. Typical material discussed includes: names, hometowns, job assignments, family, hobbies and interests, and their use of human relations skills both on the job and in their everyday life. Once the interviews have been completed, participants introduce each other to the total group using the information acquired from the interviews. This early effort at team-building also introduces members to the importance of group interaction, collaboration and cooperation.

Then, an activity designed to dramatically portray a number of common barriers to effective human relations and communication occurs. The leader tells the participants a story containing a mathematical problem. Each participant takes a position. Then the leader asks participants to attempt to convince each other of the "correct answer." Encouraging the group to communicate among themselves and arrive at a consensus, the leader is unconcerned whether or not the group solves the problem. The exercise simply allows the leader to observe participants' human relations and communication behavior during the activity. Invariably, participants exhibit a vast array of behaviors antithetical to effective human relations. They tend to explain their own positions by using volume, repetition, and expressions of anger toward those whom oppose their opinions.

When the leader calls an end to the activity and asks participants to reflect on the activity by analyzing their human relations skills, most participants display sheepish grins. The point has been made. In everyday attempts to solve problems, often we do not treat each other respectfully, frequently we do not communicate effectively. The leader summarizes the activity by reviewing a number of behaviors that most people use but which deter them in their efforts to relate effectively with others. The leader concludes the first day's session with a half-hour lecturette and discussion of a model for effective communication. This model focuses on perceptual and attitudinal "filters" which distort both what is heard and said. The theme of this presentation spotlights how participants can profit from training in listening, understanding, speaking with clarity, and attending to non-verbal cues.

Day 2. After a short review of the previous day's activities, the first major skill training activity is introduced — attending behavior. The leader recruits a volunteer willing to be interviewed by the leader, and then asks for a description of the interviewee's hometown. The leader proceeds to ignore the interviewee (by looking out the window, checking the time, reading some nearby papers, yawning, looking bored, and so on). The interview comes to a halt as the interviewee either falls silent or confronts the leader about his lack of attention.

The leader then asks the participants to pair off and replicate what they have just observed, with a promise that "we will talk about it after everybody has had a chance to experience it." After all participants have engaged in the mock interview, the leader holds a group discussion focusing on the negative aspects of these non-verbal actions.

The same format is used for three additional situations. In the first, the leader interrupts and "one-ups" the interviewee constantly. In the second, the leader makes eye contact with the interviewee and gives non-verbal clues to indicate listening when in fact such is not occurring. And in the third, the leader overwhelms the interviewee with sweet and syrupy comments, while holding or patting the participant's hand. After each demonstration, the participants repeat the interview. Then, the group discussion focuses on the negative aspects of each of these types of behaviors. This activity sets the stage for skill training in attending behavior.

Attending behavior includes comfortable eye contact, a posture in which an interviewer faces the interviewee, and attentive listening in which the interviewer concentrates upon what the interviewee has to say and responds accordingly. The leader, in a lecturette defines and describes the skill, then conducts an interview in which appropriate and effective attending behavior is exhibited. The difference between this behavior and the previous negative examples is obvious. Participants are then grouped into triads, in which they will rotate through the roles of talker (interviewee, client), listener (interviewer, helper, counselor), and observer (critic, feedback agent). This rotation is followed by participants conducting dyadic interviews, in which they begin the practice of effective attending behavior and receive feedback from their client and the observer, and the leader who moves from group to group.

After a 10-minute break, the leader briefly lectures on, "Giving and Receiving Feedback," because participants have just had their first experience with feedback from and to other group members. The leader emphasizes major points about effective feedback, including: (1) it is accurate; (2) it is specific and descriptive of behavior; (3) its purpose is to improve participant performance; and (4) it is accepted non-defensively and acted upon when appropriate. This lecturette is important because participants will offer uniformly positive and general feedback, such as, "you did fine, that was good," unless aided in developing skill in giving and receiving feedback. The leader then is interviewed by a participant in order to demonstrate the use of effective feedback.

The use of open-ended leads (Ivey, 1971) is the next skill introduced. Consistent with the training paradigm, the skill is introduced in a lecturette, followed by a demonstration by the leader, written material describing the use of the skill, participant practice of the skill in triads, and feedback. In the Air Force course, for example, participants gathered information about the nature of the interviewee's basic training. Observers were instructed to provide feedback on both attending behavior and open-ended leads. Meanwhile the leader reemphasizes the concept of accumulating skills, while circulating through the room, giving assistance with the skills under practice, and the use of feedback.

Day 3 and 4. The entire third day and half of the fourth are spent on the skill called, "Negotiation of Understanding," (roughly synonomous with paraphrasing and reflection of feelings combined). This skill involves attentive listening to what is said, attention to accompanying non-verbal cues (including facial expression, voice quality, gestures, crying, laughing, and so on), followed by a recounting to the interviewee, which communicates understanding of both the interviewee's message content and any associated feelings. The interviewer's understanding statements are generally in a shorter, more concise form than was the interviewee's original communication.

The leader then presents a number of sample statements. Participants are instructed to construct a reply, communicating understanding of both content and affect. After several trials, participants learn that they can reply in a variety of ways, while still meeting the criteria of communicating understanding. Participants are then trained to seek either affirmation or correction of their statements of understanding (the negotiation process), before continuing an interview (conversation, counseling session, etc.).

After this instruction and training, the usual format continues: leader demonstration, handout written material, and participant practice-with-feedback. Probably the most complex of the skills in the training format, six hours of separate attention are allotted to it.

Day 4 concludes as participants are trained in the use of the "Summarization Skill." This is an extension of the skill used in Negotiation of Understanding. Participants are trained to summarize whenever: (1) an extensive amount of conversation has occurred (every two or three minutes); (2) whenever their understanding of the interviewee's conversation is unclear; (3) at any natural transition point where a change of topic or emphasis occurs; and, (4) at the conclusion of any interview. The usual training format is applied to this skill, and participant practice ends the fourth day of training.

Day 5. By this time in the training, group members are anxious to begin to address the many concerns and problematic situations fellow participants have shared while serving as interviewees in the training process. Now is the time to introduce a problem-solving model applied to interpersonal communication. Oversimplified, this model requires that the interviewer use a four phase model of problem-solving, including: (1) an exploratory phase, in which the interviewee's presenting problem or concern is clearly defined (problem definition: what is the problem?); (2) a goal-setting phase, in which the interviewee attempts to specify what to do about the problem; (3) a decision-making phase, in which alternatives for problem solution are generated, evaluated, and one or more are chosen; and (4) a phase in which a plan of action aimed toward reaching each goal and, thus, the problem's solution, is designed.

Goal-setting is now introduced. After having defined and clarified some existing problem, this skill is used to help others specify how they would like matters to be different. Participants are trained to aid others in applying three criteria in the setting of a goal: specificity, personalization, and attainability. Specificity aims at stating the goal so that the interviewee will have a reasonably concrete knowledge of when a goal has been reached. For example, an interviewee might state, "I want to be happier." This is an example of a general or non-specific goal. The interviewer is trained to ascertain (specifically) "what would it take for you to be happier?" The interviewee's response, for example, "I would have to be promoted and transferred to another base," gives the specificity needed at this time.

Certainly, in this example, an individual can take actions toward being promoted, so this goal meets the criterion of being personal. But what if the goal had been, "I will be happier when *they* promote me." Participants are trained to assist interviewees to convert such non-personal statements into personal statements, e.g., "I will be happier when *I* convince my lieutenant to recommend me for promotion."

Finally, goal statements must meet the criterion of attainability. The goal is plausible when the interviewee has some reasonable chance to reach the goal. To be promoted from Airman Second Class to Technical Sergeant is a reasonable and attainable goal in the Air Force. A goal of being promoted directly from Sergeant to Colonel is not. Participants are trained to explore the attainability of goals with interviewees to ascertain if goals are within the realm of reason, or, if not, to assist the interviewee in stating goals which are attainable. As in all skill training aspects, a demonstration, a written description, and participant practice-with-feedback follows the lecturette. The initial training in goal setting requires about one hour.

The last two hours of this session are spent in training participants to aid interviewees in generating alternative methods for reaching goals. This step is followed by helping interviewees to evaluate the different alternatives relative to each other, eventually leading to a decision. Participants are trained to assist interviewees to generate alternatives when interviewees can see none of their own, or only few. Generalizing alternatives is done by asking the interviewee to state two extreme alternatives for reaching a goal. Then, other alternatives are derived from the original two. Thus, an individual's goal to get a child to do homework might be:

Alternative 1	*Alternative 2*
shower child with gifts,	take away all child's privileges,
give praise, affection;	chain to a bed, and beat severely
let child do anything	

These two extremes, one rewarding and the other punishing, are both ridiculous in terms of an acceptable alternative, but do offer a starting point for generating other alternatives. Examples of other alternatives that could be generated include:

Alternative 1	*Alternative 2*
shower child with gifts,	take away all child's privileges,
praise, affection;	chain to a bed, and beat severely

Alternative 3
take away some of child's privileges;
promise return of privileges when
child's behavior changes (homework done)

Alternative 4	*Alternative 5*
notify child that privileges	take away most of child's
will be taken away if behavior	privileges, and "ground" the child
does not improve	for a lengthy time, until
	behavior improves

Note that once the two extreme alternatives are designated, a number of alternatives can be generated by the "kind of pyramiding" shown above. In practice, such pyramiding seldom lasts longer than in this example before the interviewee begins to focus on options that are appealing. Also note that, generally, the first two options may be ridiculous in their extremity (as in the above example). Their purpose is merely to get the generation process started, not to serve as usable alternatives themselves.

Participants are then trained to assist interviewees to evaluate alternatives relative to each other. They are instructed to request interviewees to list the pros and cons, (positives and negatives) for each alternative. Each alternative is viewed in terms of its desirability to the interviewee, and of its probability of leading to the desired (goal attainment) outcome. After the lecturette on generating and evaluating alternatives, the training paradigm continues and the session ends with participants practicing and receiving feedback.

By this time a strong cohesion has usually developed among the members of all the smaller working groups. This cohesion is a result of the members having worked together toward acquiring and mastering the human relations skills. With careful monitoring and coaching by the leader, members have become quite skilled at giving and receiving feedback—a potent motivator for group cohesion. Perhaps most importantly, members by now have disclosed a great deal about themselves through role playing and practice interviews, a behavior that promotes closeness in small groups. If self-disclosure has not occurred in a small group, the leader will probably find that some of the small groups' members are displaying competitive behavior, are not giving or receiving feedback effectively, or are not committed to a group goal of learning human relations skills. If so, the leader should intervene in such a group with a problem-solving approach at this point. Two purposes can be served by such an intervention into the groups' dynamics: (1) inappropriate behavior can be identified, analyzed, extinguished, and replaced by appropriate behavior, and (2) the leader can give a "live" demonstration of the use of human relations skills used in a problem-solving process.

Day 6. This session is devoted to training in the last dyadic skill, action-plan development. This training is followed by participant practice of the total problem-solving interview. Action-planning skill aims at aiding interviewees to develop specific plan(s) for carrying out chosen alternatives. Participants learn to have the interviewee specify the who's, what's, when's, where's, and how's, the five steps of goal attainment. Applied to the interviewee whose child won't do homework, such a plan might be: (1) by Wednesday afternoon, confer with child's teachers to ascertain their perception of child's unwillingness to do homework; (2) by Wednesday evening, confer with spouse for other perceptions and opinions; talk over plan of action so that both will be consistent; and, (3) Thursday, after dinner, meet with child and review the problem; state that telephone and TV privileges are removed until homework is completed; privileges will be reinstated as soon as one week's consistent progress is noted by parents and teachers.

The above example may appear too simple a solution for what is no doubt a complex problem. However, it illustrates a training process and not an actual or even recommended solution to the homework problem.

Once participants have completed this part of their training, they next conduct a series of practice interviews. This practice allows them to use all their accumulated skills, continue to receive feedback, practice toward mastery, and further develop group cohesion and effectiveness.

Days 7, 8, and 9 of the training workshop turn attention to the use of human relations skills in small group settings, particularly to the leadership function. On day 7, participants receive training in "Basic Skills for Leading Discussion Groups." These seven skills were originally developed by Clack and Conyne (1974) to teach the rudiments of small group discussion leadership to teachers-in-training and paraprofessional counselors. Basic group discussion skills include:

1. Explanation and clarification of the task

Leaders should define and clarify the task or purpose of the group discussion in specific terms. All members are encouraged to question, state, comment, and gather reactions in an effort to arrive at a common understanding of the group's task or purpose.

2. Encouraging participation

Leaders can encourage participation in numerous ways. Initially a statement to the effect that all member's opinions are valued and desired can be expressed. As the discussion develops, individual members who are not active may be encouraged by communicating interest in what they may be thinking or feeling, e.g., "I'm really interested in what you think about this issue, Bill." On the other hand, encouragement does not include pinning a member to the wall, e.g., "You haven't said anything all day and I think it is about time you spoke up."

3. Attending and acknowledging

Interaction can be elicited by leaders by attending to members and acknowledging their participation. Acknowledgement can be accomplished in a number of ways: a nod of the head, a "thank you," or a spoken response all serve as ways to acknowledge another's efforts.

4. Clarification and summarization

Leaders can be particularly helpful in facilitating group effectiveness by clarifying and summarizing the content of the group discussion. Clarification may be accomplished by a leader restating his/her understanding of what has been said, or by asking another member to restate what they have said for purposes of clarification. Particularly if related to the task or purpose of the group, an occasional summary helps establish understanding and keep the group on course.

5. Responding to content and feelings

Verbal messages that occur in a group discussion have both content and feeling components. Leaders should be aware of both dimensions and respond appropriately to both to assure understanding.

6. Linking and pairing

Leaders may assist the group's efforts by noting similarities and differences among the statements and positions made and held by other members. This skill is used to point out common and differing perspectives toward the task of the group.

7. Closure

A leader should close each group meeting with a statement summarizing what has been accomplished, and indicating how the group will proceed. This prevents members from feeling they have been left hanging, and gives direction to future meetings.

Many, if not most, of these group discussion skills are very similar to the individual skills learned in the earlier part of this workshop. Because of this, the seven skills are presented as a unit and, as always, in the microcounseling learning paradigm. However, in this part of the training, participants are organized into groups of six members each so that each participant has a group to lead as they practice the use of the skills. In this small group setting, one person is designated as group leader, four as group members, and one as observer. Each participant leads a number of group discussions on topics they had submitted earlier to the trainer, most of which were controversial and led to lively discussion. Topics included in this case example were the Air Force evaluation system, the 55-mile-per-hour speed limit, mandatory military service, and other topics of contemporary interest. In a simulation exercise, the trainer designates himself as governor and each of the participants, in turn, gathers information about the "will of the people" with regard to the issue at hand. Thus, the purpose of first group discussion training is strictly information gathering. On the seventh day of training, after the trainer's lecturette and demonstration, each participant leads two practice groups and receives feedback.

Day 8. In this session, participants are introduced to common decision-making methods used in groups. These methods are discussed in detail in Johnson and Johnson (1975). In brief, the methods include: (1) decision by authority without group discussion; (2) decision by an expert; (3) decision by averaging opinions; (4) decision by authority after input; (5) decision by minority; (6) decision by majority vote; and, (7) decision by consensus.

As one moves through the list of decision-making methods increasingly greater group member involvement occurs in the making of decisions. A larger group discussion is conducted by the trainer, to ascertain when the different methods are appropriate and desirable and what outcomes are to be expected from the use of each. In general, the less time available and the more routine the decision, the more appropriate it is to use the methods nearer the top of the list. On the other hand, the more time available (or made available) and the more important it is to have group members feel responsible for and committed to decisions, the more appropriate it is to use methods in the lower part of the list.

Having introduced the different decision-making methods, participants lead their groups through a number of decision-making tasks based, for example, on a mythical company that has developed a revolutionary type of cooking utensil. Group decisions focus on such issues as type and style of company cars, office furnishings, fringe benefit packages for company employees, marketing strategies, and the like. Group leaders are designated as supervisors and all other members as simply employees. The leaders choose to use any of the methods available, lead a group discussion (or explanation as the case may be) and are then given performance feedback by other group members and the trainer. All participants lead a minimum of two group discussions during this activity.

Days 9 and 10 are devoted to simulations in which participants perform both individual interviews and conducted group discussions. In each activity they receive feedback regarding their performance so that they can perfect their skills.

EMPLOYMENT

Employment opportunities abound for skilled human relations trainers. In specialized consulting firms, some individuals make human relations skills training a full-time occupation. Many trainers work in consulting firms, churches, colleges, and universities and do human relations work in business, industries, political and educational institutions on a consulting basis. Increasingly, personnel departments in business and industrial organizations are employing individuals who can conduct human relations training as a part of the firm's personnel repertoire.

REFERENCES

Benjamin, A.: *The Helping Interview*. Boston: Houghton Mifflin, 1974.

Benne, K., Bradford, L., Gibb, J., and Lippitt, R.: *The Laboratory Method of Changing and Learning*. Palo Alto: Science and Behavior Books, 1975.

Berg, R.C. and Landreth, G.L. *Group Counseling: Fundamental Concepts and Procedures*. Muncie, IN.: Accelerated Development, Inc., 1979.

Bradford, L., Gibb, J., and Benne, K.: *T-group Theory and Laboratory Method*. New York: Wiley, 1964.

Carkhuff, R.: *Helping and Human Relations: A Primer for Lay and Professional Helpers, Vol. 1*. New York: Holt, 1969.

Clack, R. and Conyne, R.: Basic Group Discussion Leadership Skills. Normal, Il., unpublished paper, 1974.

Danish, S. and Hauer, A.: *Helping Skills: A Basic Training Program*. New York: Behavioral Publications, 1973.

Diedrich, R. and Dye, H.: *Group Procedures: Purposes, Processes, and Outcomes*. Boston: Houghton Mifflin, 1972.

Egan, G.: *Encounter: Group Processes for Interpersonal Growth.* Belmont: Brooks-Cole, 1970.

Gazda, G., Asbury, F., Balzer, F., Childers, W., Desselle, R., and Walters, R.: *Human Relations Development: A Manual for Educators.* Boston: Allyn and Bacon, 1973.

Ivey, A.: *Microcounseling: Innovations in Interview Training.* Springfield, IL.: Charles C Thomas, 1971.

Johnson, D.: *Reaching Out: Interpersonal Effectiveness and Self-Actualization.* Englewood Cliffs: Prentice-Hall, 1972.

Johnson, D. and Johnson, F.: *Joining Together: Group Theory and Group Skills.* Englewood Cliffs: Prentice-Hall, 1975.

Napier, R.W. and Gershenfeld, M.K.: *Groups: Theory and Experience.* Boston: Houghton Mifflin, 1981.

Pfeiffer, J.W. and Jones, J.E.: *The 1976 Annual Handbook for Group Facilitators.* La Jolla, CA., 1976.

Rogers, C.: *Carl Rogers on Encounter Groups.* New York: Harper and Row, 1970.

Solomon, L. and Berzon, B. (Eds.): *New Perspectives on Encounter Groups.* San Francisco: Jossey-Bass, 1972.

Yalom, I.: *The Theory and Practice of Group Psychotherapy.* New York: Basic Books, 1975.

SECTION II
INTERPERSONAL LEVEL OF
INTERVENTION

W HEN I ask my students what a "group" is, most of their definitions will include reference to interpersonal interaction of
some kind. In fact, a popular definition of a group, offered by the
group dynamicists Cartwright and Zander (1968), is: "A collection
of individuals who have relations to one another that make them interdependent to some significant degree. As so defined, the term
group refers to a class of social entities having in common the property of interdependence among their constituent members" (p. 46).
Indeed, interpersonal learning, cohesion, modeling, feedback, reality testing, and the concept of "social microcosm" are among the
critical interdependent phenomena occurring within group work
that are decidedly interpersonal in nature. Thus, the interpersonal
heritage and support for the widest swath of group work is located at
the interpersonal level.

The forms that interpersonal group work take are many. We begin by examining group counseling. Trotzer, in chapter 5, concep-
tualizes group counseling as a type of interpersonal problem solving.
Trotzer emphasizes the personal relational context and aspects of
group members' lives, along with group counseling as a corrective
process. His "Interpersonal Problem Matrix," comprising the dimensions of the nature of interpersonal problems, the focus of interpersonal problems, and the level of interpersonal intervention, nicely
articulates this approach.

In Chapter 6, Garvin examines group work in social control and
correctional settings. He illustrates how interpersonal dynamics can

be used in a variety of resocialization groups to correct members' performances of necessary tasks and skills.

Interpersonal growth groups abound in contemporary society. People have been very actively seeking the group medium to advance their awareness of and functioning with others since the encounter group boom days of the 1960's. Dye identifies origins for this group work type in the laboratory method and he updates the current scene, which has become much more sophisticated in the 1980's.

Hill shows how task enhancement can be addressed through interpersonal group work. His method, "Systematic Group Discussion," as well as other similar ones, illustrate how interpersonal dynamics have been harnessed in structured group discussions to help participants to increase their mutual knowledge of content material.

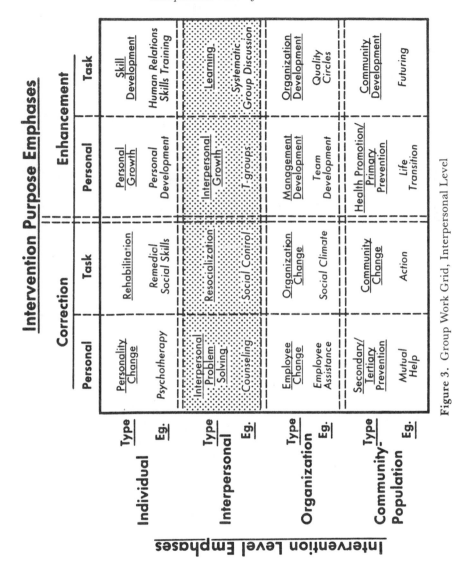

Figure 3. Group Work Grid, Interpersonal Level

CHAPTER 5

INTERPERSONAL PROBLEM SOLVING
The Group Counseling Approach

JAMES P. TROTZER

THE purpose of this chapter is to demonstrate the nature and viability of group counseling as a therapeutic tool in helping clients deal with problems which are interpersonal in origin and/or consequence.

EXPLICATION OF THE INTERVENTIVE LEVEL

The Case for Viewing People in a Social Context

The question, "What is a human?" always leads to an answer that conjures up some form of social context. Whether given extensive or minimal credit, the interpersonal environment must always be considered. William James (1890) once noted that, "no more fiendish punishment could be devised, were such a thing physically possible, than that one should be turned loose in society and remain absolutely unnoticed by all the members thereof" (p. 293). This comment underscores the crucial relevance of our interpersonal network — without it we simply would not exist. Johnson (1981) points out that "the human species seems to have a relationship imperative. We desire and seek out relationships with others, and we have personal needs that can be satisfied only through interacting with other humans" (p. 1). Harry Stack Sullivan (1953) contended that personality is almost entirely the product of interaction with other significant human beings. Who we are is forged in the cauldron of our human relationships. And, Carl Rogers (1951) pointed out, one's picture of oneself is formed "As a result of interaction with the environment and particularly, as a result of interactions with others" (p. 483). Thus the social or interpersonal context is of ultimate relevance whenever we consider human development or personal change. This being the case, it is only logical that the definition of human problems should reflect the interpersonal domain.

Nature of Human Problems

Who we are as persons is a result of the interactions between our needs (a la Maslow) which motivate us and our social relationships which provide the arena in which we must learn to meet those needs (Trotzer, 1977). Johnson (1981) concurs with this viewpoint adding that, "our identity is built out of our relationships with other people. As we interact with others we note their responses to us, and we learn to view ourselves as they view us (p. 2)." In fact, he goes so far as to state that our "psychological health depends almost entirely on our relationships with other people. The ability to build and maintain cooperative, interdependent relationships with other people is often cited as a primary manifestation of psychological health" (p. 3).

Given the perspective that individuals live and grow in a social milieu, it is then possible to construe human problems in two related but differentiated categories: problems in meeting individual needs (intrapersonal problems) and problems in social relating (interpersonal problems). In some ways these two problem categories are reciprocal, i.e., unmet individual needs will contribute to relationship problems, and relationship problems present obstacles to getting personal needs met. In most instances there is usually an interpersonal component to all human problems that must be addressed when presented in counseling. Yalom (1970) noted that in therapy, goals often shift from relief of suffering (intrapersonal) to goals that have relational implications (interpersonal). Consequently, there is both conceptual and clinical validity to viewing human problems as interpersonal in nature and for directing our attention to group counseling as a means of assisting clients in dealing with them.

EXPLICATION OF INTERVENTION PURPOSE

Conyne's Group Work Grid delineates group counseling as a form of group work that is used for purposes of corrective intervention of the interpersonal level. The focus of these groups is on interpersonal phenomena and the process relies on the personal give-and-take among members and leaders for direction and dynamics (Conyne, Personal Communication, May 19, 1983).

In order to provide a foundation for viewing group counseling as an example of the interpersonal problem solving group quadrant, the following definition (adapted from Trotzer, 1977) is presented as a reference base:

> Group counseling is the development of an interpersonal network characterized by trust, acceptance, respect, warmth, communication and understanding through which a counselor and several clients come in contact in order to help each other confront interpersonal problems or relational conflict areas in the clients' lives with the express purpose of discovering, understanding and implementing ways of resolving those problems and conflicts.

This definition emphasizes several key points. First, it identifies group counseling as an "interpersonal network." This viewpoint implies it is a human process reflective of the very domain in which group members are experiencing their problems—the interpersonal domain. Second, the traits of that therapeutic network only have meaning in a relational context. Trust, acceptance, respect, warmth, communication and understanding can only be experienced if interpersonal relationships are present. Third, there is a built-in interpersonal growth dynamic in that the process depends on members helping each other. And finally, the focus and purpose of the group are explicit. Counseling groups are initiated for the purpose of interpersonal problem-solving. As such the counseling group represents a temporary interventive modality in each group member's life, the therapeutic impact and duration of which are governed by the intention on the part of both leaders and members to dissolve the group by resolving the problems.

,XPLICATION OF SUPPORTIVE THEORY

Nature of the Group Counseling Process

Group theory, research and practice have all provided evidence to substantiate the premise that counseling groups evolve through a developmental process characterized by identifiable stages that are consistent within groups and across groups. These stages may vary in number and nomenclature, depending on the presenter, but they generally describe the same phenomena (Glass, 1978). That process, however, is a basic facilitative element of therapeutic change experienced by individual group participants. An overview of the group counseling process is presented here with particular emphasis on the interpersonal dynamics that characterize it. The model described is a summation of more in-depth information presented elsewhere (Trotzer, 1977, 1979, and 1980).

The process of group counseling is comprised of five stages that reflect characteristics of our basic human needs, qualities of therapeutic interpersonal relationships and the dynamics of problem solving. In addition, each stage includes a set of developmental tasks that must be accounted for if the group is to evolve through the various stages in a constructive manner.

Counseling groups are essentially initiated by bringing together three or more clients for a specified therapeutic purpose. Each of these clients is an individual with basic needs of trust, belongingness and esteem that must be met in the group before the motivating need for self-actualization can be mobilized, and before the specific purpose for which the group was formed can be addressed. In addition, the element of group dynamics is introduced by inclusion of the third and succeeding members (usually up to a group size of 8-12). That element, manifested in the form of potential for coalitions, more complex communication patterns, peer pressure and dynamics and loss of individual influence, must be dealt with by forming a therapeutic network with norms that facilitate self disclosure and feedback while at the same time maintaining a delicate balance between group pressure and individual autonomy. Once a milieu is established where group members can meet their individual, psychological needs, the stage is set for interpersonal problem solving using the modality of group interaction.

In some sense accounting for individual needs in a relational context (the group) has already set the problem-solving process in motion. Group members realize the group is a *safe place* to talk about their concerns and problems (step 1) and understand that even though they have problems they are still accepted by the group as persons. This *acceptance* enables them to accept their problems and concerns as part of themselves (step 2), and prepares them for taking *responsibility* for their problems (step 3). Once the problems have been owned by the person, developing and implementing a *plan* to solve them (step 4) and integrating successful *changes* into one's life (step 5) follow. Johnson and Johnson (1979) make the point that both the origin and the solution to client's psychological problems can be found in their relationships with people. Consequently, the group counseling process is a prototype for interpersonal problem solving by its very nature.

The initial stage of the group process is typically characterized by feelings of discomfort, anxiety and resistance common to forming interpersonal relationships in a new social environment. Group members, no matter how well they have been orientated, are reluctant to interact because their presence in the group is contingent on some recognized purpose that requires personal risk. This stage is referred to as the *Security Stage* because it must account for each group member's need for psychological safety. The goal of this stage is to initiate trust which is necessary for members to self disclose.

The basic developmental tasks of the security stage are 1) getting acquainted; 2) interpersonal warm-up; 3) setting boundaries and 4) building trust.[1] As these tasks are addressed, members are able to make initial contact with one another and establish a basic rapport that facilitates a deeper level of interpersonal relating.

The second stage of the group process is the *Acceptance Stage*, which is predominantly concerned with the development of group cohesiveness. This stage is a derivative of our psychological need to belong. Caring and being cared about are essential therapeutic qualities of this stage because members need to experience accep-

---

[1] Note: For elaboration on the developmental tasks in each stage of the group process see Trotzer, 1979 and 1980.

tance before they are willing to disclose parts of themselves or relational difficulties that require change. As group cohesiveness develops, a supportive milieu is formed which reinforces the norm of personal sharing and where disclosing interpersonal problems becomes an integral part of a total person perspective.

The developmental tasks of the acceptance stage are 1) personal sharing; 2) giving feedback; 3) building cohesiveness and closeness; 4) learning to accept self and 5) learning to accept others. As these tasks are accounted for, a cohesive and supportive group environment emerges where members become willing to risk individuation which prepares them for movement into the next stage of group development.

The *Responsibility Stage* of the group process reflects our psychological need for respect (esteem), which is acquired through responsible individual action in therapeutic relationships where individuals are perceived as worthwhile. The group moves from an emphasis on acceptance of self and others to evaluating self and others in terms of ownership of and satisfaction with their behavior, feelings and thoughts. Focus shifts from a group orientation to more of an individual orientation, where members are helped to explore their uniqueness and assisted in taking responsibility for themselves. Group members not only become responsible for themselves but commit themselves to helping each other work on problems as well.

The developmental tasks of the responsibility stage are 1) self assessment; 2) recognizing ownership; 3) building responsibility; 4) giving respect and 5) doing a fair share. These tasks form the foundation and impetus for working on interpersonal problems. Members realize their own initiative is necessary to solve problems while recognizing their interdependency both within the group and in society. Consequently, the stage is set for the investment of group resources and energies in the problem-solving focus of the next stage of the group life cycle.

The *Work Stage* is the central core of the group process and focuses on the basic purposes for which the group was formed. The atmosphere and relationships in the group allow individuals to a) examine their interpersonal concerns without fears of rejection or reprisal, b) explore alternatives to resolving those problems and c) experiment with new behaviors in a safe environment before risking changes outside the group. The leader, as both expert and facilitator, contributes by encouraging members to be resources to persons working on problems and by keeping the group in touch with reality. The work stage prepares group members for reentry into the world outside the group by arming them with well-thought-through plans, plausible skills or behaviors and bolstered self-confidence. Implementation and integration are emphasized through the supportive functioning of the group.

The developmental tasks of the work stage are 1) interpersonal problem solving; 2) mobilizing group resources and 3) reality testing. These tasks form the agenda for each session during the work stage. They are applied and recycled as each member addresses the specific interpersonal concerns that brought them into the group. When these concerns are resolved and/or the group approaches its time limit boundary, the final stage of the group process is imminent.

The *Closing Stage* of the group process serves a valuable transitional function for both the group as a unit and for its individual members. This stage is characterized by members actively pursuing change in their lives outside the group while at the same time preparing for disengagement from the group. Closure brings the group experience to an end by enabling members to be responsible for the work they have done, acknowledging it and reinforcing it, and then helping them effectively move back into the mainstream of their day-to-day living without the group.

The developmental tasks of the closing stage are 1) unfinished business; 2) giving support; 3) affirming and confirming growth; 4) saying good-bye and 5) follow-up. These tasks translate termination into a commencement experience where group members are able to disengage from the group without undermining any of the work that has been accomplished. They propel group members forward in their lives with added confidence and assure clarity in the closure experience.

INTERVENTION CHANGE TECHNIQUES

Group counseling is an interpersonal laboratory which facilitates social change in the clients' lives on a personal level. As such, methods must reflect two basic principles. First, group intervention techniques have merit only if they generate change activity both inside and outside the group. This is called the "bi-directionality principle" (Yalom, 1970). The second principle relates to experiential learning. Johnson (1981) points out that it takes more than explanations to help people learn interpersonal skills and solve interpersonal problems. The process must be experienced. Consequently, all group intervention techniques must contain an experiential component.

With these two principles in mind, let us look at a sample of methods that can be used. Due to space limitations only basic sketches of the techniques will be given. Others may be found in the sources listed in the references.

1. Teaching Interpersonal Skills

One primary means of resolving interpersonal problems is teaching group members appropriate interpersonal skills. The specific skills may be identified by answering the following questions:

   a. What are the interpersonal skills every person needs in order to function effectively in our society and lead a fulfilling and self-enhancing life?
   b. What interpersonal skills are clients failing to use effectively?
   c. What interpersonal skills do clients lack?
   d. Will the learning and utilization of needed interpersonal skills reduce pathological behavior and increase ability to create more productive, self-enhancing and fulfilling lives? (Johnson and Johnson, 1979, p. 213).

Answering these questions for a specific group will provide both content and method.

2. Models for Change in Interpersonal Problem-Solving

   a. **Positive Process Problem-Solving:** Otto (1967) first posited the idea that problems can be solved by starting with strengths and then focusing on weaknesses that need to be rectified. That process is particularly relevant in the interpersonal domain. The following procedure is based on Otto's basic premise:

1. Have group members make a list of accomplishments emphasizing interpersonal successes and satisfactions.
2. Have each group member write a positive paragraph about themselves emphasizing their social assets (this paragraph is not to be disclosed. It is for their personal reference only.)
3. Have group members share their list of accomplishments.
4. Positive bombardment: Have group members individually present positive feedback to each group member relative to interpersonal qualities, traits and skills.
5. Have group members identify interpersonal problem areas they want to work on.
6. The group works with each member using their positive interpersonal qualities as resources and finding ways of applying them to the problem.

b. **Behavioral Problem-Solving Process:** Many times group members have difficulty resolving their interpersonal problems because the problems lack specificity. Ask members to write down three interpersonal concerns they are struggling with and then briefly describe them to the group. Instruct them to select one of their interpersonal concerns and discuss it in detail following the four basic behavioral steps listed below:

1. Describe in behavioral terms what you do not like or what is wrong with the relationship (*problem*).
2. Describe in behavioral terms what you would like to change or how you would like the relationship to be (*goal*).
3. Discuss with the group how you might be able to accomplish your goal and develop a strategy for doing so (*plan*).
4. Try out the plan and report back to the group on your progress (*evaluation*).

c. **Role Playing:** Role playing is a particularly flexible and useful tool in the hands of a skillful group leader (Trotzer, 1977). In its simplest form it entails reenacting or acting out an interpersonal situation in the group as if it were occurring in actuality. Role playing makes use of simulation and modeling to help group members look more intensely at interpersonal areas for both deeper understanding and solutions. It provides members with a realistic basis for transfer to the real environment, making the prospect of change less threatening and the implementation of change less difficult.

Intervention techniques in group counseling always raise the issue of personal risk for the client. As such, no matter how proven, exciting, potent, innovative or relevant they may be, progress only results when group members risk changing. Seigelman (1983) notes that, "Major life change is not made easily. It usually takes some external deadline...some outrage...or burnout...or some outside pressure...to get us moving. We don't divert the course of our lives lightly or easily—at least not if we are prudent" (p. 77). This is particularly true in the interpersonal domain. Therefore, any intervention must be selected and carried out in a group with the utmost sensitivity to and respect for the individuals involved and their relational counterparts.

PRIMARY INTERVENTION TARGET POPULATIONS

Trotzer's Interpersonal Problem Matrix

Rather than enumerate specific populations for group counseling, I have opted to discuss the concept of target populations via the Interpersonal Problem Matrix presented in Figure 5. The matrix is generated by intersecting three dynamic dimensions of interpersonal problems. Level I (horizontal axis), Nature of Interpersonal Problems, depicts four categories of interpersonal problems emphasizing the dynamics involved. These are: a) problems forming relationships, b) problems maintaining relationships, c) problems changing relationships and d) conflicts in relationships.

Level II (diagonal axis), Interpersonal Problem Focus, is divided into four broadly construed categories representing the basic relational domains in which we experience our interpersonal problems. These categories are a) interpersonal skills, b) family relationships,

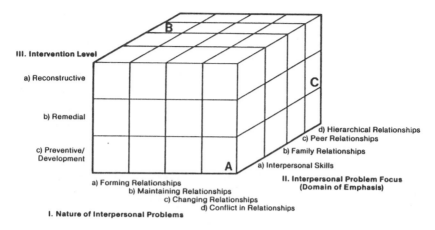

Figure 4. Trotzer's Interpersonal Problem Matrix

c) peer relationships and d) hierarchical relationships. Level III (vertical axis), Intervention Level, depicts the purpose of group counseling relative to the degree of difficulty or seriousness of the interpersonal problems and the intensity and timing of the intervention itself. The three categories are: a) Preventive/developmental — referring to the process of providing personally relevant information and skills in order to help clients prepare for, work through and/or circumvent typical interpersonal problems; b) Remedial — referring to an interventive focus that is problem-specific and designed to resolve interpersonal concerns that are impeding growth and development of the individual; and c) Reconstructive — referring to a focus which is personality-specific and designed to help clients make extensive personal changes in order to improve their interpersonal effectiveness.

The interaction of these three vectors generates descriptive cubicles that suggest the general nature of problems to be addressed (group theme or focus), the domain in which the problems occur and the basic character of the group process. For example, the cube labeled "A" in Figure 4 represents a conflict/interpersonal skills/preventive interaction. Since we know that conflict in relationships is inevitable and actually a means by which relationships grow and develop, we can propose a counseling group which teaches conflict

resolution skills as a preventive measure. Such a group would be relevant to any number of target populations. Cube "B" (Figure 4) is
forming relationships/peers/reconstructive. An example of this cube
would be a counseling group for individuals who are social isolates
that is designed to help them form friendships. The group process
would be extensive and intensive to enable the group members to
make the personal changes and acquire the interpersonal skills necessary to form friendships in their social network (peers). Cube "C"
(Figure 4) is changing relationships/hierarchical/remedial. An example is group counseling for supervisors who had been promoted to
positions of authority over former peers and who are struggling personally with this new relational pattern.

While the matrix does not produce mutually exclusive categories,
nor cover all possible permutations of interpersonal problems, it is
very useful in conceptualizing and planning group counseling programs. Combined with a particular group model for structuring
group counseling (e.g., Trotzer, 1979, 1980), it has considerable
utility.

PRIMARY GROUP LEADER FUNCTIONS

Components of Leadership

The personality of the group leader, his/her training and skills,
leader function and roles, members' needs and personalities, and the
purpose and setting of the group all interface in some way to generate leadership as evidenced in any particular group. Although an in-
depth consideration of all of these factors is beyond the scope of this
chapter, a brief accounting of the main elements is appropriate. (The
reader is referred to Chapter 5 in Trotzer, 1977 and Chapter 12 in
Hansen, Warner and Smith, 1980, for more extensive information
on group leadership).

Personality is the foundational core of group leadership style
and impact. During the initial stages of the group process, leader
personality determines how quickly rapport is established. As the
group develops, the counselor's personality is also the factor which
defines the limits of the group experience. Leader personality is

translated into a leadership style through the acquisition of interpersonal skills, group techniques and a theoretical orientation which, in turn, are manifested in the group via leader roles and functions.

Group leadership skills and techniques are the tools which enable the counselor to function effectively in the group. These skills can be broken down into three basic categories: reaction skills, interaction skills and action skills. Reaction skills are responsive in nature and aid the leader in being receptive to individuals and the group. They are particularly useful in establishing rapport and facilitating understanding. Active listening is a primary example of a reactive skill. Interaction skills provide a mediating dimension to group leadership. They provide the means by which the leader can control and guide group interaction and facilitate its therapeutic impact. Moderating discussion, linking members' comments and supporting members are examples of interactive skills. Active skills are those which enable the group leader to take an active part in directing the group process. They serve to increase the depth of group interaction and provide the means by which leaders can assert their expertise for the good of individual members or the group. Confrontation, probing, protecting and modeling are all examples of active skills.

The manner in which the group leader uses skills is dictated by the leader's personality and theoretical orientation and the nature of the group process. Which skills are used, at what time and for what purpose depict the *functions of group leadership*. Functions are the means by which leaders help the group process develop in accord with the needs of the group members and the goals of the group. The basic functions of leadership are: 1) interaction functions; 2) communication functions; 3) limiting functions; 4) conflict/impasse resolution functions and 5) mobilizing group resources functions. The *role of the group leader* is a composite of the functions performed and a manifestation of his/her philosophical biases and theoretical perspective. In actuality, the leader's role is a conglomeration of sub-roles, the most common of which are director, facilitator, participator, observer, expert and various combinations thereof (e.g. participant-observer). In addition, each group leader develops a personal *style of leadership* through training and experience. That style must take into account personality, nature of the group process, needs of the group members and purposes for which the group is formed. It must also deal with one of the major issues faced by all group leaders — the issue of structure.

Landreth (1973) defined the parameters of structure pointing out that "the basic question is not whether or not to structure but rather what kind of structuring is needed and how much to structure" (p. 371). Bednar and Langenbahn (1979) add that there is no such thing as a linear polarity of structure to non-structure because the non-imposition of expectations (ambiguity) is in and of itself a structure.

What then is the most effective structure in interpersonal problem solving groups? In my experience, interpersonal problem solving groups are most successful when there is a balance between directed and spontaneous interaction. Group members would not be in group counseling if they knew how to spontaneously resolve their interpersonal dilemmas. Consequently, structuring interaction provides both an initiating and a facilitating mechanism for the group and problem-solving processes. However, once in motion, leaders must be conscious of the danger of relying on structure and thus missing the opportunity for transferring initiative to the group. (For a more in-depth discussion of the dynamics of structure in group counseling see *The Journal for Specialists in Group Work*, 1979, *4*[4].)

PRIMARY GROUP LEADER TRAINING

Basic Requirements

Effective group leadership is predicated upon acquiring the following prerequisites:

1) Experience as a member in groups where interpersonal problems are confronted on a personal basis.
2) Cognitive knowledge relative to the theory and dynamics of group counseling, specifically including a developmental group process perspective.
3) Skills, techniques and methods that can be used in leading groups.
4) Supervised experience as a group leader.

Most training programs in counseling provide these prerequisites as part of their requirements. Acquisition of them prepares one for group leadership generally. Components described in the next section more specifically address preparedness for leading interpersonal problem-solving groups.

Specialized Requirements

Specialized training in the following areas will accentuate leader effectiveness and prove invaluable in resolving interpersonal problems in groups:

1) **Assertiveness Training.** Many interpersonal problems revolve around the issue of assertiveness. Realizing the need for and learning appropriate assertive behavior skills is one way of assisting group members in their relational dilemmas. Most assertiveness training programs use group process. For example, Lange and Jakubowski (1976) present extensive structured exercises and illustrations depicting cognitive, affective, and behavioral procedures for increasing group members' responsible assertiveness.

2) **Interpersonal Skills Training.** Training in this area includes a wide range of skills encompassing communication, relationship development, self awareness, social skills and interpersonal problem-solving. Interpersonal skills are the links that connect the individual and other people and determine the quality and satisfaction of our relationships. A major portion of those links involve communication. Satir (1972) writes that, "once a human being has arrived on this earth, communication is the single largest factor determining what kinds of relationships he makes with others and what happens to him in the world about him" (p. 30). Miller, Nunnally and Wackman (1975) add that communication is both a vehicle for creating relationships and an index of relationships" (p. 279). Consequently, knowing how to assist group members in acquiring interpersonal skills is vital. In fact, Yalom (1970) points out that socializing techniques are a curative factor which operates in all helping groups.

   Several excellent sources for content and techniques in this area are Johnson (1981), Miller et al. (1975), Satir (1972), and

Tubbs and Moss (1978).

3) **Social Learning Techniques and Behavior Modification.** A wide range of methods and techniques based on social learning theory and behavioral principles is applicable to interpersonal problem solving. Techniques that stress imitative, cognitive, emotional or operant learning all provide helpful tools to the group leader. Helpful resources in this area are Agras (1978), Krumboltz and Thoreson (1976), and Kanfer and Goldstein (1975).

4) **Marital and Family Processes and Dynamics.** Many of the interpersonal concerns members bring to group emanate from their family relationships. Yalom (1970) notes that, "without exception patients enter group therapy with a history of highly unsatisfactory experience in their first and most important group—their primary family" (p. 12). Satir (1972) states simply that, "troubled families make troubled people" (p. 18). Seigelman (1983) adds that the greatest interpersonal risks are related to marriage, separation and divorce, confronting family members and raising children. It stands to reason, then, that extensive knowledge and understanding of the dynamics of marital and family relations are vital in group counseling. A background in family systems theory related to nuclear and extended family interaction, understanding family constellation and ordinal position, and knowing other concepts drawn from marriage and family therapy are useful.

5) **Conflict Resolution.** Conflict in relationships is inevitable and often surfaces as the focus of attention in counseling groups. Johnson (1981) points out that, "an interpersonal conflict exists whenever an action by one person prevents, obstructs or interferes with the actions of another person" (p. 195). Effective conflict resolution, therefore, is often the key to not only solving the presenting problem but future problems as well. (Chapter 9 in Johnson, 1981 is an excellent resource on resolving interpersonal conflicts.) Developing expertise in teaching conflict resolution strategies is another valuable asset to the group leader.

6) **Values Clarification.** Many interpersonal difficulties stem from a lack of understanding of one's values or values conflicts. Knowing values clarification strategies and techniques will prove useful

in group counseling. Helpful sources here include Kirschenbaum (1977) and Simon, Howe and Kirschenbaum (1972).

EVIDENCE OF INTERVENTION EFFECTIVENESS

One assessment method that has great promise and utility for evaluating interpersonal problem-solving groups is called Goal Attainment Scaling (GAS). Developed by Kiresuk and Sherman (1968), and adapted to group counseling by Paritzky and Magoon (1982), this procedure requires that each group member identify specific interpersonal behaviors they want to achieve or diminish. For each goal the counselor determines a realistic estimate of "expected outcome" and assigns it a value of 0 on the Goal Attainment Scale. "Better than expected" outcome estimates (assigned values of +1 and +2) and "worse than expected" outcome estimates (assigned values of –1 and –2) are then generated to complete the scale. The group member's current behavior relative to the Goal Attainment Scale is then plotted and quantified by interpolation. At the end of group counseling each member's behavior relative to their goals is again determined, plotted and quantified resulting in a score indicative of change that has occurred. This procedure accounts for individualized group member goals and when combined across all group members also demonstrates the overall effectiveness of the group counseling process.

ILLUSTRATIVE INTERVENTION CASE EXAMPLE

An Interpersonal Problem-Solving Group in a Mental Health Center

The counseling group described occurred in a mental health center. The group consisted of 10 adult members, six of whom were female and four male, and it was facilitated by a male-female co-leadership team. All group members were referred to group counseling by their individual therapists at the center. Group members had become involved in individual therapy for a variety of reasons but were referred to the group to work specifically on the interpersonal dimensions of their lives. The group met for a total of 30 hours including an intake/orientation interview, an exit interview and fourteen two-hour group sessions over a four month period.

Overview of the Group Counseling Process

Orientation/Intake Interview: The co-leaders conducted an intake interview with each prospective group member for purposes of screening, orientation and goal-setting. During this one hour interview clients were helped to identify interpersonal problem areas in their lives and asked to specify particular problems they wanted to work on in the group. Ground rules for the group were explained and questions were answered. The client was introduced to the Goal Attainment Scaling (G.A.S.) process described earlier in this chapter, and a commitment to participate in the group was obtained.

Based on the content of the intake interviews, the leaders determined to use a semi-structured approach to the group introducing specific activities related to relevant topics, as well as providing for open-ended interaction. The nature of the clients' interpersonal problems indicated that attention to four specific interpersonal skill areas would be a helpful adjunct to the group counseling process. These areas were communication skills, social skills, assertiveness skills and conflict resolution skills. Consequently, two sessions were devoted to each of these areas. (Refer to Trotzer, 1979, for a specific format for organizing a group counseling program.)

Sessions 1 and 2: These sessions were primarily devoted to the forming aspects of the group. Members became acquainted with one another through structured activities and began engaging in self-disclosure and giving feedback. Group rules were reiterated and clarified, and time was devoted to making contact on a person-to-person basis.

Sessions 3 and 4: The focus of these sessions was on communication skills. Members engaged in lab activities related to active listening and practiced various forms of interpersonal communication (Miller, et al., 1975). Time was also spent identifying the various interpersonal problem areas in the clients' lives, which served as content for the process of learning effective communication skills.

Sessions 5 and 6: Social skills were emphasized in these sessions combining the use of role playing and behavior rehearsal with out-of-group tasks and assignments to facilitate the learning of social skills. The principle of in-group and out-of-group connectedness was thus established prior to any intensive consideration of interpersonal problems.

Sessions 7 and 8: Assertiveness principles and techniques were integrated into these sessions. Members practiced assertiveness skills in the group and targeted situations where they could use them outside the group.

Sessions 9 and 10: Lab activities were used to teach the various strategies of conflict resolution and to help group members identify their own tendencies in conflict situations. Conflict situations in each client's life were identified and analyzed from the viewpoint of effective conflict resolution. Contracts were drawn up for each member with respect to a conflictual relationship outside the group.

The approximate ratio of structured activity to spontaneous interaction for the first ten sessions was 1-1 ½ hours structure and ½ -1 hour open-ended. The last four sessions, however, were heavily oriented toward the open-ended form of interaction following the lead of members as they zeroed in on the specific problems in their lives.

Sessions 11-14: The focus of these sessions was directed by the content of the problems on which group members were working. A check-in system was used where members updated the group about their progress and indicated whether they wanted specific attention (time) during the session. A goal board was also constructed so that members could be quickly apprised of each other's goals and progress. Sessions were primarily work oriented and devoted to making plans, testing them in the social laboratory of the group and reporting on their success or failure outside the group. The final session involved reviewing individual and group progress, making commitments to continue working individually and saying good-bye.

Exit Interview: An exit interview was conducted by the co-leaders with each group member and centered around the Goal

Attainment Scaling procedure that had been introduced in the orientation session. Each individual was helped to assess and take credit for his/her own efforts and change and the overall effectiveness of the group counseling process was determined.

Application Possibilities: Employment

The applications of group counseling and the employment prospects for trained group leaders particularly in the area of interpersonal problem-solving are almost unlimited. I make that statement, however, with one qualification: program administrators and counselors themselves still need to be convinced of the efficacy of the group approach. Given the ability to explicate the merits of group counseling, the courage to stand by one's convictions relative to groups, and the expertise to effectively set up and run groups, my first statement will be validated.

Group counseling has relevance in all educational settings. Counselors can develop group programs that not only further the goals of the learning enterprise but increase the relevance of the counseling process to the institution and students.

Counseling groups are becoming standard operating procedure in a wide variety of community mental health programs. Mental health agencies use counseling groups in various forms to service a broad spectrum of client problems. Most special population treatment programs such as alcohol and chemical dependency rely heavily on the group modality. Corrections has endorsed the group approach both within institutions and as part of the reentry and social rehabilitation process. Group homes and halfway houses for populations that benefit from a transitional situation between institutionalization/treatment and full scale involvement in society, often use group counseling as an integral part of their programs.

Business and industry is another potential arena for implementation of group counseling. Skilled group leaders working through personnel departments and, more recently, through Employee Assistance Programs (EAP), are beginning to find a niche. Companies are realizing the merit of providing mental health services to their employees as a cost effective means of insuring and increasing productivity. As that attitude expands, interpersonal problem solving groups will become more prominent in the private sector.

Finally, group counseling has relevance for professionals engaged in providing training and consultation in the human services. Group methods can be adapted and implemented in a wide range of settings in the private and public domain. In fact, being an effective group leader may be an essential requirement in this area regardless of content and purpose.

SUMMARY

This chapter has reviewed the nature and process of group counseling as exemplified in interpersonal problem-solving groups. A perspective for viewing the group process with respect to interpersonal problems was presented along with models, techniques and examples. It should be evident from reading this chapter that the content and therapeutic utility of groups falling under the rubric of "Group Counseling" must be broadly construed. The process certainly overlaps with many of the other modalities posited in the Group Work Grid. But, at the same time, group counseling is an entity—in its own right—that the skilled group worker will value and become adept at using.

REFERENCES

Agras, W.S. (Ed.): *Behavior Modification: Principles and Clinical Applications* (2nd ed.). Boston: Little Brown, 1978.

Bednar, R.L. and Langenbacn, D.M.: Structure and Ambiguity: Conceptual and Applied Misconceptions. *Journal for Specialists in Group Work, 4:*170-175, 1979.

Conyne, R.K.: Personal Communication, May 19, 1983.

Glass, S.: Group Work for the 80's: What Next After Encounter Groups? Luncheon Address at the meeting of the Association for Specialists in Group Work, Washington, D.C., March, 1978.

Hansen, J.C., Warner, R.W., and Smith, E.J.: *Group Counseling: Theory and Process.* Chicago: Rand McNally, 1980.

James, W.: *The Principles of Psychology, Vol. 1.* New York: Holt, 1890.

Johnson, D.W.: *Reaching out: Interpersonal Effectiveness and Self-Actualization* (2nd ed.).

Englewood Cliffs: Prentice-Hall, 1981.

Johnson, D.W., and Johnson, F.P. The Use of Counseling Groups to Improve Interpersonal Skills. *Journal for Specialists in Group Work, 4*:211-215, 1979.

Journal for Specialists in Group Work: Group Counseling and the Dynamic of Structure (Special Issue). Author, 1979, *4*(4), whole issue.

Kanfer, F.H., and Goldstein, A.P. (eds.): *Helping People Change.* New York: Pergamon Press, 1975.

Kiresuk, T.J., and Sherman, R.E.: Goal Attainment Scaling: A General Method for Evaluating Community Mental Health Programs: *Community Mental Health Journal, 4*:443-453, 1968.

Kirschenbaum, H.: *Advanced Value Clarification.* LaJolla: University Associates, 1977.

Krumboltz, J.D., and Thoreson, C.E. (eds.): *Counseling Methods.* New York: Holt, 1976.

Landreth, G.L.: Group Counseling: To Structure or Not to Structure. *The School Counselor, 20*:371-374, 1973.

Lange, A.J., and Jakubowski, P.: *Responsible Assertive Behavior: Cognitive/Behavioral Procedures for Trainers.* Champaign, IL.: Research Press, 1976.

Miller, S., Nunnally, E.W., and Wackman, D.B.: *Alive and Aware: Improving Communication in Relationships.* Minneapolis, MN: Interpersonal Communication Programs, 1975.

Otto, H.: *Guide to Developing Your Potential.* New York: Scribner's, 1967.

Paritzky, R.S., and Magoon, T.M.: Goal Attainment Scaling Models for Assessing Group Counseling. *Personnel and Guidance Journal, 60*:381-384, 1982.

Rogers, C.R.: *Client-Centered Therapy.* Boston: Houghton Mifflin, 1951.

Satir, V.: *Peoplemaking.* Palo Alto: Science and Behavior Books, 1972.

Seigelman, E.: *Personal Risk: Mastering Change in Love and Work.* New York: Harper and Row, Publishers, 1983.

Simon, S.B., Howe, L.M., and Kirschenbaum, H.: *Values Clarification: A Handbook of Practical Strategies for Teachers and Students.* New York: Hart Publishing, 1972.

Sullivan, H.S.: *The Interpersonal Theory of Psychotherapy.* New York: Norton, 1953.

Trotzer, J.P.: *The Counselor and The Group: Integrating Theory, Training and Practice.* Monterey, CA.: Brooks/Cole Publishers, 1977.

Trotzer, J.P.: Developmental Tasks in Group Counselilng: The Basis for Structure. *Journal for Specialists in Group Work, 4*:177-185, 1979.

Trotzer, J.P.: Develop Your Own Guidance Group: A Structural Model for Planning and Practice. *The School Counselor, 27*:341-349, 1980.

Tubbs, S.L., and Moss, S.: *Interpersonal Communication.* New York: Random House, 1978.

Yalom, I.P.: *The Theory and Practice of Group Psychotherapy.* New York: Basic Books, Publishers, 1970.

CHAPTER 6

RESOCIALIZATION
Group Work in Social Control and
Correctional Settings

CHARLES D. GARVIN

INTRODUCTION

M ANY of the other chapters in this book describe work with groups that individuals join voluntarily in order to enhance or change some aspect of their individual or social functioning. These groups are usually found in agencies in the community and individuals seek them out for these purposes. Other groups are created by a community, organization, or educational institution to improve the functioning of that system as well as of individuals within it. In all of these cases, however, the *voluntary* nature of group participation is, at least in principle, protected.

There is another type of group that is also created and conducted by human service professionals in which participation is initially often involuntary. This category consists of groups whose purpose is to prevent or reduce the incidence of behavior that is viewed as deviant by society. The determination of what is deviant has usually been made by such institutions as courts and legislatures. These bodies have consequently created or used prisons, probation services, training schools, and halfway houses to control or modify deviant behaviors and, within these settings, a variety of groups are conducted to control the behavior of members and to resocialize them to enact non-deviant behaviors. The term "resocialization" is often used in this context to refer to replacing anti-social values and behaviors with pro-social ones through processes of interpersonal influence.

These groups, therefore, can be thought of as instruments of social control and as extensions of the social control purposes of the sponsoring institutions. This is the rationale for groups conducted in prisons for adults and training schools for youth. While we shall focus on such groups in this chapter, we believe that virtually all groups in the human service system have social control purposes to some degree and that social control represents a continuum and is not solely a property of groups for criminals and delinquents.

Social control exists as a phenomenon in groups because it is impossible to discuss beliefs and behaviors without introducing norms — normative development is a feature of all groups. Some group norms are relevant only to functioning of the specific group such as those embodied in rules about attendance, participation in group activities, and conduct during group ceremonials. Others, however, have implications for behavior outside of the group as members intentionally or unintentionally develop a consensus about how each is to behave in the community.

While one does not usually think of psychotherapy groups as instruments of social control, when the group discusses such topics as a member's use of violence, alcohol, or deception of others these behaviors tend to be proscribed by the group. A number of groups are also conducted in institutions in which the social control purposes are only thinly veiled. Groups are created in schools, for example, in which a main group purpose is to convince the students to work harder at their studies or to cease distracting others from their school tasks. In psychiatric institutions, groups also fulfill social control purposes when they seek to prevent members from interfering with hospital personnel or misusing hospital resources.

Nevertheless, we recognize that there are quantitative, if not qualitative, differences between these groups and those comprised of people labelled as actual or potential criminals or delinquents. The latter groups are our focus in this chapter.

Five differences that have implications for group services in these settings and that we shall discuss throughout this chapter are:

1. **Involuntary Membership.** Group members, as we have stated, are not likely to enter the group voluntarily. At times they are

explicitly ordered to attend the group, such as when a court states attendance in a group is a condition of probation or an institution for delinquents indicates that group participation is a compulsary part of the program. On other occasions, group membership is less compulsary but occurs as a result of either substantial pressure from others or a promise of substantial rewards for participation. Thus an abused wife might threaten to divorce a violent husband unless he joins a group for male batterers.

A consequence of this point is that the group members and worker must, as a first task, respond to the members' reactions to the involuntary nature of the group. While all efforts at helping individuals change meet with resistance, the resistance produced by involuntary group membership is greater than that produced by other groups and it must be reduced if the processes and procedures employed by human service professionals can be used.

2. **Value Issues.** Groups in social control situations require practitioners to develop a set of values that are responsive to both the social control purposes of these groups as well as professional ethics. We believe that this is possible when the practitioner has come to terms with the idea that society has a right to establish consequences for breaches of acceptable behavior and that individuals can choose to suffer these consequences. The practitioner is the instrument for helping individuals make this choice.

3. **Social Forces Maintain Deviance.** The kinds of deviant behaviors we refer to in this chapter result from social forces. The group process, therefore, must not only help members to acquire new behaviors but to cope with such forces. These forces include those created by anti-social subcultures as well as those due to the absence of opportunity structures such as jobs and education for former criminals and delinquents.

4. **Inmate Code.** When group work is practiced in an institution for criminals or delinquents, the processes of the group are strongly affected by the inmate code. This code, according to Kassebaum, Ward, and Wilner (1971) requires the inmate to uphold solidarity with other inmates by refusing to divulge information about them and by siding with them rather than staff. Some of the behavioral consequences of this code are that members resist discussing their reactions to each other as well as knowledge that they have of the be-

havior of other group members. As demonstrated throughout this book, these interactions are sought by most group workers and their absence is a major hindrance to the use of many group work procedures.

5. **Organizational Forces.** All group work is affected by the organizational sponsorship of the group. As we have stated elsewhere (Garvin, 1981) organizational forces include those that affect the purpose, membership, role of worker, access to resources, and activity of the group. If the barriers to group progress imposed by the inmate code are to be reduced, there must be some complementarity between the character of the organization and the group. Correcional institutions are often coercive and punitive, and through these and other means alienate their inmates.

The preceding points must make the undertaking of group service in a social control setting seem a formidable one. Nevertheless, such services are widespread. According to Arnold and Stiles (1972), there has been a sharp upswing in the uses of groups with inmates of correctional institutions. Their survey showed that 35 percent of institutions had such groups in 1950, 79 percent in 1966, and 62 percent in 1972. While we do not have more recent statistics, we believe that inmate groups have achieved a firm place in the program of the majority of prisons.

GROUPS FOR SOCIAL CONTROL:
RATIONALE AND THEORY

For several decades many writers on deviant behavior have conceived of such behavior as produced by the social, and more specifically group, circumstances of the deviant. Behavior change, therefore, can also be produced through groups having a strong interpersonal orientation. As Studt, Messinger, and Wilson (1968) state, "Whether the offender is seen as a distingrated personality unable to respond to group norms, or as a member of delinquent groups in an anomic society, treatment by the group method is proposed as a specific for the problem."

Sutherland and Cressey (1978) outline a series of postulates that expand upon this perspective on deviance. They state that criminal behavior is learned through interaction with other persons; that this learning occurs within intimate personal groups; and that the learning includes both techniques for committing crimes as well as the direction of motives, drives, rationalizations and attitudes. A major factor, according to these authors, in being subjected to these group forces is differential association in that when deviant groups exist in one's environment the probability of exposure to them is high. The implication of this theory for treatment is that the same group processes that have been used to "educate" people for deviance can be used for the opposite effect.

Another group phenomenon that makes group work a viable tool in social control situations is that of surveillance, that is, the opportunity group members have to observe and give feedback to each other. It is almost impossible for inmates to conceal their problems from each other as well as their progress or lack of progress in resolving these. (Inmates may, nevertheless, conceal from each other their past, present, and future outside the institution but many clues are picked up regarding these realities, also.)

A third group condition that is a factor in the effectiveness of groups in these settings is the use members can make of each other as models. In such groups, members will vary from each other in attitudes, motivation to change, social and problem-solving skills, and associational patterns. This offers members an opportunity to learn by imitation. Practitioners, therefore, will seek to compose groups so as to be able to use imitational processes for pro-social purposes (the opposite is, of course, an ever present possibility in these groups) and to "seed" groups with positive models — often those who have been socialized through a previous group experience.

Another important and yet controversial contribution groups can make in this environment is that they can be a more potent force for social change than can either inmates, or even staff, acting as individuals. Institutional conditions that can inhibit resocialization include a strong custodial orientation of the staff or a strong inmate code against disclosure and confrontation. The type of group contribution, however, will be hindered if the inmates are convinced that their norms are functional in buffering them from an unnecessarily oppressive institutional environment.

PRACTITIONER FUNCTIONS AND TECHNIQUES

The practitioner's functions include all those that apply to any group situation as well as several that relate to the social control purposes of the groups discussed here. Those that apply to working with all groups include securing members for the group, helping the group to accomplish the tasks of group formation, assisting the group to accomplish its goals, and supporting the group as it faces termination. Some techniques for accomplishing these functions are highly relevant to social control situations and these will be emphasized in this discussion.

Worker functions that are unique to social control situations are responding to member reactions to pressure to join the group so as to achieve at least a minimum degree of voluntariness; serving as a mediator between members and the custodial aspects of correctional systems; and seeking to humanize the correctional system. A pervasive function of all group workers in such settings is that of defining and seeking the members' compliance with pro-social norms. When and how to fulfill this latter function constitutes the most important question facing these workers.

Every approach that has been used with groups in other settings has been used in the correctional field although there are some, such as Guided Group Interaction (Stephenson and Scarpitti, 1974), that were developed uniquely for this field. As with any setting the practitioner should select an approach based upon the needs of the specific group members, the circumstances of specific institutions, the phenomena present in the group due to its stage of development, and the change targets that are appropriate in the light of the aforementioned conditions.

Change Targets

Change targets place a heavy burden on a group worker in a social control setting but, in many ways, this burden is no greater than that placed on any group worker. The paradigm we have used to conceptualize the forces that confront members that might be selected as change targets in this type of setting is as follows: The forces that are relevant in these settings consist of *peer groups* and *social structures*. Peer groups exist both *within* and *outside* of the institution and the same is true for social structures. The task of the worker, consequently, is to help the member to use the group (1) to change how she or he behaves toward peer groups and social structures or (2) to change the effects of those peer groups and social structures on himself or herself, or both.

This use of the group, therefore, proceeds through a phase in which such forces are assessed followed by a phase in which a change plan is developed and carried out. A brief example of this approach follows:

Example

John is an inmate of a prison; his offense was stealing in order to support a drug habit and these problems still concern him. The use of the above paradigm suggests the following targets for John's work in the group:

1. John's behavior toward peers in the institution —
   John tries to establish very dependent relationships with other inmates.
2. John's behavior toward the social system of the prison —
   John views the institution as the enemy and avoids making use of its resources.
3. John's behavior to peers in the community —
   John seeks to gain favor with members of a drug sub-culture.
4. John's behavior toward the social structure of the community —
   John has avoided contact with such community institutions as schools and places of employment.
5. Behavior of institutional peers to John —
   They reject him for his efforts to be dependent on them.
6. Behavior of institutional social structure to John —
   Institutional staff have labelled John a "dead-beat" and few resources for change are offered him.
7. Behavior of community peers toward John —
   Anti-social peers seek to include him in their interactions; pro-social peers have long rejected him.
8. Behavior of community social structure to John —
   John has been rejected from community job training program

because of irresponsible behavior while in program; community lacks adequate drug treatment programs.

Change Approaches

We shall briefly portray the approaches that have been most frequently used with groups in social control settings and we shall note the most relevant target for each approach as it is used in a social control setting.

Analytic Group Psychotherapy

This approach may be used in a social control setting when the appropriate target is the individual's behavior as it is molded by the impact of her or his emotional development on ways of coping. Rappaport (1977), in his thoughtful discussion of the use of this approach in prisons, recognizes that this creates a paradox. As he states, "This 'rehabilitative setting,' the classical prison environment, is the least likely media upon which to culture and grow new life....There is no less fertile ground for the growth of the human ego, for the betterment of man's condition, or for the resurrection of human character" (p. 116). Nevertheless, he believes that in some situations it is possible to transform the institution's punishment function into one of psychotherapy.

Rappaport developed unique strategies in order to function as an analytic group therapist in a prison environment. These included incurring no obligations to either staff or inmates that would restrict the therapeutic process; avoiding becoming an advocate for inmates outside of the therapeutic situation; defending the group's existence; and avoiding any participation in corrupt acts. He emphasized that the therapist must make a "special effort toward reducing the fear of retribution by favoring exposure of feelings and interpretation of their origin" (p. 124). Unlike the traditional analytic group therapy situation, at times Rappaport introduced prison personnel into the groups as actual members. He also sought to include family members as discharge time approached.

Behavior Modification in Groups

Behavior modification may be used in a social control setting when the appropriate target is the individual's behavior, particularly social skills. This is a very valuable component of rehabilitation as many inmates are hindered by their inability to secure employment, friendships with pro-social peers, and satisfying, non-violent family relationships. Behavioral procedures that have been used with both youths and adults in prison groups include the use of models, the use of tokens as reinforcers for pro-social behavior, reinforcement, in the form of feedback from other group members, and the creation of practice situations to try out new behaviors.

A major issue with the use of these procedures in prisons is whether inmates voluntarily participate in the groups and select the behaviors for change. Nevertheless, evaluative studies of behavioral groups in social control settings have shown the effectiveness of this approach. Among studies of adolescent groups are those of Jesness, DeRisi, McCormick, and Wedge (1972), Sarason and Ganzer (1973), and Ollendick and Hersen (1979). Studies of the effectiveness of this approach with adult offenders have included those of Novotny and Enomoto (1976), Mills (1978) and Bornstein, Weingardner, Rychtarir, Paul, Naifeh, Sweeney, and Justman (1979).

A recent review of Group Assertiveness Training in correctional settings demonstrates that this procedure has had many positive consequences for this population. These include a reduction in undesirable behaviors in the setting as well as an improvement in measures that simulate social behaviors.

Enhancing Problem Solving Through Groups

When the appropriate target of change is the member's ability to identify and solve his or her problems within or outside of the institution, problem-solving groups may be used. These are usually referred to as counseling groups to distinguish them from the analytic group therapy referred to earlier. While the literature on counseling in correctional settings describes such groups as providing opportunities for expression of emotions, feedback from peers, and reinforcement of reality testing, a central theme is problem-solving (Hatcher, 1978; Kassebaum, Ward, and Wilner, 1971).

These groups focus on member concerns about relationships with other inmates, prison conditions, family relationships and plans for discharge. The typical group does not usually seek to help the inmates to acquire specific problem-solving skills; problem-solving occurs through a variety of means such as securing suggestions from peers, testing one's solutions against the reaction of others, and learning how to give and take help in group situations.

A thorough evaluation of group counseling in a prison was conducted by Kassebaum, Ward and Wilner (1971). These authors point out the complex problems that emerge when one tries to assess the forces imposed by the heterogeneity of inmates, the functions of the prison, the "outside" forces that act upon inmates, the inmate culture, and the training and orientation of group counselors. This strengthens our idea that a group treatment program in a correctional setting must take into consideration (and possibly seek to change) conditions present in the institution and community. We now turn to approaches that specifically attend to organizational conditions.

Guided Group Interaction

Guided Group Interaction is an approach to modifying deviant behavior that is directed at the norms of the peer group. It has been evaluated through a number of studies conducted over the last twenty-five years and has been found to be more effective in reducing recidivism than "typical" reformatory programs. These programs, usually directed at adolescents, also have improved the inmates attitudes toward peers, program, and staff. Mixed findings, however, prevail when various attitudinal and personality measures are employed and when institutional treatment is compared with treatment in the community. (Elias and Pilnick, 1964; Empey and Erickson, 1972; Empey and Lubeck, 1971; McCorkle, Elias, and Bixby, 1958; Stephenson and Scarpitti, 1974.)

The group is conducted by the members albeit with facilitation provided by a staff member. The group evolves a set of "down-to-earth" terms for common problems of members such as lying, low self concept, and substance abuse. Members, through "telling their story" are helped to identify their problems. Members "check" each other for manifestations of the problems both within and outside of the group. This behavior is seen as a demonstration of "caring" and members who fail to confront a member are accused of not caring.

Members make recommendations for increased privileges and

eventually for discharge from the program but these recommendations may be rejected by staff. The staff facilitator also adopts a confrontational style and typically redirects questions to the group, thus cultivating a sense of ambiguity as to where the staff stands.

Guided Group Interaction programs, as well as the closely related Positive Peer Culture ones (Vorrath and Brendtro, 1974), do not only depend on daily group meetings but on orienting the entire staff to the philosophy and methods of the approach. Staff meet as a team to strategize on inputs to the group and also on how these can be reinforced when staff members interact with inmates in other institutional programs such as school, workplace, and living unit. Guided Group Interaction, therefore, resolves some of the problems we have alluded to stemming from the contradictions inherent in conducting therapeutic groups in repressive settings. We conclude this discussion, therefore, with a consideration of turning a prison into a therapeutic community in which work with groups plays a significant role.

Group Work in a Therapeutic Prison Community

While there have been many efforts to create therapeutic communities within residential programs for adolescent delinquents, parallel developments in penal institutions for adults are rarer. One of the most carefully developed and researched programs for adults was developed by Studt and her colleagues in a California institution (Studt, Messinger, and Wilson, 1968). In their well documented book *C-Unit: Search for Community in Prison*, these investigators report in detail on all aspects of the program, including its history from inception to demise. We shall summarize here the group aspects.

The core concept in the program that pervaded its groups was problem-solving. As the authors state:

> The project's first task was to get prison inmates to experience legitimate problem-solving as rewarding in and of itself. This could not be accomplished by telling them about the satisfactions they were missing, by instructing them in the process, or by providing them with material rewards for behaving in the desired fashion. Only a problem felt strongly enough to motivate action, a process for successful problem resolution; and the actually experienced rewards of pride in self, safety with others, accom-

plishment and fellowship, would be sufficient to establish effective community values to govern action in prison (p. 61).

The focus of the program at first was upon common problems. These included conflicts between two types of inmates with different statuses, disorder in the TV room, and poor communication between staff and inmates. Problem focussed groups developed in a serendipitous manner out of "Bull Sessions" participated in by staff and inmates.

In these Bull Sessions, staff became familiar with the inmates' world. This included ethnic group conflicts, conflicts between project staff and prison administrators, and the view that project personnel were exploiting inmates. Practical inmate concerns were also expressed such as boredom, program ideas, changes in prison facilities, and rumors of riots.

Out of these Bull Sessions, a number of specialized groups were created. These included committees for special events and ad hoc groups to solve specific problems. Ultimately a "program" began to emerge that was jointly created by project staff and inmates. This group oriented program consisted of (1) Community groups to deal with mutual concerns of staff and inmates; (2) Task groups to do specific jobs for the unit; (3) Counseling groups for discussions of personal problems of inmates; and (4) Interest groups focussing on leisure time interests.

The above description of the program and its groups does not do full justice to the way staff worked with inmates to develop it. All interactions were governed by a spirit of compassion, a sense of common humanity, and a desire to create a community in which all members, including staff, could develop their capacities to cope with the realities of the situation.

One way of making decisions as to an appropriate approach is to examine stages of group development and the facilitation required at each stage. We now present a discussion of this issue.

Phases of Group Development

Pre-Group Phase

Prior to work with a group in a social control setting, the worker should seek to assess the potential members. This will help the worker to anticipate the approaches that are likely to be helpful as well as the group composition that will be compatible with the approach.

The worker, therefore, should gather information on the peer group interactions of potential members, both within the institution as well as prior to admission. In many cases the worker will take on a "natural" group such as a section of a prison, or a cottage in a training school. While this choice precludes much impact on group composition, it allows for some advance study of the nature of the group.

An interactional assessment should be sensitive to value issues, especially to value conflicts among inmates that might be predictive of motivation in the group to examine values relevant to change. When assessing this aspect of individuals, the worker should ask about times they have pursued alternative goals and whether family members and others in their social networks will be supportive of this pursuit in the future.

Group composition in a social control setting poses some problems because a prison population may be relatively homogeneous in life experiences, behaviors, and values. Nevertheless, there are many social types in prisons and this should be well understood by practitioners. Kassebaum, Ward, and Wilner (1971), for example, present an excellent discussion of such types as "square john," "right guy," "con-politician," and "outlaw" as well as means for assessing individuals in relationship to a typology of prison types. Workers should carefully consider the particular mix that will be most conducive to their purposes.

Group Formation

Our discussion of group development during formation and after draws heavily from the Guided Group Interaction literature. Our own experiences suggest that the processes described there can be generalized well beyond the uses of that model (see, particularly, Empey and Erickson, 1972: 96-103, for such an analysis).

When beginning a group in a social control setting, it is important to overcome the initial distrust and hostility of the members toward the group experience. Empey and Erickson (1972) assume that members will behave in a manner that is "erratic and defensive" and they recommend that the group leader should foster interaction among group members and seek to instill some confidence that the group will ultimately be valuable.

Another way of promoting interaction during the process of group formation is to ask members to "tell their stories." The worker need not fear that this process will continue indefinitely as it produces much material that can be drawn upon to help members choose goals, confront each other on repetitive dysfunctional patterns, and seek changes in their behavior.

As members find themselves behaving in stereotyped ways during the formation period, the worker should confront them with the fact that this way of using the group will not lead to any desired benefits such as a discharge from the program. This further promotes the idea that the group can be used for problem-solving activity.

The content of discussions during this period must be open to an examination of institutional conditions that are harmful to group members. When this is done with the support of the worker, it encourages members to also examine themselves as contributing to their problems. The kinds of conditions that are examined include institutional resources such as those devoted to education, recreation, and job training. Staff behaviors, as well as policy decisions, are also appropriate topics here. These discussions are likely to lead to critiques of disciplinary actions and sexist and racist attitudes.

The formation period is likely to be drawing to a close when the worker and members have a viable *contract*. This contract reflects an agreement on the purposes of the group, a developing trust between worker and members and among the members, and at least an intellectual understanding of the procedures likely to be used in the group for problem solving.

Goal Pursuit — The Middle Phase

Empey and Erickson (1972) find that the middle phase of the group begins with the group still engaging, to a degree, in stereotyped problem-solving. As they note, members begin to raise concerns but are still well defended in the way that this is done. They ask the kinds of questions that they think they are expected to ask and they give answers of similar quality (p. 103). The group worker should be patient at this point in order to prevent a reemergence of the resistance manifested earlier. Nevertheless, some genuine problem-solving discussions will begin to occur and these should be reinforced. This must be done tactfully as some members of the group are likely to move in this direction while others oppose this and subtly seek to punish such members. Thus, conflict is inevitable at this point and the worker should seek the role of mediator rather than advocate for one side.

As Empey and Erickson note, members during this period begin to take responsibility for making judgments rather than being the targets of judgments made by others. This introduces members to a "reformation role" and begins to make the group a medium for change. Another group phase begins to emerge as members begin to challenge each other's characteristic defenses.

If this period is well handled, more members begin to focus on individual differences and needs. This leads to problem-solving around current issues. That allows the worker to also initiate problem-solving discussions around issues of which he or she is aware. Gradually, the degree of cohesiveness and trust that have emerged permit the members to become more conscious of their own group and to deal with internal issues that impede progress.

Termination

When members terminate, an individual evaluation should take place and this evaluation should become part of the individual's institutional record. This evaluation should examine changes in the individual's goals, behaviors, values, and emotions. This should be linked to how the group has helped or harmed such outcomes. The typical social control group will seek to add new members to replace those departing so that the positive norms of the group may be perpetuated. This requires the group to become skillfull in helping members to deal with membership losses as well as the socialization of new members.

Gender Issues

Thus far we have discussed group work in social control settings with no reference to whether members are male or female. Gender in such groups is a topic, nevertheless, about which more research must be done (for a start in conceptualizing the relevant gender issues, see Reed and Garvin, 1983). We believe that gender of group members in these, as in all, settings makes a great difference in how group processes are understood and facilitated. Many men in prisons, for example, are likely to be imprisoned for offenses that are typically committed by males such as those related to violent behaviors. They are likely to bring to groups a desire to maintain and protect a masculine image of strength that includes nonattention to affects and a facade of independence. These reactions must usually be confronted in any social control group for progress to take place. Men are also likely to be competitive with each other and with the worker and this can impede progress.

Women, on the other hand, may be more likely than men to take and give help to each other initially in groups in such settings. On the other hand, they have often been harmed by sexist responses and these may be associated with the deviant paths they have taken. A keen appreciation of these issues, and particularly of the way society has responded to female assertiveness, must be maintained by the worker. Rehabilitation of women in such settings must be accompanied by a realistic awareness and confrontation of the barriers to women in the society, particularly women who have been labeled as deviant.

An Example

As an example of some of the processes and procedures, we present a segment of a meeting of a prison group. The group, as can be seen, had progressed past the phase of group formation and had entered the early middle phase of development.

The group was composed of twelve men (eight black and four white) whose offenses included murder, armed robbery, and rape. The group had been meeting for four months.

The group worker, as shown in this episode, introduced a variety of group approaches drawn from group counseling and psychotherapy, including behavioral as well as insight-oriented techniues. An innovation that he had created for this and other groups is the use of an inmate as co-therapist. Such inmates had been selected and trained by him based on their participation in groups in which they demonstrated talent for helping others. I refer to the psychologist as Dr. S. and the inmate co-leader as F.

At this meeting, two new members were present for the first time, Bill and Ted. They had learned from informal discussions with group members outside the group that they would be expected to tell something about their "problems" and background at this meeting and this had been reinforced in a screening interview they held with Dr. S. Bill began talking when the group convened, as if he had been cued to do this. He stated that his offense had been armed robbery but that his was not the usual case. He had come from a "good" family and had not been in trouble as a teenager. He had been married when he was seventeen to a woman whom he loved and with whom he had a close relationship. He had received training as a musician and earned his living playing with bands. The group discussed Bill's story. In this example, however, we shall describe Ted's subsequent input and the group's reaction to it.

Ted told his story without any prompting. He had been involved since he was a young teenager in a series of thefts. When he was seventeen (about three years before), he and a "Rap-buddy" (partner in committing crimes) had been engaged in a burglary. While it was in progress, the owner returned and drew a gun. Ted grabbed a hammer and hit the owner on the head. The man was in a coma and was expected to die. His rap buddy "snitched" on him and he was arrested. The buddy was not sentenced but Ted was given a seven to fourteen year sentence. The victim survived but, because of the seriousness of his crime, Ted was tried as an adult and placed in adult institutions.

Ted indicated that he had a problem with violence and several men asked him to elaborate on this. He said that he had been involved in at least a dozen fights in several institutions in which he had been an inmate before being transferred to this one because his fighting had diminished. Nevertheless, he had been placed in solitary confinement a number of times. His first fight occurred when his rap-buddy, in jail on a new charge, had been transferred to the same institution in which Ted was a prisoner. Ted said that he was justified in attacking the buddy but he had been wrong in his earlier attack on the person he robbed. He explained that several fights had occurred as he sought to ward off homosexual advances.

F. commented that Ted seemed to present himself as a "victim" who was forced by others to be violent. Within this institution, it was clearly understood that "victim" meant that one abdicated responsibility for one's own actions. Ted did not respond to this and this theme was picked up by several other men. One commented that he thought Ted was a danger to other people and was not ready for a release to the community. Another asked Ted if he still would attack his rap-buddy and Ted said he wouldn't as this matter was now settled.

A discussion took place in the group that lasted only five minutes as a digression from dealing with Ted. The substance of the discussion was what constitutes "snitching." Several men said they had come to the conclusion that it was not "snitching" if you told the truth about something even if another person was implicated in a crime. These men said that snitching should only be thought of as telling lies that falsely implicate others when the liar is the culprit. This discussion was in reference to Ted's attack on his rap-buddy for "snitching."

Another man in the group who is black (Ted is white) asked Ted about his recent actions to relieve himself from his work assignment in the kitchen. Ted stated he had not liked kitchen work. The other man said that he knew Ted had secured relief from this assignment by writing a letter to the supervisor stating that he was being "pressed" by others on this work detail and he could not handle pressure (probably a reference to his known violent reactions). The other member stated that Ted had "manipulated" a situation to his own benefit in a way that could cause others to suffer. He went on to point out that since Ted was white and the others on the detail black, the charge of the white man would be believed, as it was often alleged, that black inmates, who were in a majority of all inmates, harassed white inmates. Ted denied this charge and a lengthy discussion ensued in which black group members (supported by one white member) sought to convince Ted of the implications they saw in his actions. These also were linked to the earlier assertion that Ted tended to play the "victim" when he actually provoked others.

At this point the time allocated to the meeting had expired. Dr. S. indicated to Ted that his anger at others and the way he handled it may have been the result of some of his earlier experiences, perhaps family ones. He asked Ted to think about this and to discuss his reactions to it at a future meeting.

This example illustrates several processes that are typical of groups in social control settings. We see the new members encouraged to "tell their stories" as a way of introducing themselves to other members, initiating interactions, and identifying problems to be worked on in the group.

Even though this is Ted's first meeting, the other members sense that he may be open to confrontation, which they proceed to offer. It is also likely that the other members confronted him because his actions not only harmed himself but were detrimental to his fellow inmates. That this is not a beginning group is evidenced by the fact that the members were willing to confront one another and to deal with such problems as racism in the institution. The inmate code usually prevents the former in new groups. Members, as well, are likely to be pessimistic that confrontation of racism will accomplish anything if they are still discovering the purposes of group work.

EVIDENCE OF INTERVENTION EFFECTIVENESS

There have been a number of studies of group work in social control settings that indicate its degree of effectiveness. We begin this section, however, by noting, somewhat defensively, that the effectiveness of the use of group work in such settings has not been conclusively demonstrated. This reality, however, is true of the use of group work in all settings, to say nothing about the effectiveness of psychological helping in general.

One review of group treatment of juvenile delinquents (Julian and Kilmann, 1979) concluded that behavioral and modelling groups were the most effective. A study that compared behavioral treatment and transactional analysis with delinquents found that both were effective at the time of the termination of service but, as is true of many institutional programs, did not produce substantially better results than those attained by controls at follow up, when community influences were again operative (Jesness, et al., 1972).

A massive work by Lipton, Martinson, and Wilks (1975) surveyed virtually every research evaluation of any kind of treatment of offenders completed by the late 1960's. This work has often been cited by correctional officials who wish to dismantle psychological programs. In this compendium, however, group treatment "comes off" fairly well and we now cite some representative studies from this work.

Harrison and Mueller found that group counseling conducted in an adult institution for more than a year with a single leader was more effective than such counseling led by more than one leader and was more effective than no treatment at all provided that the institution does not emphasize security or the program does not become routinized. Stable group counseling is less likely to be effective in institutions that provide more intensive custody and less likely to be effective with offenders with longer sentences.

Shelley completed a study of counseling that comprised 52 hours a year in group and 38 hours a year in individual counseling. The subjects were first offenders in a Michigan prison camp. The group led to decreased anti-social attitudes of members compared to controls who received routine camp treatment.

Other similar findings were reported in studies by Kessemeier, Aleranes and Mandel. Not all studies generated positive findings, however. Examples of the latter were Heim and Kassebaum.

The above studies demonstrate the failing of many studies of group work outcomes. They seldom specify the details of the group program to the degree required for replication of the study. They also do not usually answer the vital question as to which kind of treatment is best for which kind of offender with which problem and, in which type of setting. They, nevertheless, show the value of group work in such settings, particularly when goals are clear, when members realistically can profit from change and when professional leadership is consistent.

TRAINING

We believe that work in social control settings has some unique requirements. These include the following:

1. An understanding of the forces in the society that produce deviant behaviors.
2. A comprehension of the nature of prisons: their structures,

methods, staffing patterns, and inmate careers.

3. An awareness of the nature of inmate culture, how it manifests itself in group work, and how its negative forces may be overcome.

4. A knowledge of the ways that prisons must change in order to make it likely that inmates may receive benefits from incarceration beyond protecting the public from their acts *and* a possession of the techniques that may be employed to create changes in the prison, itself.

EMPLOYMENT

We believe that the future is bright for workers who seek employment in these settings although such work will always be fraught with frustration and hard work. The members of prison communities and correctional programs are not the easiest people to work with but they *are* among the most needy of services. A caring society must be one that places an emphasis on helping such people rather than simply punishing them and a caring professional must be open to this type of employment.

REFERENCES

Arnold, W.R. and Stiles, B.: A Summary of Increasing Use of Group Methods in Correctional Institutions. *International Journal of Group Psychotherapy, 22*:77-93, 1972.

Bornstein, P., Winegardner, J., Rychtarir, R., Paul, W., Naifeh, S., Sweeney, T., and Justman, A.: Interpersonal Skills Training: Evaluation of a Program with Adult Male Offenders. *Criminal Justice and Behavior, 6*:119-132, 1979.

Elias, A., and Pilnick, S.: The Essexfields Group Rehabilitation Project for Youthful Offenders. *Correction in the Community: Alternative to Incarceration.* Monograph No. 4, Board of Corrections, State of California, 1964 (51-57).

Empey, L., and Erickson, M.: *The Provo Experiment: Evaluating Community Control of Delinquency.* Lexington: Heath, 1972.

Empey, L., and Lubeck, S.: *The Silverlake Experiment: Testing Delinquency Theory and Community Intervention.* Chicago: Aldine-Atherton, 1971.

Garvin, C.: *Contemporary Group Work.* Englewood Cliffs: Prentice-Hall, 1981.

Jesness, C., DeRisi, W., McCormick, P., and Wedge, R.: *The Youth Center Research Project.* Sacramento: American Justice Institute, 1972.

Julian, A., and Kilmann, P.: Group Treatment of Juvenile Delinquents: A Reveiw of the Outcome Literature. *International Journal of Group Psychotherapy,* 29:3-37, 1979.

Kassebaum, G., Ward, D., and Wilner, D.: *Prison Treatment and Parole Survival: An Empirical Assessment.* New York: Wiley, 1971.

Lipton, D., Martinson, R., and Wilks, J.: *The Effectiveness of Correctional Treatment.* New York: Praeger, 1975.

McCorkle, L., Elias, A., and Bixby, F.: *The Highfields Story: A Unique Experiment in the Treatment of Juvenile Delinquency.* New York: Holt, 1958.

Mills, C.: The Use of Modelling, Coaching, and Behavior Rehearsal in Assertive Training as Therapy with a Group of Men at a Correctional Institution. Unpublished Doctoral Dissertation, Kansas State University, 1978.

Novotny, H., and Enomoto, J.: Social Competence Training as a Correctional Alternative, *Offender Rehabilitation, 1*:45-55, 1976.

Ollendick, T., and Hersen, M.: Social Skills Training for Juvenile Delinquents. *Behavior Research and Therapy, 17*:547-554, 1979.

Rappaport, R.: Group Therapy in Prison: A Strategic Approach. In Seligman, Milton, (Ed.), *Group Counseling and Group Psychotherapy with Rehabilitation Clients.* Springfield, IL: Thomas, 1977.

Reed, B., and Garvin, C. (Eds.): *Group Work with Women/Group Work with Men: An Overview of Gender Issues in Social Group Work Practice.* New York: Haworth Press, 1983.

Sarason, I., and Ganzer, V.: Modeling and Group Discussion in the Rehabilitation of Juvenile Delinquents. *Journal of Consulting Psychology, 20*:442-449, 1973.

Stephenson, R., and Scarpitti, F.: *Group Interaction as Therapy: The Use of the Small Group in Corrections.* Westport: Greenwood, 1974.

Studt, E., Messinger, S., and Wilson, T.: *C-Unit: Search for Community in Prison.* New York: Sage, 1968.

Sutherland, E., and Cressey, D.: *Principles of Criminology* (10th ed.). Philadelphia: Lippincott, 1978.

Vorrath, H., and Brendtro, L.: *Positive Peer Culture.* Chicago: Aldine, 1974.

CHAPTER 7

INTERPERSONAL GROWTH
Learning and Change Through
Interpersonal Process

ALLAN DYE

S ELF-disclosure, taking the risk of saying whatever seems important at the time, is the single most important behavior in a laboratory group. Thus, it seems appropriate to begin this chapter with a
statement about purposes and objectives, the things I hope to accomplish in the following pages. The fundamental goal is to provide
an operational description of how learning and change occur
through the interpersonal process. Specifically, I hope to describe
the laboratory group in a comprehensive manner so that it can be
distinguished in important ways from other types of groups. An additional goal is to discuss the interpersonal process in a way that will
enable practitioners to conduct this form of group work with maximum effectiveness.

Several questions will be addressed. Who participates in laboratory groups and for what reasons? In what ways does change occur?
What is the nature of such change? What role do leaders play and,
specifically, what do they do? How does one become competent in
conducting a laboratory group? What are the usual outcomes, and
in what ways can laboratory groups be used?

From one point of view it could be accurately stated that there are
as many particular forms of group work as there are practitioners
and combinations of circumstances. Just as an individual is unique,
so is each group. From another perspective, however, all group work

stems from only two origins, therapy and enhancement. That is, all group work is conducted either for the purpose of correcting something that has gone wrong or as a way of improving a tolerable but less than desirable situation. Neither form is particularly new. Group therapy was conducted as early as 1905, according to some authors (for an excellent historical overview, see Gazda, 1982), while the generic form of the enhancement group, the T-group, first appeared in 1946 (see Yalom, 1975). Of these two formidable ancestors in the group work family, those groups in the enhancement category, e.g., laboratory, T-group, training, sensitivity, human relations, encounter, and personal growth, have touched more lives, been a part of more training and service programs, and have undoubtedly spawned more creativity in the use of the group setting to serve a vast array of purposes.

The valuable properties of the laboratory group were recognized by Lewin and his associates during the formative years of the National Training Laboratory. The findings of this original group, and of a large number of successors, were quickly transmitted through an informal network of professionals in education, business and industry, psychology, social work and religion. By 1970, following a decade of spectacular growth, group work for the purpose of enhancement had become a widely popular modality for achieving gains in personal and interpersonal awareness. Moreover, massive gains had occurred at the meta level; that is, the laboratory group movement had itself become a laboratory for learning about learning and interpersonal processes, the effects of which have influenced the entire spectrum of the behavioral and social sciences. A great deal has also been learned about teaching in the study of interpersonal learning. Skills training, for example, is a major activity that is a direct outgrowth of the laboratory group movement.

INTERVENTION LEVEL

The primary focus of the laboratory group is upon the *interpersonal* process, matters pertaining to the exchange of information between two or more persons. In addition, an explicit assumption is held that learning and change will occur reciprocally between individual members who are peers in the laboratory environment.

Laboratory groups are highly interactive. Members are encouraged and implicitly expected to be active in thinking, feeling, being aware of motivations, and speaking as both initiators and reactors. The term *interpersonal process* implies the participating of two or more people in a sequence of two or more actions that are progressive in nature. A *process*, the basic unit in a laboratory group, consists of two persons, a bit of information from one, and a reaction to the bit of information from the other. The expectation in a laboratory group is that both individuals may learn something about themselves, the other, and how they learned from one another.

THE ENHANCEMENT EMPHASIS

Enhancement can be interpreted literally to mean improvement. In comparing remedial with enhancing groups, therefore, a distinguishing feature of the latter is that no assumption of deficit is made. Rather, the purpose is taken to be generative not rehabilitative, creative as opposed to adaptive. The motto might be, "Making a good thing better," or, in humanistic vernacular, "Becoming more of who you already are." At the same time, it must be acknowledged that there is not always a clear distinction between what is remedial and what is enhancing. Many practitioners, the author included, contend that the dynamics of learning and change vary only slightly between the two environments.

If one accepts the notion that behavior is purposive, first in surviving and then in improving one's lot in life, than it is relatively easy to account for the popularity of group experiences having an enhancement focus. All of us are eager to understand more fully, to be more aware, skillful and in control. These are precisely the objectives of the laboratory group.

THEORY AND ASSUMPTIONS

In addition to the assumption that behavior is purposive, a second foundational assumption of the laboratory group is that social behavior is learned. This learning is acquired in two ways, operant conditioning (so-called trial and error) and social modeling (so-called imitative learning). In both cases, the learner discerns what is appropriate or correct by noting the responses of significant others. That is to say, there is no such thing as absolute certainty where social behavior is concerned. Each act depends for verification upon one's own judgement or, if available, the opinion of others. Feedback, knowing how we are perceived by others, is an essential component of the learning process. Yalom (1975) has identified it as one of the most powerful of the curative factors in group psychotherapy.

Inevitably, each of us must decide what is correct or most appropriate for us and act on this basis. In becoming able to do so, we first observe others' behavior, watching and listening for evidence that they have acted successfully. In our own subsequent attempts to behave similarly, we infer approval or disapproval, success or failure, according to the responses of others whom we value. We literally compare the outcome of our actions with one or more criteria that we have first (often unknowingly) selected. Thus, we can use as criteria our own judgments, those of others, or some absolute criterion such as specific task performance. Because social learning requires feedback, it can be concluded that we learn complex behaviors through a sometimes elaborate process of making comparisons. All that passes for knowledge, but is actually no more than personal belief (or opinion, judgment, assumption), is the net result of comparing one's own judgments and reactions with those of others. Thus, what a person "knows" and subsequently uses as a basis for action is limited by several factors. Among these are the availability of models, opportunities for experimentation, encouragement, reward, and skill in choosing models, making comparisons and evaluating outcomes. Both the quantity and quality of learning are directly proportionate to the supply of these ingredients.

It seems appropriate to observe that most cultures value accomplishment, pay relatively little attention to learning how to accomplish, and leave the matter of learning how to learn largely to chance. These priorities follow a different order in the laboratory group, where learning *how* to be more effective receives primary attention, followed by insight concerning the learning process. Accomplishments are taken largely for granted, being regarded as natural by-products of an enriched climate.

CHANGE TECHNIQUES

How does change occur in laboratory groups? It is too simple to say that change occurs as a result of the interpersonal process, though there is a great temptation to do so. The interpersonal process is inherent in all groups, however, and for this reason it is not possible to distinguish with precision among the varieties of group experience. Rather, in identifying one sort of group from another it is necessary to speak in terms of emphasis, focus and function. What are the goals? To what, in particular, is attention given? What action is taken?

The emphasis in a laboratory group is upon enhancement of both knowledge and skill in interpersonal relations. This enhancement includes the fundamental communication processes of attending, observing, listening and expressing one's own thoughts and feelings. A desire to understand more fully develops, to become more acutely aware of one's experience — thoughts, sensations, perceptions, and so on — and those of others. Correspondingly, focus is given to the communication and exchange among members, the discussion of perceptions of self and others, of values, goals, and assumptions, and of immediate and previous experience. While there may be some attention placed on an individual member's intrapsychic processes and also of the group's dynamics, these dimensions are of less prominence than in remedial or training groups, and typically are not used as either evaluational or decision-making criteria.

The members of a laboratory group talk to each other rather than to a leader, trainer or therapist. In the beginning they talk about their frustrations in the absence of agenda, conventional structure, and authority. They next begin to offer perceptions of one another that have been formed during the initial period. Later on, they have learned to describe individual learning goals and to ask for help in their attainment. Finally, they talk about what they have learned, how they learned it, and the roles each member has played. They may even discuss such topics as group processes, leadership and power, patterns of decision-making, and other related subjects.

To talk about change techniques in the laboratory group seems almost a contradiction of terms since techniques, per se, are conspicuous by their absence. Or so it would seem. The more accurate statement is that laboratory group techniques may be difficult for the inexperienced observer to detect, partly because they are so different from such other group techniques as didactic instruction and active remedial intervention. The categories of change techniques will be briefly described here, followed by a discussion of specific techniques in the Leader Functions section.

The single most obvious and vital technique, for example, is an attitude characterized by understanding that a group of emotionally healthy, appropriately motivated individuals who, when given the freedom to do so, can learn a very great deal from one another. Conducting a laboratory group requires a certain amount of restraint in the use of conventional techniques, especially for those who are adept in using active methods in counseling, training and therapy groups. It must be kept in mind that change occurs in the laboratory group as a result of member interaction rather than active leadership. Beyond the attitudinal dimension, techniques consist, in general terms, of providing an appropriate setting and facilitating interpersonal conversation. Trying to do anything more is either a mistake or an attempt to conduct some other type of group experience.

Learning in a laboratory group is characterized by a sequence of intention, motivation, situation, risk, observation, action, reaction, evaluation, encouragement, autonomy and responsibility. These elements must be present, either spontaneously or by design, if learning is to occur. The laboratory group is a special case in which the situational elements, those external to the learner, are intentionally provided to create a unique combination of environmental circumstances and personal characteristics of the learners.

Provision of these conditions constitutes the second major change technique. It consists of several separate tasks. Included is obtaining a meeting room that is comfortable and free of interruption. Another task is the selection of a group of individuals who are motivated toward enhancement rather than remediation, are informed concerning the group's goals and activities, and are committed to participation.

Changing old behaviors or acquiring new ones first requires being able to freely and directly confront oneself, to realize what is and is not true, what one does and does not want, and to assess self-perceptions, motives and current behaviors. It is often the case that individuals require encouragement from others to behave in these challenging ways. At the very least, they will be more successful in the company of others who also seek change. Thus, another change technique involves the promotion of inquiry, freedom of expression, and the capacity to take risks and give non-judgmental feedback.

The final change technique of major proportion is that of facilitating the interpersonal process. Having brought together individuals who want to learn and who are capable of participating in the mutual inquiry teaching-learning process, the task now is to assist the group members in obtaining full value from the available personal and environmental resources.

It must be pointed out that the term *facilitating* reflects leader behavior that is located midway along a continuum of a leader's use of personal authority, falling between didactic teaching on the far right and peer influencing on the far left. Didactic teaching is not only intrusive, but it is predicated on the assumption that members will learn when the leader imparts expert knowledge in an authoritative manner. This concept contradicts the principle of interpersonal learning and it can obstruct the interpersonal process. The peer influencing concept, conversely, assumes that whatever may happen is for the best, that no prior understanding of group process is necessary and that, in fact, no form of leadership or facilitation is required. Neither of these orientations is appropriate for a laboratory group.

TARGET POPULATION

Historically, laboratory groups have been populated by representatives of two professional fields, the applied behavioral sciences and business and industry. Work titles of participants include manager, counselor, trainer, psychologist, religious professional (minister, priest, nun, rabbi), social worker and teacher. This form of group work is most well suited to those whose professional effectiveness depends on knowledge of self, understanding of others, and skill in interpersonal communications. To a large extent, persons in management, human relations and the applied behavioral sciences rely on the self in instrumental ways. Success depends more on knowledge of human behavior and being able to work cooperatively with others than upon subject matter or technical expertise. The laboratory group has been shown to be an ideal milieu for such multidimensional learning.

Those who are most likely to gain from learning via interpersonal process can be described in several ways. They are well educated, having typically completed a baccalaureate or equivalent degree; advanced degrees are commonplace. The typical member is dedicated to achievement and excellence, though these dimensions are often unrelated to prestige or income. They usually possess a willingness to engage in introspection, to be critically aware of personal motivations, perceptions, values and behaviors. Most laboratory group members demonstrate relatively high levels of ego development and personal maturity. They are individuals who make rapid progress in counseling and psychotherapy as clients, but are most likely to seek help only for situational crises. Most productive members demonstrate a clear sense of personal responsibility and are free of affective disorders.

The age range is typically from approximately 17 to 55 years. Persons below the age of 17 have usually not achieved the necessary levels of personal and professional identity. Persons beyond the age of 55 have ordinarily completed the exploration process that is the group's primary enterprise. In spite of age or sex differences, members are alike in seeking some sort of enrichment. In the majority of instances, this ambition will be described in vague and general terms. It is common practice, for example, to invite members during the first meeting to describe personal goals and expectations. It is to the chagrin of inexperienced leaders that the standard response may be a mixture of silence and brief statements about goal uncertainty.

How is it that bright, well-educated, energetic people are consistently inarticulate regarding their presence in what they expect to be a challenging experience? The answer can be found in the nature of enhancement. It is a relatively simple matter to know that something in particular is wrong and to have some idea of what changes must be made. However, most of us know relatively little about how to become more creative, healthy, perceptive, or wise. Since no direct route to such destinations seems to exist, we simply choose a reliable vehicle, trusting that progress in a forward direction will result. For some, the journey is more important than the destination.

While intelligence, by itself, is not a selection criterion, it is necessary that members be able to conceptualize and generalize. These abilities are requisite in comparing one situation with another, in noting similarities and differences, and in making comparisons. These are relative competencies, of course, and difficult to evaluate during a brief selection interview. Consequently, the level of education or career achievement is ordinarily used as an indicator of cognitive ability.

In a perfect world every member of every group would be fully qualified for totally productive participation. The present world and its inhabitants being as they are, however, several exclusion factors need to be observed in a careful selection process. Interpersonal interaction in a laboratory group is frequently intensive with regard to emotional honesty, the candid expression of thoughts and feelings. Members should be personally secure, able to be responsible for themselves, and able to be helpfully responsive to others. As will be discussed later, a minimum of protective intervention by the leader(s) occurs in this group form. Therefore, individuals seeking personal psychotherapy should not be included. Considerable risk exists, such that self-preoccupied people would be unable to attend to others. In the give and take process of the laboratory group, these people would be able to do only the latter. Those in either situational or chronic crisis are also poor risks for the same reason.

In addition, the laboratory group is an improper place for making important life decisions calling for immediate action. It should be kept in mind that laboratory learning is concerned with voluntary rather than forced choices, that the experience is exploratory rather than definitive, and that the amount of learning time is relatively brief. Those in crisis may tend to react with haste in adopting new perspectives and behaviors, only to discover that such pseudo-change is neither effective nor lasting.

Some personal styles and behavioral orientations are incompatible with the laboratory process. Those who are unable or unwilling to be introspective should be excluded. They tend to become frightened or angry whenever their behavior is the focus. Further, their understanding of others may be superficial. Persons with a high need for either superiority or control are likely to dominate conversations and exert an inhibiting effect on others. Conversely, a severely inhibited member not only does not participate but may eventually come to be resented by others. A marked tendency toward aggression, either psychological or physical, as a way of responding to tension can have ruinous effects for both aggressors and their targets.

It must be acknowledged, again, that we are speaking of relative matters and that all of us are capable of behaving in these ways under certain circumstances. In deciding whether someone is a good candidate for a laboratory group, therefore, the focus is placed upon characteristic behavior, the manner in which the person customarily behaves. It is necessary to rely on common sense and clinical judgement in deciding whether a person's behavioral orientation falls within an acceptable range in comparison to other prospective members.

LEADER FUNCTIONS

The leader's primary responsibility is to facilitate the interpersonal process, the way in which members talk with each other. It is from the discussion of goals, perceptions, and behaviors that members become aware of new behavioral options, form tentative objectives, and then act in achieving them. The leader's role consists of performing five specific functions: attending, modeling, encouraging, protecting, and making process observations. It is assumed that those who aspire to lead a laboratory group will have obtained previous training in counseling and/or communication skills, so that brief definitions of these functions will be sufficient for present purposes.

Attending means to give exclusive attention, to watch and listen, to understand, and to communicate understanding. The leader can convey understanding by either verbal or nonverbal means including eye contact, nodding, facial gestures, postures or verbal responses.

Modeling is comprised of consistently using the attending and communication behaviors that promote clear expression by the speaker and full comprehension by the listener. Modeling is a non-intrusive way of teaching. It is based on the assumption that learners are capable of observing what does and doesn't work, then deciding whether to behave similarly.

Encouraging, verbally or non-verbally, is a way of acknowledging that learning involves risk. Further, it is a message that the risk is worth taking, that the leader has confidence in the person, or merely that the leader values and wishes them well. It also implies a willingness to assist if called upon.

Protecting is unique to the group setting and, at least initially, is the responsibility of the group leader(s). People who are inexperienced in open interpersonal exchange sometimes behave in ways that are not helpful or that pose a danger to their own and others' well being. It is incumbent upon the leader to monitor the rate and nature of personal disclosure and exchange, using prior experience and common sense as guidelines.

Making process observations that call attention in useful ways to themes, metaphors, similarities and differences, unfinished conversations, and other group dynamics and events, also requires training and practice. This is the leader's unique contribution; that is, creating an interactive fabric from separate conversational strands. In addition to being aware of each individual member and noting the relationships among members, the leader views the group as an entity, a social organism with character, energy and initiatives. The leader's observations from this perspective provide a valuable form of feedback and an additional source of comparison and reference.

Beginning Stage Functions

During the opening stage of a laboratory group the leader's goals are to create an environment in which members feel safe and free to talk about themselves and to exchange perceptions. An additional goal is to make contact with all members, to acknowledge their presence, and to endorse their participation. Thus, the most important and frequent functions are *attending* and *encouraging*. Examples are as follows: An opening statement is made about common objectives, length and number of sessions and such basic guidelines as freedom of expression and authenticity. Some leaders provide description of their background and a statement describing their immediate thoughts and feelings. Any such statement should be brief, the purpose of which is to start the session, to identify oneself as the leader, and to invite members to begin speaking.

Unobtrusive eye contact lets members know they are noticed. Listening carefully, and occasional nodding, communicates understanding of member statements, as do minimal verbal responses, reflections and restatements.

Requests for clarification are appropriate at this time. However, pointing out contradictions or mixed messages, challenging, or asking for additional information should be deferred because doing so at this time may preempt voluntary disclosure, deprive members of an opportunity to be useful to each other, and suggest that the leader will henceforth continue to play a central, active role.

Inviting members to discuss immediate thoughts and feelings is a simple and effective way of starting the session. Saying anything more or specifying the manner of the conversation, however, should be avoided because this, too, may imply an intention to direct and control.

Early Stage Functions

The primary leadership objective for the early stage is the creation of productive norms such as disclosing, attending and offering feedback. This period is crucial for initiating interpersonal conversation among members. The central leadership functions in this stage are *modeling, encouraging,* and *protecting.*

The consistent use of observing, listening, clarifying messages, and giving feedback demonstrates the laboratory group's criterion skills. The group leader should acknowledge, verbally or nonverbally, all disclosive statements during this stage and provide a verbal response to those that are unclear or incomplete, especially if no one else does. It is neither necessary nor desirable to respond to every statement or to explain how members should respond to each other. The objective is to positively reinforce and encourage appropriate disclosure, and to illustrate what to attend to and how to respond. Other behaviors are negatively reinforced by disregarding them.

In this new environment populated by strangers, where clear guidelines and directions do not yet exist, each person commits a minor act of courage in merely speaking. Because risk is a constant factor in learning and change, the leader enriches the process by acknowledging the great effort that is sometimes required.

During this time it is common for members to feel enthusiastic and eager to proceed. Some may react dramatically and with a great deal of intensity, either in talking about themselves or in reacting to others. Excessive personal disclosure, monologues, and rude and aggressive behaviors, all of which may be tolerable later on, can have severely impeding effects during a laboratory group's beginning. The wise leader will intervene, not so much to monitor content as to offer guidelines concerning the timing and format of disclosure and feedback. The protective function is directed toward individuals with the underlying objective of establishing and maintaining effective patterns of communication.

Middle Stage Functions

Attaining the middle stage is evidence that the beginning and early stage goals generally have been met. Members have learned attending and responding skills so that there is less need to concentrate on personal communication. Instead, the leader's focus is now upon interpersonal and group processes. The most important function during this stage is *making observations* about interactions, in addition to commenting upon group themes and patterns. The intent is to provide feedback that will invite members to notice the effects of behavior on both simple and complex interactions. Process observation comments should be descriptive rather than interpretive, more tentative than declarative. Calling attention to these processes is more important than being correct in explaining them.

Members will perceive and discover the meaning of events in idiosyncratic ways. In a laboratory group there is no need for a common reality or consensus. By the same token, a group that has reached the working stage will rarely contain members who express a need for either conventional leadership or counseling services. Such leader interventions as suggesting an agenda, challenging member statement, and conducting training activities are inconsistent with the learning model. Put another way, the leader's responsibility for developing productive communication norms has been met prior to this time. It is now necessary to be less prominent, thus enabling members to call upon their individual and collective resources.

Ending Stage Functions

The goals of the ending stage are to bring the experience to a close, to identify what has been learned, to consider ways in which learnings may be applied and, in some instances, to rehearse applications when success will depend on behaving in new or different ways. The amount of time to be devoted to each of these goals is often decided by the group. However, it should be noted that learning requires action and that the best evidence of learning is behavior change. Group members are frequently reluctant to leave the working stage, thereby attempting to avoid facing termination. It is the leader's responsibility to anticipate these reactions and to invite the consideration of applications well in advance of final sessions. It is ordinarily appropriate to suggest during the working stage that the matter of applications be discussed and that a commitment be made to spend an adequate amount of time, perhaps one hour per member, to this vital activity.

In addition to making provision for sufficient time, other functions become pertinent during this stage. These include modeling, encouraging, process observation, helping members see relationships between their behaviors in the group and in their other life contexts, suggesting rehearsal formats and participating in them, and acknowledging efforts to act in different, more satisfying ways.

LEADER TRAINING

Evidence of concern regarding the quality of small group leadership is available in the form of ethical standards which have been published by the National Training Laboratory Institute for Applied Behavioral Science (NTL, 1970), the Association for Specialists in Group Work (1980), the American Association for Counseling and

Development (formerly the American Personnel and Guidance Association, 1974), the American Psychological Association (1973), the American Group Psychotherapy Association (1978), the National Association of Social Workers (1960, 1967), and the American Association of Marriage and Family Therapists (formerly the American Association of Marriage and Family Counselors, 1975).

How one becomes able to perform in ethical ways is usually not specified. Two exceptions are the training outline described by the American Group Psychotherapy Association (1978) and the training requirements recently published by the Association for Specialists in Group Work (1983). These products tangibly demonstrate the considerable interest being given to professional accountability for group work. However, several formidable dilemmas need to be overcome when defining competency in training terms.

What follows is an arbitrary description in generic terms of the knowledge and competencies required for laboratory group leadership. Because it is often impossible to distinguish the practice of psychotherapy, personal growth, and training, either methodologically or in interpersonal dynamics, it follows that leadership training should include experience in all these modalities. This is a controversial issue, however, and it should be recognized that some training programs focus exclusively on only one group form.

In knowledge terms, laboratory group leadership training includes the didactic study of individual, interpersonal and group processes, containing such topics as human development, personality, counseling and psychotherapy theory and technique, and group dynamics. In addition, aspiring leaders should also study learning theory and associated formats as applied to psychotherapy, development, training and organizational-systems dynamics.

Several basic competencies can be described. Perhaps the single most important skill is communication discrimination, the ability to detect and understand verbal and nonverbal messages according to content, meaning, affect and intention. A group leader should be a communications specialist, so there is a corresponding need to acquire a considerable repertoire of skills in this area. The need for facility in making therapeutic interventions varies according to several factors, but it is clear that there is utility in being able to recognize personal distress and to respond accordingly. Also useful are small group leadership skills in working with task groups, discussion groups, and those constituted for teaching or training purposes.

The laboratory group is an intimate environment, full of candor and intensity, in which people talk about matters of great personal importance. Effective leaders cannot rely exclusively on technique; a need exists for them to be personally authentic and secure, well aware of their own motives and ways of perceiving and behaving. Along with self-knowledge there is a need for skill in communicating and relating to others.

A comprehensive training program would include the following sequence of activities:

1. Study of human development, personality, social systems, individual and group counseling/therapy, personal growth and training groups;
2. Individual counseling and therapy training;
3. Participation in various types of groups, at least one of which provides for extensive self-exploration;
4. Observation of experienced leaders, with opportunity for post-group discussion and consultation;
5. Co-leadership with an experienced practitioner, including opportunity for personal supervision and consultation;
6. Individual leadership with supervision and consultation.

EVIDENCE OF EFFECTIVENESS AND APPLICATIONS

Good evidence of something's value is the uses to which it is put. Even this criterion, however, runs the risk of begging the quality issue. The most popular model is not always the best. The validity dilemma is inherent in behavioral science research. While many data-based reports of laboratory group effectiveness have been published, the studies have often been plagued by a host of design, methodological and statistical insufficiencies. For a thorough review of group research history with attention to laboratory groups, see *The Journal of Applied Behavioral Science* (1979).

Meanwhile, the popularity of the laboratory group continues.

Massive amounts of clinical evidence exist that the laboratory group is effective, well beyond its statistically demonstrated value. (In the publication just mentioned, see especially the articles by Argyris; Bednar and Kaul; and Zander.) However, researchers have been less than fully articulate in explaining how this is so. One of the most literate and believable discussions of this matter has been provided by Yalom (1975) in describing the curative factors in group psychotherapy.

Laboratory group experience is virtually always a part of training for group leadership or therapy. A study by Davis (1979) indicated that some form of personal growth experience in a group setting was included in approximately 70 percent of master's level counselor training programs. It might be expected that the same is true for doctoral programs in counseling and counseling psychology and related specialities in the behavioral sciences.

In spite of using what first appeared to be a clumsy, unwieldy format, the laboratory group is a relatively simple and, apparently, a remarkably efficient way of achieving personal awareness, communication skills and an understanding of group processes. It can be used whenever these outcomes are vital to professional effectiveness.

REFERENCES

American Association of Marriage and Family Counselors: Code of Professional Ethics. Claremont, CA.: Author, 1975.

American Group Psychotherapy Association: *Guidelines for the Training of Group Psychotherapists.* New York: Author, 1978.

American Personnel and Guidance Association: *Ethical Standards.* Washington, D.C.: Author, 1974.

American Psychological Association: Guidelines for psychologists conducting growth groups. *American Psychologist, 28 (933),* 1973.

Argyris, C.: Reflecting on laboratory education from a theory of action perspective. *Journal of Applied Behavioral Science, 15(3):*296-310,1979.

Association for Specialists in Group Work: *Ethical Guidelines for Group Leaders.* Alexandria, VA.: Author, 1980.

Association for Specialists in Group Work: *Professional Standards for Training of Group Counselors.* Alexandria, VA.: Author, 1983.

Bednar, R., and Kaul, T.: Experiential group research: What never happened? *Journal of Applied Behavioral Science, 15(3):*311-319, 1979.

Davis, S.: The training of entry level group counselors: A descriptive survey. Unpublished doctoral dissertation, Purdue University, 1979.

Gazda, G. (Ed.): *Basic Approaches to Group Psychotherapy and Group Counseling,* 3rd ed. Springfield: Thomas, 1982.

Journal of Applied Behavioral Science, (special issue): What's happened to small group research? *JABS, 15(3),* 1979.

National Association of Social Workers: *Code of ethics.* Adopted by the delegate assembly of the National Association of Social Workers, October 1960, and amended April, 1967.

National Training Laboratory Institute for Applied Behavioral Science: *Standards for the Use of Laboratory Method.* Washington, D.C.: Author, 1970.

Yalom, I.: *The Theory and Practice of Group Psychotherapy,* 2nd ed. New York: Basic Books, 1975.

Zander, A.: The study of group behavior during four decades. *Journal of Applied Behavioral Science, 15(3):*272-282, 1979.

CHAPTER 8

LEARNING
Systematic Group Discussion Method (SGD)

WM. FAWCETT HILL

THE prototype for the Systematic Group Discussion (SGD) method will be recognized by many students of group discussion as a paraphrase of our Learning Thru Discussion, or LTD method (Hill, 1982). The latter publication is a culmination of a number of revisions going back to the original version, Learning and Teaching Thru Discussion (Hill and Hill, 1958). The main reason for changing the title here is that an emphasis in this book and in this chapter is on "systematics," although the basic technique of LTD remains unaltered, albeit somewhat updated. Also, there is a personal predilection for moving toward stressing systematics. We now refer to our work in a parallel field, group therapy, as Systematic Group Therapy or SGT (Hill, 1974). Thus, the change in title to SGD gives an aura, at least in retrospect, of consistency in the development of our work with groups. Certainly a reader would more fully understand what is presented here by examining the more detailed accounts to be found in the first two referenced works.

The case for a systematic approach to group work has already been made in previous chapters. We persist in the matter, even though it may seem superfluous, as there is considerable resistance on the part of group discussion leaders to use systematic approaches. Many practioners act as if knowing what they are doing or following some plan of action is subversive and deters the free flow of information, dampens spontaneity and eliminates potential for insight.

Being a Lewinian by training and disposition, I subscribe to categorization and feedback. To paraphrase Lewin, "A poor system is better than none at all."

In our approach to discussion groups, we expect the members and the leader to share a common understanding of the objectives for the discussion and, also, to have an agreed upon method for achieving these objectives. The next section deals with objectives and a technique for realizing them.

THE SGD METHOD

A few unkind references have been made by others about practitioners of a laissez-faire type who break up their class into small groups and say, "Let's discuss." There are those more structured types of leaders who may go so far as to propose a set of discussion questions. Students come mostly from a lecture-dominated educational culture and have little knowledge of group process, group dynamics or group development theory. The same statement could also be made of many instructors. Discussion groups, therefore, rarely achieve solid learning of course material. They are often viewed as a waste of time, although they may be subscribed to for the wrong reasons, e.g., to avoid a dull lecture, to meet others, to ventilate, etc. As a matter of fact, the critics of discussion groups may be right in many instances when they claim the groups are a case of the blind leading the blind.

A structural analysis of a discussion group indicates that logically the following three conditions (called Type A, B, and A/B) could obtain in regard to learning about some topic we will call X.

Type A: Everyone in the group understands X.

Under this condition a group will often elaborate the obvious ad infinitum, and sometimes, ad nauseam. As everyone understands X, then everyone feels secure while it remains the topic of discussion.

Type B: No one in the group understands X.

Interaction under this condition also may be sustained, for as every student of politics knows, ignorance of a topic is no deterrent to the making of public statements about it. Interaction in this mode may become quite intense but it should be pointed out that more heat than light is generated by this kind of friction. In some groups, Type B may also be perceived as safe to participate in as no one really knows what they are discussing.

For our purpose, the important point is that no new learning of subject matter X can occur under these conditions and persisting in the discussion is what we call Type A and Type B error. For learning to take part in a group the following condition must obtain.

Type A/B: Some members understand X and others do not.

This is the situation where some group members need help in understanding the topic of discussion, as they are Type B, while the Type A members hold the potential for helping in understanding the topic. Thus, Type A/B provides the crucible for profitable group discussion. While this condition obtains frequently, it does not usually yield beneficent results. Type A members often wish to keep others in a state of ignorance, particularly where the class is graded on the curve, and Type B members are reluctant to display their ignorance to their peers or the instructor. Thus, a method is needed in discussion groups that rewards members for seeking knowledge and dispensing it.

Beyond the all-important transmission of knowledge, another potent learning dynamic can take place under A/B conditions. A member may play the Type A role, attempting to explain X to the members, and in the course of his or her presentation come to the realization that he or she does not really understand the material. This is a very insight-provoking experience, particularly for verbally facile and superficially bright students. This outcome is consistent with the old maxim, "You don't really know a subject until you have taught it." On occasion the obverse occurs where a member, in trying to state why he or she is having difficulty with a concept, will obtain insight into the problem. This is consistent with another old maxim that, "If you can formulate the question you are half-way to answering it." As indicated, group members can enjoy very effective group discussions if they come to the meeting prepared with their understandings and difficulties concerning the assignment and are willing to share these with each other.

CONCEPTUAL DERIVATION OF SGD

The idea that a group can be conceived of as a system is taken to-day as being almost self-evident. That a group can be conceived of as an entity with particular characteristics and forces is a notion evolving mainly from Lewin's work on what he called Group Dynamics. Hugh Coffee, one of Tolman's students and a colleague of ours at the National Training Laboratory in Group Development (NTL), presented the concept that a decision making group could be conceived of as an entity. He suggested that such a group could follow a four-step cognitive map and, thereby, efficiently realize its stated goals. This concept was applied by the authors to discussion groups, resulting in a nine-step cognitive map.

The thought that group members needed training in group dynamics, group process analysis, and in group development theory in order for the discussion group to be effective was a revolutionary one in the Forties. Back then, Jack Gibb, another NTL colleague, had developed a training manual for students in his discussion-oriented Psychology classes. Our Learning Thru Discussion book is primarily, although not exclusively, a training manual. The approach is based on the premise that members need familiarity and training in the three areas presented in the next section.

As students in classes conducted by Bruno Bettelheim, the original authors were subjected regularly to the admonition that, "A classroom is a small group." The authors, who were both group dynamicists, incorporated this notion into their derivation of the method and at every point attempted to include techniques that would tap the unique potentials and forces within the small group.

THE THREE FUNDAMENTAL AREAS OF SGD

Unfortunately, it takes more than coming to the group well prepared and with a spirit of cooperation to assure effectiveness. In terms of a general systems approach, group process, group dynamic, and group development problems are inherent in all small groups. These problems cannot be resolved by good intentions alone. For the purpose of simplifying (read systematizing) a vast array of problems that small groups fall heir to we have reduced them to three areas: I) Group Cognitive Mapping; II) Member and Leader Skills; and III) Criteria of a Good Group. The inherent and inevitable problems in these areas are discussed below and solutions are proposed for ways to train prospective group members so that these problems are minimized or become capable of solution by the group members.

GROUP COGNITIVE MAPPING

Let us consider a hypothetical discussion group in which all the members are highly motivated and imbued with enlightened self-interest and altruism. Furthermore, no saboteurs are present in this group. These conditions make this group hypothetical, as the educational system seems to be at its best in training students in techniques that can sabotage the educational enterprise. The point here is that even this ideal group will founder.

The main reason for this prediction is that individuals, in their zeal to make the group work, will each try to move it in a different direction. It is as though an airplane were being navigated by all the crew and each member had a different map. Either one person prevails, and has the correct map, or disaster ensues.

Here, we talk not of geographical maps but of cognitive maps. This concept, as previously indicated, is borrowed from Tolman. In the discussion group context we are stating that all members of a group share in and operate with the same cognitive map. Such a situation would minimize confusion and make it possible for members to cooperate more readily in moving toward their objectives. In fact, these objectives should be built into the steps of a cognitive map. Again, to paraphrase Lewin, "A poor cognitive map would be better than none at all." Incidentally, the reason this statement is true is that any systematic approach is subject to improvements in the light of subsequent usage, but a random or unknown process cannot be readily improved upon.

A group could develop its own cognitive map, which could be highly advantageous, but this process would be very time consuming. Hence, a cognitive map suitable for discussion groups, a prototype, is presented to a group and the members are instructed in its use. The steps of this Cognitive Map are presented below, followed by a detailed discussion:

Step One.   Definition of terms and concepts
Step Two.   General statement of author's message
Step Three.   Identification of major themes or subtopics
Step Four.   Allocation of time
Step Five.   Discussion of major themes or subtopics
Step Six.   Integration of the materials
Step Seven.   Application of the material
Step Eight.   Evaluation of author's presentation
Step Nine.   Evaluation of group and individual performance

Step One — Definition of Terms and Concepts

One objective of the group cognitive map is to lessen the possibility of the group becoming involved in useless argument. It is now standard operating procedure to define terms before discussing any subject. This avoids the so-called semantic trap which ensnares so many groups. Also, the act of defining terms, in itself, constitutes learning. An additional reason for beginning with this step is that it makes for an easy and relatively non-threatening way to begin the discussion.

Step Two — General Statement of Author's Message

The purpose of this step is to obtain some sort of grasp of the overall meaning of the assigned reading. Enunciation of a general statement is meant to accomplish this goal. It also demarcates the area to be discussed, that is, it zeros in on the topic for discussion, and serves the purpose of launching the group into the discussion.

Step Three — Identification of Major Themes or Sub-topics

Most material can be readily broken down into a number of important sub-topics. Often this is already done by the authors in their use of sub-headings. The group needs a consensus as to what these major sub-topics are and usually this can be accomplished without excessive debate.

Step Four—Allocation of Time

Allocation of time is a crucial step in the method. The common complaint of discussion group members is that they never cover the material, spending too much time on one aspect to the neglect of all the rest. To meet this real difficulty, the group must budget its time, allocate it wisely, and then conduct the discussion accordingly. These processes are particularly important, in this case, when one considers that time must be made available not only for the topics identified in Step Three but also to fulfill the requirements of Steps Five, Six, Seven, Eight, and Nine. Step Four is significant because the group sets its own time limits and gains some grasp of the scope of the areas to be discussed. Thereby, the group can regulate itself accordingly.

The results obtained by omitting this step are not hard to visualize. All readers have had unfortunate experiences with groups that have no regulatory clock and could not pace themselves appropriately. While this step is crucial, however, it is also the most difficult one of all for groups to master. The discussion period should be used only to deal with those parts of the material that the members, for one reason or another, feel it would be most profitable to discuss. By doing so, the members avoid or minimize Type A and Type B error. Learning to exercise this selectivity is not easy. At the outset, groups have difficulty in determining, with any degree of confidence, what needs and does not need discussing. Sometimes the least understood parts are nominated for exclusion in order to avoid the embarrassment of exposing ignorance and a group will prefer to discuss that which is already known. Also, the group cannot estimate accurately how much time is needed in Steps Five, Six, Seven, Eight, and Nine until it has had some experiences with the method.

Step Five—Discussion of Major Themes and Sub-topics

The discussion proceeds within the structures established in Step Four, whereby the topics have been selected and the amount of time to be spent on them has been assigned. As might be anticipated, groups will become frustrated with their inability to execute their own decisions in regard to allocation of time, and this will negatively affect the quality of the discussion. What is to be done in this step is clear, but it is easier explained than conducted. The method does not create these problems; it only pinpoints them.

In the first five steps of the Cognitive Map, the emphasis is placed on the content and not on the personal opinions of the group members. As has been indicated, the personal reactions of members have so far been suppressed by the method. This is not because thoughts and feelings of group members are considered to be insignificant. Quite the contrary, it is only because we have found in our experience that groups rarely discover what the author had to say if members begin by first giving their personal opinions on the material. Invariably, such practice leads to some form of disagreement with sides being drawn up; what the author has to say becomes only of incidental importance. Thus, in this method, personal reactions are inserted only after the group has discussed what is to be learned from the assignment.

Step Six — Integration of the Material

An oft-heard criticism of the educational system is that learning is too fragmentary and too much concerned with the acquisition of isolated bits of information. It is a well-known fact of learning theory that isolated, unassociated facts are the first to be forgotten. Even if they are retained, they still may be unattached to any corpus of knowledge and, therefore, are of limited value.

To counteract this possibility, Step Six requires group members to allocate time and make a conscious effort to relate learnings in the assignment to ideas and concepts acquired in previous meetings or in other learning situations. As the course proceeds, the student should be able, at least, to relate and integrate the learnings of later chapters to earlier ones, if not to outside readings. Thus, the end result should be that the materials form a gestalt rather than result in isolated learnings from each chapter. Ideally, students should make connections to all sorts of knowledge and form a habit of relating newly acquired knowledge to the greater corpus that he or she already has acquired. Our experience has been that professors automatically operate at this level but that students find that it does not come naturally to them.

Step Seven — Application of the Material

The criticism of educational systems raised above occurs again here in a slightly altered form. Knowledge should not only be accumulative and integrated, but it also should have personal value or significance for the student. Subject matter mastery should enhance feelings of ego mastery. Acquired knowledge that is not internalized and remains ego-alien is either readily forgotten, or if it is retained, results in the creation of arid scholasticism or mere pedantry. To counteract this possibility, we require group members to allocate time and make a conscious effort to assess the possible applications and implications in the material.

Step Eight — Evaluation of Author's Presentation

At long last, the personal reactions of the student are programmed in to the method. When Steps One through Seven have been covered first, criticism often has less affective loading and resembles more of what we call constructive criticism. If learning is to be served, criticism should become critique and, rather than being eliminated, it should be raised to a level of incisive and insightful criticism. The development of the ability to apply critical thinking may well be more important than the learning of the material itself, as it will serve the student well in all future learning and life situations.

Step Nine — Evaluation of Group and Individual Performance

This step is essential for the method to work. As a matter of fact, for any group to be effective some time must be devoted to evaluating the inevitable individual and group process problems that have occurred. In this method, it is expected that approximately the last 15 minutes of a two-hour discussion be devoted to diagnosing and evaluating group and individual effectiveness.

While group process is a highly technical subject it has been found that raising questions about the group's ability to move through the cognitive map, play the group roles, and meet the criteria provides sufficient insight into process problems to improve group operation and learning. Also, in this step post-meeting reaction sheets might be introduced and results interpreted. These data are stimulating, sensitizing, and often diagnostically useful.

Evaluation of the Group Cognitive Map is a difficult matter, and the case for it rests on its "face validity." To this writer, it is evident that implementing such a program could achieve most important educational goals.

Testimonials are about as valuable as "face validity" and we have in our files many enthusiastic endorsements. Unfortunately, no two are alike. Some educators praise our emphasis on subject matter mastery while others overlook this factor and praise the incorporation of the student's personal reaction to the material. One or two were ecstatic about the idea of getting a student beyond the confines of the discipline being studied and connecting the material to the larger world of knowledge (Step Six). Some of our colleagues approved of the notion that the course material should be directly related to the experience of the student (Step Seven). One noted educator indicated that the only worthwhile point to the Group Cognitive Map was that students might be able to develop a critical capacity (Step Eight) and that was what education should be all about.

The Group Cognitive Map programs the group discussion so that most of the significant goals of education are included, providing for a balance between subject matter mastery and personal involvement. Nonetheless, it does not always yield a satisfactory result. Naturally, if the majority of members come unprepared the results can be disastrous. However, even when students are keen and follow the Group Cognitive Map religiously, the process can be depressingly boring.

The Group Cognitive Map is, in reality, the anatomy of the discussion, without the accompanying physiology. To switch metaphors, the Group Cognitive Map is the structure, with the function being provided by incorporating the other two areas—Group Roles and Members Skills and Criteria for a Good Group—into the process.

GROUP ROLES AND MEMBER SKILLS

For a discussion to be successful there must be recognition that a group is operating. Principles of group work should apply. One important principle is that for any group to be effective certain roles have to be performed and members must have the interpersonal skill to perform them. Ever since Benne and Sheats' (1948) original article on group roles, workshops and laboratories in human relations training have been developing lists of group roles. No complete or final list can be prepared, and the one presented here is selective, not exhaustive. The selection has been guided by the learning theory inherent in the method, as well as by group theory.

Group roles are usually classified as "group maintenance," "task accomplishment," or both. This distinction is observed in our organization of group roles. In it we have followed the standard nomenclature that is to be found in group work literature. Usually, much overlap and repetition occurs, which we have tried to deliberately minimize by grouping the overlapping roles into three functional clusters:

A. Sequence of Task Roles Specific to Discussing a Topic
B. Overall Task Roles Needed by a Discussion Group
C. Group Maintenance Roles Needed by a Discussion Group

An effective group member can and should perform many, if not all, the group roles with some finesse. A member playing only one role consistently and persistently will be more of a hindrance than a help. The concept of appropriateness is inherent in the exercise of group roles and a need for member sensitivity is indicated.

Group Roles and Member Skills

A. Sequence of Task Roles Specific to Discussion of a Topic

1. Initiating
2. Giving and Asking for Information
3. Giving and Asking for Reactions
4. Restating and Giving Examples
5. Confronting and Reality Testing
6. Clarifying, Snythesizing, and Summarizing

B. Overall Task Roles Required in Method

7. Gate-keeping and Expediting

8. Time-keeping
9. Evaluating and Diagnosing
10. Standard Setting

C. Group Maintenance Roles Needed by a Discussion Group

11. Sponsoring and Encouraging
12. Group Tension Relieving

D. Nonfunctional Roles

1. Aggressing
2. Blocking
3. Self-confessing
4. Competing
5. Seeking Sympathy
6. Special Interest Pleader
7. Horsing Around (Playboy)
8. Status Seeking
9. Withdrawing
10. Dominating

One role that is not included in the regular lists of group roles, and that is of particular importance in the method, is listening. The magazine supplements of Sunday newspapers invariably include an article on the importance of being a good listener. It seems as if this role is completely mastered, all one's ambitions will be realized. Our claims are more modest. Good listening will promote good interaction and learning. The distinction to be made is between active and passive listening. If members are actively listening their chances of learning something are greatly improved. If their "hearing aid" is turned down, not only will they not learn anything, but their passivity will exert a very depressing effect on the actively participating members.

The significance of group roles is apparent. If many of these roles are missing from the discussion, it will inevitably bog down, and the learning potential of the discussion group will not be realized. These roles are absolutely necessary functions to be performed, according to general group theory. These roles are present in untrained or in uninitiated groups, but the leader, not the members, performs these functions.

CRITERIA FOR EFFECTIVE FUNCTIONING

Typical trainees, because of years of academic exposure, know all too well what is expected of them and what they can expect from the traditional lecture situation. Yet, they have no similar set of expectations when confronted with the group discussion approach. This problem is compounded by the fact that not only are trainees' previous academic experiences of little help but, also, their other experiences with formal groups have in all probability not been too satisfying. Thus, even the most highly motivated student has difficulty being effective because he or she holds no conceptual model of a good group nor a clear image of the kind of behavior that would contribute to building a good group. Consequently, what is needed is an idea of the group ideal which can be shared by the group members.

The instructor's task, therefore, is to help the group members to formulate some concept of what constitutes a good group learning situation. Much of what has already been said in the previous sections on the group cognitive map and on group roles and member skills points to the requirements for an effective democratically-oriented discussion group. A group must have some notion of how it should operate, some standard of performance, or, in our terms, it needs a list of criteria. The criteria serve the function of a goal and, also, as a standard against which to measure current performance.

A List of Criteria is presented which is not by any means exhaustive, but which is intended to cover the major conditions that are required for the efficient operation of the method. All groups should be encouraged to add to this list as their experience in the group dictates:

Prevalence of a warm, accepting, non-threatening group climate.
Learning is approached as a cooperative enterprise.
Learning is accepted as the raison d'etre of the group.

Everyone participates and interacts.

Leadership functions are distributed.

Group sessions and the learning task are enjoyable.

The material is adequately and efficiently covered.

Evaluation is accepted as an integral part of the group operation.

Members attend regularly and come prepared.

SUPPLEMENTARY TECHNIQUES AND MATERIALS

In order to get the group discussion off to a good start the following activities are suggested:

- Assign the LTD book as required reading.
- Give a brief lecture on the method and remarks on how groups will be formed, what texts will be used, grading, etc.
- Show a video tape (20 min. color) that is available which shows a discussion group going through the steps of the cognitive map.
- Make forms available which summarize the tasks to be performed when a member is either a group discussion leader or observer (these assignments are rotated). Also, a sheet can be distributed which outlines what is involved in completing the preparation sheet prior to the discussion. Incidentally, these sheets are graded on a scale of one to 10 and become part of the marks obtainable in the class. The preparation sheets are used by group members in the course of the discussion and are in the same format as the group cognitive map. Textbooks remain unopened during the discussion.
- The observer gives his or her evaluation of the group, the leader, and the members' performance during step nine. Various post meeting reaction sheets have been devised for this purpose. An observer can check off the ratings as the meeting progresses. A check list on group skills also can be employed to provide feedback about how well members participated in the various roles.

We require the observer to rate each participant on a scale of one to 10 to describe the quantity and quality of participation. These quantitative evaluations also contribute to the accumulated marks that determine a student's grade, along with performance on quizzes and on any other evaluations.

These supplementary practices noted above are not central to the method itself and certainly can be omitted. Clearly, they are aimed at providing extrinsic motivation. While they may be counter-productive with a small seminar-type class, they have been found useful in large classes which are broken down into several sub-groups.

RESEARCH AND EVALUATION

The independent variables most used in group discussion studies are measures of satisfaction with the experience, and grades obtained. In terms of the latter, the findings for this method are consistent with other studies. To wit, no significant differences have been found in grades obtained through the discussion method, when compared to the lecture method, although there is a promising trend.

For instance, one unpublished study used two psychologists in a crossover design, where one psychologist lectured to a class and the other conducted a discussion group for a quarter-long introductory psychology class. In the second quarter, the procedure was the same except that the psychologists reversed roles. The same quizzes were given to the classes. It was found that at the first midterm there were slightly higher marks obtained in the lecture classes, which washed out by the second midterm; in the final quiz, the discussion group obtained higher marks than the lecture classes. These differences were not statistically significant. This finding suggests that if the time spent on instruction were equivalent, and the students came to the class already sophisticated in the discussion method, there might be a real advantage in subject matter mastery for the discussion method.

In terms of student reaction to the method, all of our extensive data, based on over 3,000 participants, show that over 85 percent rate the experience as very good or excellent. Even higher satisfaction indices were found in a carefully conducted doctoral dissertation (Gutzmer, 1969; Gutzmer and Hill, 1973).

While this kind of data is reassuring, it still requires closer scrutiny. Preliminary investigations showed that there were differences in satisfaction indices from course to course taught by the same instructor as well as differences from instructor to instructor teaching the same course. In particular, Downs (1972) found that within a large class considerable variation occurred from sub-group to sub-group. As one might expect, the quite positive molar satisfaction ratings mask considerable individual variance in reaction to the method.

A large-scale study was launched through a grant from the Chancellor's Office of the California State Universities (Hill and Hill, 1975). Two not-surprising findings became evident early in the study. We found that upper division classes showed more satisfaction with the method than lower division classes and that considerable differences appeared in satisfaction indices between engineering courses and those in liberal arts, with the latter being, as expected, higher.

The major thrust of the study was to determine the effects of group composition variables on the discussion groups. In particular, it was hypothesized that some students hold a positive response bias toward groups while others tend to be defensive and are reluctant to be involved in group activities.

The Total Acceptance Score (TAS), derived from the Hill Interaction Matrix (Hill, 1969), was used as a dependent variable in this study. The Hill Interaction Matrix itself is a grid designed to deal systematically with important group therapy variables. One of the scales associated with the Hill Interaction Matrix is the HIM-B, a 64-item paper and pencil test that yields scores for the cells in the matrix. By adding up these scores, a total score can be obtained called the Total Acceptance Score (TAS). As the items of the HIM-B deal with typical therapy group situations, a high score is presumed to indicate an overall "acceptance" of group participation, while low scores (less "acceptance") have been found primarily in testees who are reluctant to be involved in group situations. Groups were comprised of members having high TAS scores, called Homogeneous High (HoHi) groups, those consisting of members with low TAS scores, called Homogeneous Low (HoLo), groups, and those comprised of high, low, and medium TAS scores called Heterogeneous (HiLoMed) groups.

One of the independent variables in this study was a measure of member satisfaction with the discussion group experience. An instrument to evaluate the class experience was developed and it was administered at the completion of the course. The student was required to give a rating on 22 different aspects of the group discussions. A total score, called the Satisfaction Score, was obtained. It was found that the HoHi groups had the highest Satisfaction Scores. Conversely, the HoLo groups obtained significantly lower Satisfaction Scores. The Heterogeneous groups, HiLoMed, were found to produce Satisfaction Scores that were almost as high as those for the HoHi groups. Because instructors in public education must work with a broad spectrum of students, it is important to know that properly composed Heterogeneous groups are able to function at high levels of satisfaction. The SGD method does not depend for its success on an educationally elite group of students. In our use of this discussion method we administer the HIM-B to all students in a class and comprise our small discussion groups as heterogeneously as possible in order to avoid including in one group a disproportionate number of members who, at the outset, are negative to participating in group interaction.

One final study, by Barker (1982) on group size, found a significant difference in Satisfaction Scores between discussion groups of seven or eight members and those of 10 or 12 members. While it was anticipated that the more traditional size group of seven or eight members would yield higher satisfaction indices, it was not anticipated that the differences would be so clear cut and robust.

SUMMARY

If a bumper sticker were to serve as a summary for this chapter, it would say "Think Systematics." This chapter emphasizes the need for a systematic approach in the use of group discussion. Furthermore, it is meant to serve as an antidote to the laissez-faire style of many (read "most") instructors who expect learning in the classroom to occur by uttering the magic words, "Let's discuss." If the antidote has had its desired effect, then the reader will push on to discover how to approach discussion groups in a systematic fashion.

It is claimed that for discussion groups to be effective members must have some knowledge of group process, group development, and group dynamics. An even more radical suggestion is made that instructors might also gain some expertise in these areas. As it is unlikely that students will first take some training in these areas prior to participating in a discussion group, some method needs to be introduced that will help the group participants to be aware of (diagnose) and do something about (treat) the inevitable group process, group development and group process problems they will encounter.

One method for systematically conducting discussion groups is presented which is, for obvious reasons, called Systematic Group Discussion (SGD). This method involves a wholesale borrowing from the author's *Learning Thru Discussion* method (Hill, 1982), with an intended emphasis on systematics. A careful reading should reveal how a group might successfully negotiate the learning process by following the steps of the group cognitive map while also employing the member roles and the criteria for a good group. In all systematic approaches there is not only an awareness of the procedure being followed, but also the existence of the cybernetic principle of feedback, so that optimizing the process on the basis of experience with it becomes possible. The chapter also contains some "How To" tips.

In the final section, there is a brief account of the research and evaluation that has been conducted on the method. Most of the development of SGD has not come from research investigations but from trial-and-error experiences. However, some research, much of it unpublished, has been conducted and reported here. These more carefully conducted investigations indicate not only that the method has been very favorably received by students, over 3,000, but also that it can yield results in terms of student satisfaction indices with the average classroom population and it is not restricted to use with the exceptional student. Furthermore, evidence is presented that indicates the importance of group size and group composition for the method. The Hill Interaction Matrix is proposed as a way of insuring that groups are balanced in terms of ability and willingness of members to participate. This is, of course, of great importance where the instructor is faced with the problem of breaking a large class into several small discussion groups.

The long-term benefits to a student experiencing a successful small group learning experience have not been dealt with in the chapter. To engage in an active role during the learning process and to discover first hand that cooperative, as opposed to competitive, approaches have value is an important learning in itself. Finally, for students to obtain insight into how learning can take place in the classroom and how they, in turn, could teach a class is probably more important than learning the subject matter itself.

REFERENCES

Barker, S.: *Analysis of Evaluation Instruments of Discussion Groups.* Senior Project, California State Polytechnic University, Pomona, 1982.

Benne, K. and Sheats, P.: Functional roles of group members. *J. Social Issues,* 412, 1948.

Downs, P.: *Study of Discussion Groups.* Senior Project, California State Polytechnic University, Pomona, 1972.

Gutzmer, W.: A Study in Structured Discussion. Unpublished Doctoral Dissertation, University of Utah, 1969.

Gutzmer, W., and Hill, W.F.: Evaluation of effectiveness of the Learning Thru Discussion method. *Small Group Behavior,* 4:1, 1973.

Hill, I.S. and Hill, W.F.: *Learning and Teaching thru Discussion: Notes and Essays –21.* Center for the Study of Liberal Educationf or Adults, Chicago, 1958.

Hill, Wm. F.: *Supplement to Hill Interaction Matrix (HIM): Test Manual.* California State Polytechnic University, Pomona, 1969.

Hill, Wm. F.: Systematic Group Development: SGD therapy. In A. Jacobs and W. Spradlin (Eds.), *The Group as an Agent of Change.* New York: Behavioral Publications, 1974.

Hill, Wm. F.: *Learning Thru Discussion* (3rd ed.), Beverly Hills: Sage, 1982.

Hill, Wm. F. and Hill, P.S.: *Final Report: Optimizing Learning Thru Discussion Method.* California State Polytechnic University, Pomona, 1975.

SECTION III
ORGANIZATION LEVEL OF
INTERVENTION

W ORK is central to our lives in this society. For many, work involves membership and participation in an organization of some sort. This membership and participation in organizational life requires employers and employees alike to become involved in a number of groups, whether these be task or social in nature, formally or informally structured.

Many managers have recognized the important role group involvement plays in their organizations by establishing organization groups that are meant to change or to further improve selected aspects of the worker-organization relationship. Primarily important to these managers is that organizational effectiveness increases through such group activity. A desired secondary goal, or even by-product, that these managers hope for is that employees themselves will become increasingly effective and satisfied, thus leading, in turn, to a more effectively functioning organization.

Cherniss discusses a significant and new organizational group type, the employee assistance group, in Chapter 9. Where clinical, out-of-work settings have historically dominated as the treatment settings for employees with personal problems, many contemporary organizations themselves include employee assistance programs to provide such care. Cherniss describes two major forms of employee assistance groups, which he terms "palliative" and "problem-solving," with an emphasis on the latter.

Sometimes the organization may itself be in a state of despair, disruption, or destruction. Such organizations may be able to profit from corrective group treatment that attends to techno-structural organizational properties, such as organization arrangements, policies, procedures and the organizational climate that is perceived. Discussed in Chapter 10, is an innovative approach to organization change called the "social climate group." This change technique uses a representative group drawn from the organization to assess its social climate. Resulting data are used within a general group problem-solving model to positively change certain dysfunctional organizational properties, such as techno-structural components that are thought to be contributing to that climate.

Prominent among the innovations occurring at the organization level have been "organization development" and its latter day spin-offs: quality of work life, human resource development, and organizational transformation. Within these umbrella labels is a group-based organization improvement technique called, "quality circles," which Rapin describes in detail in Chapter 11. This group procedure, associated with the so-called Japanese influence on American organizations, provides opportunities for the introduction of novel ideas by line staff for organizational adoption.

Intervention Purpose Emphases

		Correction		Enhancement	
		Personal	Task	Personal	Task
Individual	Type	Personality Change	Rehabilitation	Personal Growth	Skill Development
	Eg.	Psychotherapy	Remedial Social Skills	Personal Development	Human Relations Skills Training
Interpersonal	Type	Interpersonal Problem Solving	Resocialization	Interpersonal Growth	Learning.
	Eg.	Counseling	Social Control	T-groups	Systematic Group Discussion
Organization	Type	Employee Change	Organization Change	Management Development	Organization Development
	Eg.	Employee Assistance	Social Climate	Team Development	Quality Circles
Community-Population	Type	Secondary/ Tertiary Prevention	Community Change	Health Promotion/ Primary Prevention	Community Development
	Eg.	Mutual Help	Action	Life Transition	Futuring

Intervention Level Emphases

Figure 5. Group Work Grid, Organization Level

CHAPTER 9

EMPLOYEE CHANGE
Employee Assistance Groups

CARY CHERNISS

T HIS chapter deals with an organizational intervention, the
Employee Assistance Group, which is provided to workers who
are experiencing work-related problems. Thus, it is an organizational level group intervention with an emphasis on employee
change. The social context of this kind of group makes it very different from several of the other kinds of group interventions
described in this volume. Group developers and leaders probably
will be more effective if they are sensitive to these unique aspects of
the employee assistance group.

INTERVENTION LEVEL AND PURPOSE

Group interventions at the organizational level are unique in that
they occur within highly structured settings. Work organizations are
different from families, communities, and personal growth settings
in the extent to which activities are structured around a clear task focus. This high degree of structure and control imposes significant
constraints on both group members and leaders. For instance, managers have the right—and the need—to monitor the behavior of
workers to a degree that would be considered excessive in a voluntary community group. Also, standardized policies and procedures
usually are developed to assist this monitoring function, an arrangement that would be highly unusual in a family.

The source of this high degree of structure derives from the fact that work organizations are created to pursue goals and accomplish tasks. At least in theory, there tends to be a balance between individual and group needs in families and other less formal settings. The group exists in part to help individuals grow. But in a work organization, the organizational task is primary, and independent of individual needs and goals. When there is a conflict between organizational goal attainment and individual preferences, the latter will be subjugated to the former. This essential characteristic of life in most organizations is the source of much personal malaise and interpersonal conflict; it also creates problems for those who wish to deal with these conflicts within the organizational setting.

Nevertheless, it is possible to help individuals within a work organization. But to do so, one must be familiar with the setting and sensitive to the problems of making employee assistance compatible with the goals and structures of the work context.

Compared to other kinds of organizational group interventions, those with a personal corrective purpose are particularly vulnerable because organizations traditionally have not seen personal correction as part of their responsibility. In the past, the prepotent response to problem employees has been to remove them through termination, rather than attempt to correct the problem. Clinical settings have been seen as the appropriate site for corrective action. Until the development of the community mental health model in the 1960s (Bloom, 1977; Rappaport, 1977), the helping professions tended to support this approach.

Fortunately, many changes in society during the last 20 years have helped to make the climate more favorable now for personal corrective intervention within work organizations. Most significant has been an expansion in the definition of the organization's responsibility to society. Environmental protection and affirmative action programs imply that organizations must attend to values other than their own productivity and profit. In fact, organizations now are expected to reduce pollution and promote racial justice even if it means a decrease in profit and organizational effectiveness.

Interest in Japanese management methods also has contributed to support for employee assistance efforts. One feature of Japanese management that seems to have contributed to high performance has been a greater concern for the quality of life of Japanese workers (Ouchi, 1981). Employee assistance programs in American companies represent one way to express such a concern.

Spurred by these social forces, many large organizations have developed employee assistance programs. And they have discovered that these in-house programs actually enable the organization to exert more control over the assistance function than it could when personal correction occurred off-site in clinical settings. This fact is something of a mixed blessing for those who administer and provide such services. It means that management is supportive of the employee assistance effort, especially if it can be shown to be cost-effective. On the other hand, it can lead to complex ethical conflicts. Such conflicts, however, are not inevitable if those who are directing the employee assistance effort are careful, skillful, and highly knowledgeable about the culture of the setting in which they must work.

SUPPORTIVE THEORY

Employee assistance groups generally can be tied to one of two overarching theoretical approaches. These approaches can be termed *palliative* and *problem-solving*. (In practice, a group can follow both of these approaches, but usually one is dominant because of the leader's own theoretical inclinations.) The palliative approach seeks to help the workers deal with the disturbing emotional and behavioral effects of stress. Group support, behavioral prescriptions, cognitive restructuring, and other kinds of activities are used to reduce depression, anger, and anxiety that impede the workers' functioning. Edelwich and Brodsky (1980), two proponents of this approach, suggest that the workers need help in recognizing and accepting reality, for little can be done to change that reality. Once the disturbed workers accept that reality as a given, they can be helped to find a satisfying adjustment within the existing framework.

The problem-solving approach, on the other hand, seeks to help workers change the source of the stress. The goal is to help individuals to develop attitudes and skills necessary for changing salient aspects of the work environment. Some relief for the symptoms of stress may be offered, but only so that the workers will be able to develop sufficient strength to change the stresses contributing to those symptoms.

Undoubtedly both theoretical approaches can be valid, depending upon the particular situation; however, the problem-solving model seems to have more theoretical and empirical support, and that is the approach that will be presented here. Theoretically, the work of Seligman (1975) on learned helplessness supports a more problem-solving type of intervention. As the result of numerous studies with both animals and humans, Seligman has concluded that people with psychological problems will best be helped when they directly experience a sense of mastery and control over their environment. Depression, excessive aggressiveness, anxiety neuroses, and many other kinds of psychological problems develop when people perceive that they lack control over significant reinforcers in their environment.

Empirical studies of stress and burnout in the work place have tended to support the view that problem-solving interventions directed at the sources of stress will be more effective than palliative ones. Both Shin and Mørch (1983) and Newman and Beehr (1979) have provided evidence suggesting that palliative approaches to coping with stress in the work setting are less effective than problem-solving ones. Work-related stress seems to be unique in this respect; Newman and Beehr (1979) found that palliation was effective in non-work contexts, such as marriage relationships, but not in the work place.

Thus, the most effective approach to reducing stress and its psychological concommitants in the work place appears to be one that seeks to reduce "learned helplessness" by increasing the organizational problem-solving skills of the worker. This problem-solving model is the theoretical basis of the employee assistance group described in this chapter.

MAIN INTERVENTION CHANGE TECHNIQUES USED

The problem-solving employee assistance group relies heavily on two change techniques. The first is a set of procedures for group problem-solving first developed and tested by Maier (1963). Many variations have appeared since this pioneering work (e.g., Easton, 1976; Kepner and Tregoe, 1968; Napier and Gershenfeld, 1981), but most involve the nine steps listed in Table 2.

Table 2
GROUP PROBLEM-SOLVING PROCEDURES

Step	*Activity*
1	Air feelings
2	Identify problems
3	Prioritize and select one problem to work on
4	Explore contributing factors and causes
5	Brainstorm solutions
6	Examine likely consequences of each alternative
7	Select solution to implement
8	Develop action plan: time lines and responsibilities
9	Evaluate

In the first step, the leader encourages group members to air their feelings. Their personal concerns about the problem are accepted in a nonjudgmental atmosphere. No argument, criticism, or other kind of attempt to influence the group members is accepted at this stage. This process of ventilation helps reduce the strong emotionalism that can interfere with constructive problem-solving. When the ventilation process has accomplished this task sufficiently, the group is ready to move to the next step in the process.

In step 2, the group identifies the problem or problems. The leader and group members help each other to identify the real problem as clearly as possible. Maier (1963) provides a number of guidelines for accomplishing this goal. For instance, it is important to discriminate between real problems, and solutions that are posing as problems. ("How to terminate a problem employee" would be an example of a solution posing as a problem.)

Frequently a group will identify several different problems or aspects of a larger problem; thus, in step 3, the group must decide which problem it should focus on first. In the fourth step, the group goes beyond the obvious, superficial aspects of the problem and explores contributing factors and causes. For instance, if the problem is a supervisor, the group is encouraged to explore factors that may cause the supervisor to behave in the problematic ways that the group has discussed.

In step 5, the group pools its creative potential by "brainstorming" solutions to the problem. In brainstorming, the group members are encouraged to think of as many different solutions as possible. The goal is quantity at this stage, rather than quality. The pace should be quick, and no criticism of ideas is allowed at this stage. Various techniques have been developed to help groups increase divergent thinking (e.g., Gordon, 1961; Prince, 1970; Rickard, 1974).

Once the brainstorming of solutions has progressed sufficiently, the group is ready to go back and examine each one more critically. In this sixth step, the likely consequences of each alternative are examined. In step 7, the group is ready to select a solution. Often this involves a combination of ideas generated during the brainstorming phase. The leader helps group members choose a solution that is both meaningful and feasible. Also, care must be taken that the group not take on too much at this stage.

Many good solutions never are implemented and the problems remain unsolved because step 8, the development of an action plan, is skipped. Unless the group examines what will be required to implement the solution and clearly assigns responsibility and time lines for the essential tasks, success is unlikely. The ninth and last step involves evaluation: the group agrees to meet again at some specified date in the future to review what progress has been made in dealing with the problem and modify the strategy where it appears necessary.

In practice, problem-solving groups rarely proceed in such an orderly, step-wise fashion. Frequently, underlying feelings about the problems, the organization, the group, or the leader erupt and interfere with the process. The group leader must be sensitive to this possibility and ready to stop the process to explore these interfering attitudes and feelings as they occur. Thus, the "airing of feelings" described under step 1 often needs to occur several more times during the course of the problem-solving process.

The second change technique useful in the employee assistance group is networking. In networking, resources inside and outside of the group are identified and tapped to help deal with the work-related problems. At the root of much work-related stress is an imbalance between resources and demands (Cherniss, 1980). The employees are asked to accomplish tasks for which they lack time, knowledge, skills, etc. Creative use of resources in the organization and the larger community can provide the additional resources necessary for accomplishing the job (Sarason and Lorentz, 1979). Also, in the process of networking with others, group members often experience a psychological sense of community that helps reduce the sense of helplessness which is central to so many psychological problems at work.

Many other techniques are useful in employee assistance groups, but group problem-solving and networking are two particularly salient ones for this type of intervention.

TARGET POPULATIONS

The employee assistance group described in this chapter is intended for workers who are experiencing work-related personal difficulties. They may have other types of problems (e.g., marital) that are contributing to stress, but it is assumed that the primary source of stress for them at this time is job related.

The kind of employee assistance group described here would be counter-indicated for workers who are manifesting a particularly high degree of depression and/or alienation, particularly if the majority of group members fall into this category. The employee assistance group also is not advisable when the organizational climate is particularly negative. For instance, in one school setting there was a high degree of animosity between the director of the school and the teachers. The director believed that many of the teachers were "lazy, incompetent, or worse." She saw her mission to be "cleaning house." She requested some kind of group for the teachers because morale had become such a serious problem, and some of the "good" teachers were suffering. However, she was particularly concerned that the group leader not allow the "bad" teachers, whom she was trying to fire, to talk in the group. She was afraid that the group would give them "reinforcement" and encourage them to stay on rather than re-sign. In this kind of situation, an employee assistance group would be a questionable intervention.

The credibility of the leader within the organization is particu-larly important. The employee assistance group may not be viable if the group leader does not have the support and confidence of both management and workers. In general, organizations will be most re-ceptive when the leader has high credibility and the organization is facing serious pressures (e.g., an excessive amount of employee ab-senteeism or evidence of widespread alcohol abuse).

PRIMARY GROUP LEADER FUNCTION

Given the potential for conflict between the goals of the employee assistance group and those of the organization, one important func-tion for the group leader is to serve as an advocate for the program within the system. To do this effectively, the leader should engage in extensive diagnostic activity before the group begins to meet. Some important questions to address include: Who requested the program or group? What is that person's position and power in the organiza-tion? What are the attitudes of the employees' supervisors toward the group? What are the initiator's goals and expectations for the group? Are they congruent with those of the participants? What are the po-tential barriers to developing trust among the participants? Scully (1983) has noted that the answers to these and similar questions will determine how the system responds to the employee assistance group. An important function of the group leader is to anticipate this response and develop the program in ways that minimize con-flict.

During group sessions, the leader should guide the group through the problem-solving process outlined above, using flexibil-ity and judgment in determining how closely to adhere to the se-quence. Also, the leader needs to monitor the group process, noting who talks to whom, about what, what the safe topics are, how nega-tive feelings are handled, what implicit or unwritten rules exist, etc. (Scully, 1983). It is the leader's responsibility to help the group ex-amine its process if it begins to impede the problem-solving.

Another important function of the leader is to help the group gain access to resources and facilitate the networking process.

Given these multiple functions, it is desirable that the leader be familiar with the organizational system. But it also is helpful for the leader to be an outsider, in order to enhance objectivity. Scully (1983) suggests that the ideal arrangement is for the group to have co-leaders, with one drawn from outside the system and the other being an insider. Finding an insider with the requisite skill and credibility can be difficult, however. For instance, a lower level person may be seen as lacking the necessary skill, stature, and organizational role for serving as a group leader for employees at his/her level and above. On the other hand, a high level person may be in a supervisory and evaluative position vis a vis members of the group, and this relationship could cause the members to "hold back" in the group. Also, another difficulty is that the outside leader may not have the amount of time and access necessary to sufficiently assess a large organization in order to identify the right insider. Nevertheless, the insider-outsider combination is valuable, when feasible.

LEADER TRAINING

Besides the usual training in group dynamics and group leadership skills, it is useful for the leader of an employee assistance group to know about the organizational culture — the history of that field or industry, the core problems and conflicts facing the field, and so on. An effective group leader in private industry settings may not be effective in schools, and an effective group leader in schools may not be prepared to lead a group of workers employed in health care organizations.

For instance, Kouzes and Mico (1979) have suggested that unlike business organizations, human service programs contain three distinct domains: the policy, managerial, and service domains. Many interpersonal conflicts, particularly between caregivers and administrators, tend to be coded as "personality conflicts" by those involved. However, the root cause is the difference in organizational perspective found in the different domains. Thus, administrators tend to be most concerned about cost efficiency and effectiveness, for these are the criteria on which they are evaluated. Caregivers tend to be more concerned about quality of service and good standards of practice. They want to do the best job possible with each individual client, while the administrator wants to do the best—but also the cheapest—job possible with an entire client population.

An employee assistance group leader who is aware of these systems dynamics can help members of an employee assistance group to view their work-related problems more objectively. Such a leader also can suggest more viable strategies (e.g., negotiation and conflict resolution) for dealing with these problems. But his "domain" perspective may not be a valid framework for analyzing employee problems in a business organization. Each type of setting has a unique culture and set of dynamics.

The complex relationships between the group and the larger system also make it desirable that the leader receive training in consultation skills and planned organizational change. This kind of training will prepare the leader to function as an effective advocate for the group.

For instance, in any organization, an administrator's permission may be necessary before a group can be formed. Many administrators will be reluctant initially to grant such permission because they are concerned about the potential unintended negative consequences that might be associated with the project. Consultation and planned change theory can help a group leader to anticipate and recognize resistance in such a situation. The theory also can help one to identify the sources of the resistance, even when these are not stated directly. Consultation skills also may assist one in interacting with administrators in a way that facilitates the working through and resolution of these concerns. Thus, training in consultation and planned change skills is valuable preparation for leading employee assistance groups in work organizations.

EVIDENCE OF INTERVENTION EFFECTIVENESS

Employee assistance groups are a relatively new kind of intervention, and thus there is not a solid base of evaluative research concerning their effectiveness. As noted above, there is research supporting both the theory and techniques used in problem-solving employee assistance groups. However, good evaluation studies are needed, particularly those that examine the differences between groups based on a palliative and problem-solving approach.

ILLUSTRATIVE CASE EXAMPLE

This example of an employee assistance group involved employees of a state department of mental health. These workers were experiencing extremely high levels of stress because of various organizational changes that had occurred. Through the employee assistance group, they were able to assume a more active stance toward their jobs. Initially, they were helped to design a strategy for collective action. When the situation deteriorated and budget cuts proffered massive lay-offs, the group helped the workers plan positively for the possibility of termination. Thus, the example demonstrates how an employee assistance group can help workers to cope even in a turbulent, changing environment. It also demonstrates how changes in the larger organization may require changes in the format and focus of the group.

The Context

The "prehistory" of the group was significant. I had been working in the system for over two years, providing training workshops and consultation on a variety of issues, including stress and burnout. As the result of this work, I was known to many important actors in the system, had considerable credibility with both workers and management, and knew the system and its problems quite well.

Like many state mental health systems, this one had been attempting to reduce the census of the large residential institutions (state psychiatric hospitals and developmental centers for the mentally retarded). A key staff person in this process was the client services worker, a state employee who worked out of a regional office and who served as a liaison between the institutions and the community. The client services workers received referrals from the community and attempted to find non-institutional placements for clients.

They also worked with institutional staff to prepare institutionalized clients for return to the community. They needed to know about the resources available for clients in the community, and they often had to be creative and persistent in finding new resources. Their backgrounds were varied, as were their skills. Most had the equivalent of a bachelors degree and some graduate training.

The role of the client services workers was a stressful one even in the best of circumstances, for they were often the person in the middle, caught between various demands, pressures, and constraints. However, during the months prior to initiation of the employee assistance groups for them, the situation had become considerably more difficult. A large state budget deficit was discovered shortly after a gubernatorial election; consequently, department administrators were told that they would not receive the funds that they had anticipated receiving for that year. To avoid bankruptcy, the department had to curtail or eliminate many programs.

For the client services workers, this meant that they did not have enough funding to place clients in community programs. At the same time, they were required by law to place any clients who needed services. Thus, it was literally impossible to meet the legal and moral requirements of their jobs. Their supervisors recognized this dilemma, but many of them chose to let their subordinates resolve it on their own. Presumably, it was the client services workers who would be the scapegoats when laws and regulations concerning client placement were violated.

Origin of the Employee Assistance Groups

The idea of providing employee assistance groups to the client services workers in one region of the state emerged from a committee. The committee consisted of a group of administrators who advised the regional training coordinator on training needs. During one of their regular meetings, they discussed the problems faced by the client services workers and decided that some kind of training in "stress management" might be helpful to them. The regional training coordinator took the responsibility for developing the program. He contacted me and asked me if I would be willing to provide some kind of workshop on stress management. I told him that in this kind of situation I preferred to use problem-solving groups which would help workers develop resources and tools for dealing directly with the sources of stress, rather than simply help them adjust to the situation through palliative measures such as relaxation training or exercise programs.

Fortunately, the training coordinator responded positively to the change in approach. In fact, he initially had been dubious about a workshop on stress management. The problem-solving approach seemed to be a more effective way of dealing with the stress problem. One idea he suggested was to involve a group of resource people: administrators in the system who had worked as client services workers in the past and who could provide insights on how to deal with the problems. We arranged for me to meet with some of these resource people before the workshop at which the groups would be initiated.

The meeting with these resource people was the major diagnostic activity. It was during this meeting that the nature and scope of the client service workers' problems became clear. The meeting also was used to plan the resource people's role in the first workshop.

Twenty-five client service workers attended the first workshop. They were divided into three groups, and each group was led by a trained group leader. I had worked with all three leaders in previous projects. Two had received considerable training in group problem-solving before we began working together. I had trained the third. My role now involved starting and ending the workshop ("official greeter"), and I floated among the groups throughout the day in order to monitor what was occurring. During breaks, I gave the leaders feedback on their groups, and helped them to debrief and plan for the next phase.

The groups were to follow the problem-solving sequence outlined above. Although the groups were formed in a random fashion, their atmospheres differed considerably. Two of the groups were able to work through their feelings of depression, anger, and impotence with little difficulty, but the third group was less willing to attempt this activity. It was hard for the leader of this group to move the members beyond the ventilation stage into active problem-solving. However, by lunch time all of the groups had progressed through the initial stages of the process; problems had been identified and one of the groups had reached the brainstorming stage.

After lunch, the resource people came in to hear what the groups had identified as problems during the morning session and to offer insight and suggestions. Unfortunately, this segment of the program did not work out as planned. The groups were ready to identify their own solutions and resented the presence of the outsiders. Also, the resource people were higher level administrators and thus were identified as part of the system that was creating so many of the problems. Most of the resource people handled this difficult situation well; they kept their poise, adopted a supportive stance toward the client services workers, and did not become defensive or argumentative. This part of the workshop did not seriously disrupt the process, but we certainly would not repeat it in the future.

When the resource people left at the scheduled time, the problem-solving groups resumed their work. The afternoon went much better. By the end of the day, all of the groups had identified a number of promising strategies for dealing with the focal problems. These three problems, stated in terms of goals, were: 1) To create mechanisms to facilitate resource sharing and networking across sectors of the region; 2) To create mechanisms to increase knowledge of resources and procedures; 3) To devise ways to motivate staff and keep them from getting burned out.

During the last half hour, the three groups came together and discussed a plan for having a second workshop at which they would decide on the best solutions and formulate action plans. The workshop was scheduled to occur in three weeks. The group also identified some tasks that needed to be done in preparation for the next workshop. The group leaders assumed the responsibility for doing many of these tasks.

Between the first and second workshops, the situation took an unexpected turn for the worse. The budget problems in the state department of mental health worsened, and more drastic measures for dealing with them were ordered. Among them was the decision to lay off two-thirds of all client services workers employed in the region. We considered cancelling the next workshop but decided that the workers might need it even more than before. However, we were prepared to alter the plan for the session.

We expected a very poor turnout due to the impending lay-offs, and we were surprised that half the participants returned for the second workshop. I began by summarizing what had happened during the last workshop and then brought up the topic of the lay-offs. I identified four options for the day: 1) do what we originally had planned, 2) discuss how the group might mobilize to fight the lay-offs, 3) identify ways of coping with the current situation on a more personal level, or 4) adjourn. Because the group was smaller, we did not break down into smaller groups as we had previously. Thus, I became the primary group leader, and the other group leaders functioned as co-leaders.

The group then spent some time discussing the lay-offs. Depression was the dominant tone. Their attitude about the workshop and what to do during the day resembled their feelings about their work in general: they came, but they did not know why they came. They had no expectation that the workshop would do any good or that they could make any difference in their jobs. Gradually, there was some expression of anger against the state system, but apathy and resignation were the dominant responses.

Timing was critical at this stage. If we continued with the discussion of feeling too long, the group would have become too depressed to do any constructive problem-solving. Yet we had to give them an opportunity to ventilate and acknowledge how they felt, or there would be no commitment to moving ahead with the problem-solving. Eventually, I sensed that the group was leaning toward discussing how to cope personally with some of the difficult problems that arose in the current uncertain climate.

With a little encouragement, one of the members presented a specific problem. A mother had recently became widowed, and she had two children who both needed residential services. The client services worker had told the mother three months ago that she could not place the children then, but that she would be able to within three months. Now, however, there was no money left to place the children, and the worker herself could be laid off any day. What could she say to the mother?

The group discussed this case and came up with some good ideas. The case helped show that serving a client in this kind of situation could involve more than just providing tangible placements. Providing the mother reassurance and up-to-date information about what was happening, and checking back with her at predictable intervals, could be a meaningful service for the worker to provide.

The group was feeling much better by lunch time, but during the lunch break new rumors surfaced. It was reported that the lay-off plan was to be announced at staff meetings later in the afternoon. The depression and apathy had returned by the time we reconvened after lunch.

During lunch, the group leaders decided that we had to assume a more active and directive stance toward the group. We hastily devised a plan for mobilizing political support against the lay-offs, and when the group came back from lunch we presented it to them. The plan involved contacting major organizations in the state that were organizing a political fight against the department's budget cuts in order to find out how the client services workers, individually or as a group, could help. The workers also would contact some local journalists to try and get them to run stories about the budget cuts and their impact on services. Finally, the workers who were present would try to recruit co-workers to come to a meeting the next week to help plan more strategies for dealing with the lay-offs.

The group members were not immediately enthusiastic about this plan; but after some discussion, support for it developed. During two more meetings, a small group worked on the action plan and made some headway. Eventually, however, the lay-offs were approved and many of the workers received their notices. At that point, we sensed that they were ready to give up the fight and prepare for termination.

When the lay-offs became inevitable, the group members needed help in thinking about how to handle termination. Many of them had worked for the department for ten years or more, and they had not had to look for a job in the competitive job market since joining the department. Also, their backgrounds were in the human services, and there were few jobs available in this sector. Further, the unemployment rate in the state was over 10 percent, so jobs in the private sector also would not be easy to find. Now the major source of stress involved the prospect of unemployment and the search for a new job.

Given this shift in need, we decided to use the employee assistance groups to provide "job search" aid. The participants were helped to think about job options that had not occurred to them before. As well, concerns were dealt with in resume writing, interviewing, and other aspects of finding a job.

Thus, this example illustrates the varied ways in which a problem-solving employee assistance group can help its members to confront work-related personal stress. In the first phase, we attempted to help the members find new ways of dealing with job-related problems in a situation characterized by high demand and few resources. In the next phase, we helped the group to respond to a major political and economic crisis in an active, organized fashion. In the last phase, we helped the members to take stock and manage the stressful process of termination. Although our activities and goals varied considerably, in each instance we were guided by a theoretical model which emphasized active coping in response to work-related stress. The group helped its members overcome the depression and apathy that immobilized them and prevented them from dealing effectively with stress at work. When the members suggested that they had no control over the external forces acting on them, the employee assistance group challenged this perception. Organized activity directed toward changing those external forces was encouraged when it seemed appropriate. Engaging in such activity seemed to be "therapeutic" for the members in the sense that they felt better about their work and themselves. On the other hand, the group also helped its members to withdraw from the political arena and plan for their own personal futures when this seemed warranted. But even in this last stage, the emphasis was on active coping rather than palliation.

APPLICATION POSSIBILITIES: EMPLOYMENT

Although there are no data concerning opportunities for employment in the employment assistance field, the potential seems to be present. Community mental health centers, for instance, are finding this a promising area to move into as funding for activities in the public sector has been reduced. While employee assistance programs encompass many activities, such as diagnostic evaluation and individual therapy, the employee assistance group certainly seems to be a particularly useful component for any program.

Another setting in which employee assistance groups can be developed is human resource development departments in large corporations. Traditionally, these units of the corporation have been concerned with activities such as personnel selection and placement, job training, and labor relations. But, in recent years, there has been much interest in expanding the scope of their activities. Sponsoring employee assistance groups now seems to be a legitimate part of the human resource department's mandate in many large companies.

The example presented in this chapter suggests that employee assistance also is possible in the public sector. Management practices in schools, mental health programs, and health care settings often have been borrowed from private industry, which can be a mixed blessing. However, the employee assistance program is one management practice that public sector agencies would do well to emulate. As private corporations invest more heavily in this area in the coming years, we probably will see growing interest in the public sector as well.

Therefore, the employee assistance group is a promising new intervention for personal correction at the organizational level. However, any activity intended to help individuals which is conducted within a highly structured work organization must confront paradoxes and problems. In many ways it is easier to provide such assistance in the community or in counseling programs that have a clear mission to offer such services. Yet the work place is the source of much of the stress that contributes to psychological difficulty in our society. The main virtue of employee assistance programs is that they deal with work-related stress much closer to the source. In the employee assistance group, workers help each other to confront and overcome the forces that generate so much stress in their lives. In doing so, they can experience a psychological sense of community which enhances their ability to deal with stress in the future.

REFERENCES

Bloom, B.L.: *Community Mental Health: A General Introduction.* Monterey, Ca.: Brooks/Cole, 1977.

Cherniss, C.: *Staff Burnout: Job Stress in the Human Services.* Beverly Hills, Ca.: Sage, 1980.

Easton, A.: *Decision-Making: A Short Course in Problem Solving.* New York: Wiley, 1976.

Edelwich, J. and Brodsky, A.: *Burn-out.* New York: Human Sciences Press, 1980.

Gordon, W.J.: *Synectics.* New York: Collier Books, 1961.

Kepner, H. & Tregoe, B.: *The Rational Manager.* New York: McGraw-Hill, 1968.

Kouzes, J.M. & Mico, P.R.: Domain theory: An introduction to organizational behavior in human service organizations. *Journal of Applied Behavioral Science,* 449-469, 1979.

Maier, N.R.F.: *Problem-solving Discussions and Conferences: Leadership Methods and Skills.* New York: McGraw-Hill, 1963.

Napier, R.W. & Gershenfeld, M.K.: *Groups: Theory and Experience* (2nd ed.). Boston: Houghton Mifflin, 1981.

Newman, J.E. & Beehr, T.A.: Personal and organizational strategies for handling job stress: A review of research and option. *Personnel Psychology, 32:*1-43, 1979.

Ouchi, W.G.: *Theory Z.* Reading, Ma.: Addison-Wesley, 1981.

Prince, M.: *The Practice of Creativity.* New York: Collier Books, 1970.

Rappaport, J.: *Community Psychology: Values, Research, Action.* New York: Holt, 1977.

Rickard, T.: *Problem Solving Through Creative Analysis.* London: Halsted Press, 1974.

Sarason, S.B. & Lorentz, E.: *The Challenge of the Resource Exchange Network.* San Francisco: Jossey-Bass, 1979.

Scully, R.: The work-setting support group: A means of preventing burnout. In B.A. Farber (Ed.), *Stress and Burnout in the Human Service Professions.* New York: Pergamon, 188-197, 1983.

Seligman, M.E.P.: *Helplessness.* San Francisco: W.H. Freeman, 1975.

Shinn, M. & Mørch, H.A.: A tripartite model of coping with burnout. In B.A. Farber (Ed.), *Stress and Burnout in the Human Service Professions.* New York: Pergamon, 227-240, 1983.

CHAPTER 10

ORGANIZATION CHANGE
The Social Climate Group

ROBERT K. CONYNE

ORGANIZATIONAL problems are common across all contemporary work settings. This chapter addresses the role of group work in efforts to produce positive, intentional change in organizations that are currently dysfunctional in some important way. Further, it will focus on the social climate group, one example of organization change groups.

INTERVENTION LEVEL

As Rensis Likert (1961, 1967) formulated in his linking-pin theory, organizations can be conceptualized as systems of interdependently functioning groups. His model of organizations is compatible with the basic direction of this chapter, where group phenomena are recognized as the basics of organizational behavior. Thus, leadership, group goals and standards, cohesion, social climate and other group level dimensions all assume great importance in understanding and in positively altering organizational group behavior.

Acceptance of group phenomena as a primary means for providing desired change in an organization builds upon the tradition established by group dynamicists such as Cartwright and Zander (1968), Lewin (1947), and White and Lippitt (1960). As well, group organization change emerges from a range of empirical studies that

Murray. In shorthand, social ecology is concerned with describing the "personality" of an environment, the way in which it is perceived by its members or by others.

Rudolf Moos and his colleagues at Stanford University's Social Ecology Laboratory have created a family of psychometrically sound social climate scales as one method for describing the social ecology of different environments. Irregardless of the organization of reference (e.g., family, residence hall, work group, or correctional facility) these social climate scales all are comprised of three basic opportunity dimensions: Relationship, Personal Growth, and System Maintenance/System Change. These three dimensions each contain subscales that, when taken together, provide for a description of task, personal, and contextual aspects of an assessed environment.

The basic notion is that these dimensions cut across all environments. Once measured accurately through self perceptions, the social climate of an environment can be described. This information allows for an understanding of how a particular environment may affect an individual's, "...attitudes and moods, (his) behavior, (his) health, and overall sense of well being and (his) social, personal, and intellectual developments" (Moos, 1974, p. 3). Further, such information can be used for organizational change. This activity is where social climate groups become important.

Change Techniques Used in Social Climate Groups

Setting aside leader functions until a later section, the change techniques necessary within social climate groups are the following seven, derived from the work of Aulepp and Delworth, 1976; Cochran, 1982; Conyne, 1978; Conyne and Clack, 1981; Dahrer, Corazzini, and McKinnon, 1977; Huebner, 1979; Insel and Moos, 1974; Moos, 1979; Moos and Lemke, 1983; and Schroeder, 1979:

1. Entry into and contracting with the organization by a social climate facilitator (a group leader and consultant).
2. Formation and development of representative *social climate group.*
3. Systematic assessment of the environment (real vs. ideal discrepancies).

4. Data feedback to members.
5. Organizational decision making on how to proceed.
6. Program development and implementation.
7. Reassessment of the social climate.

The representative social climate group is formed in step two of this process. Along with the social climate facilitator, the group becomes responsible for conducting all subsequent steps, numbers three through seven, of the process.

In addition to reflecting the organization members representatively, members of the social climate group need also to possess or acquire a variety of competencies in order for them to function effectively throughout these steps. These competencies include team building and interpersonal skills in step two (Aulepp and Delworth, 1976), environmental assessment skills in steps three and seven (Conyne and Clack, 1981), data feedback skills in step four (Hausser, Pecorella, and Wissler, 1977), obtaining a large group decision in step five (Zander, 1982), and program development and implementation skills in step six (Craig, 1978; Moore and Delworth, 1976).

Acquisition and maintenance of this complex set of competencies by group members requires sufficient training and supervision by the social climate facilitator. The investment of time and effort, however, is worth the price paid and is, moreover, an ethical imperative. The ethic involved is that of "user participation," where environmental change is planned and conducted, not by some expert external to a system, but by representative members of the system itself. Besides satisfying the ethical constraint mentioned, following this practice increases the chances for a successful change effort.

Leader Functions

The leader of social climate groups has been referred to previously as either a "social systems change facilitator" (Insel and Moos, 1974, p. 187) or an "environmental educator" (Moos, 1979, p. 245). I use the term, "social climate facilitator" in this chapter. The facilitator functions to assist the social climate group in promoting greater environmental competency (Steele, 1973), or perceived personal control, throughout the organization.

The facilitator of a social climate group needs to hold an ecological perspective to change. Among other points, this means that the facilitator keeps informed of the group and organizational context, and of the balance between task (e.g., organizational structure, policies and procedures, physical arrangements) and the more familiar personal dimensions. Because the assessed social climate of an organization is premised on an ecological orientation, the fit between assessment data and facilitator perspective is a close one.

Initially with the social change group the facilitator performs interpersonal and procedural training functions through team building experiences and discussion. The goal is to help members to develop a free-flowing working relationship that is characterized by mutual trust and clear procedural guidelines.

Later, but still in the team building stage, the facilitator trains members in the task skills of test administration, data feedback procedures, decision making, and program development and implementation. These task skills are then used by the group as it works with the entire organization in steps three through seven of the social climate change project. Throughout the group's life, the facilitator provides supervision and support to assist members with the handling of issues and problems that arise.

The general purpose of a social climate group is to assist an organization in correcting its task functioning. The modal leader function required for this purpose is that of *executive function* (Lieberman, Yalom, and Miles, 1973). The facilitator guides and mediates group formation, awareness, interaction, and action (Gill and Barry, 1982; Trotzer, 1979) by engaging in such behaviors as:

> ...limit setting, suggesting or setting rules, limits, norms, setting goals or directions of movements, managing time, sequencing, pacing, stopping, blocking, interacting, as well as such behaviors as inviting, eliciting, questioning, suggesting procedures for the group or a person, and dealing with decision-making (Lieberman, Yalom and Miles, 1973, p. 239).

In addition, to continue the Lieberman, et al. (1973) group leader function terminology, social climate facilitators place great importance on the function of *group-oriented meaning attribution,* that is, he or she demonstrates consistent interest in helping group members to understand and relate more effectively to the social system of the organization. These facilitators exhibit a moderate amount of the *caring* function, through providing relatively high levels of support and affection. Last, again in terms of the Lieberman, et al. group leader function model, social climate facilitators exercise relatively little of the group leader function, called *emotional stimulation.* They are low in charisma but high in peer orientation.

This pattern of group leader functions (high executive function, high group-oriented meaning attribution, moderate caring, and low emotional stimulation) is called a "social engineer" leader type. The social engineer is one of six empirically-derived types identified in the group research of Lieberman, et al. (1973). This label of "social engineer" fits the social climate facilitator very well, as demonstrated by the following examples of specific behaviors a facilitator might be called upon to provide during a social climate group:

- Coordinate and direct team (group) activities.
- Conduct facilitative procedures such as brainstorming, field force (sic) analysis, and consensus making.
- Give systematic, positive feedback and reinforcement to team members.
- Confront team members who are not doing their contracted work.
- Deal openly with conflicts and disagreements as these occur.
- Lead resolution of conflict between team members or team factions.
- Prepare meeting agendas if necessary.

(Aulepp and Delworth, 1976, p. 16).

Leader Training

The facilitator of a social climate group must draw from a complex competency base that extends beyond group facilitation. The other important areas include competencies in a social ecological perspective, communication, applied research, consultation, training and supervision, and action research. Space disallows a discussion of these areas and of appropriate training, but competency in each area is necessary to allow social climate group facilitation to successfully occur. Readers may wish to examine these areas in greater depth (Conyne, 1983; Conyne and Clack, 1981).

As we have seen in the previous section on group leader function, the social climate group facilitator can be considered a "social engineer of task correction groups," one who actively guides and mediates group behavior, relates this behavior to the larger social system, and supports members. The *group leader* training necessary to prepare an individual to competently perform the role of social climate group facilitator includes both generic group leader knowledge and skill competencies (Kottler, 1981) and specific competencies appropriate to task groups (Schindler-Rainman, 1981).

The critical generic knowledge and skill competencies, as well as a suggested supervised experience training program, have been officially approved by the Association for Specialists in Group Work (ASGW) as "...providing a minimum structure for standardizing the knowledge and skill competencies unique to the practice of group work" (Kottler, 1981, p. 129). Included among the 26 competency areas are knowledge of the major theoretical approaches to group work, of basic group dynamics, and of specific ethical problems. The qualified group leader also would demonstrate skills in such areas as making use of major strategies, techniques, and procedures, facilitating potent group therapeutic forces, and using basic group leader interventions. The reader may wish to refer to the most recent issuance of these ASGW standards (ASGW, 1983) for elaboration.

Schindler-Rainman (1981) has studied task group leaders specifically. She has identified seven areas that she considers as being significant for the training of task-group leaders. These areas for training, which have direct relevance for social climate group facilitators, include: helping the group make decisions; dealing with and using differences among members; giving feedback and guidance to improve the work of the group; mobilizing and using the resources that are needed to do tasks; formulating and clarifying goals; implementing goals; individualizing members' abilities, needs, and skills to fit the tasks at hand; and sharing leadership appropriately with members.

Trainees learning to facilitate social climate groups need to develop knowledge and skills in both therapeutic and task group approaches. Further, trainees need to learn how to form and manage the social climate group as well as how to connect it to the larger social system of the organization itself.

Didactic and practical experience would need to be interdisciplinary to accomplish these training needs. A typical counseling group course or series of courses, for instance, would represent a partial approach. Course work in groups drawn from social work, management, and social psychology also could contribute effectively to the breadth of knowledge and skills necessary.

Illustrative Intervention/Case Example

Several case examples of social climate change projects now exist in the literature. For instance, Moos (1979) has summarized a number of educationally-based efforts that have occurred in university student living groups and classroom settings. A number of these, and other, projects have used the social climate (often called, restrictively, "planning") group as a central change vehicle. Typically, however, the associated group phenomena are left largely unarticulated.

Some especially good treatments of the social climate group process have been provided by Cochran (1982), Dahrer, et al. (1977), and Schroeder (1979). Of these projects, Cochran's case study of the planning group approach in a student affairs organizational consultation provides the most concrete information about group phenomena.

Cochran and his facilitator formed a social climate (planning) group representative of the organization. It was comprised of four administrative staff, two line staff, one support staff, and the two facilitators. The group used a 10-step social climate group technology, a variation of the seven-step model presented earlier. Progression through these steps covered 18 group meetings over a six month period, prompting the group members to begin facetiously referring to the steps as, "ten steps to heaven." These steps were: Form a representative planning group (four sessions), discuss issues to assess (three sessions), select assessment methodology (four sessions), gather data, interpret and disseminate results (four sessions), design supported Lewin's (1951, p. 228) observation that, "It is easier to change individuals formed into a group than to change any of them separately."

INTERVENTION PURPOSE

Groups can be used in an organization to correct existing problems or to further develop an organization that is generally functioning adequately. The purpose of the groups described in this chapter is to correct problems existing in an organization. I refer to this class of groups in terms of "organizational change."

Problems are endemic to all systems. An organization is susceptible to an especially complex array of them. These problems can be experienced in the personal or task sides of the organization. In the personal side, for example, communications among organizational members may be poor, while in the task side the organization's physical arrangements might restrict proper functioning. The presence of these kinds of organizational problems can lead to undesirable outcomes, such as a "cold" social climate existing in the organization, where members feel unwelcome, and/or to lowered organizational productivity, where the "bottom line" of the organization is negatively affected. As we shall see later, the trend in organizational change efforts today is to place greater emphasis than previously on *task* correction, a direction that represents an emphasis away from a preoccupation with people-process elements in the organization. Organization change groups, then, are conducted to ameliorate identified problems and to assist the organization to become able to meet its stated tasks and goals.

A variety of organization change approaches have been developed that make use of group activities. These approaches include process consultation (Schein, 1969), action research (Lewin, 1951), survey guided development (Hausser, Pecorella, and Wissler, 1977), TORI (Gibb, 1978), encounter (Rogers, 1970), social climate (Moos, 1979), and environmental design (Holahan, 1977), among others. Some of them, such as encounter and TORI, are more advanced in specific group application than are others, such as environmental design. Yet, all these approaches have been used to remedy organizational deficiencies, and they all contain group work applications holding promise for organizational change.

THEORETICAL SUPPORTS

No distinct, integrated theory exists for organization change groups. Rather, supportive theory and research derives from three general sources, and practitioners have joined aspects of these sources in different ways. These sources are organizational psychology, group dynamics, and the therapeutic group helping process.

Organizational psychology is a branch of the discipline of psychology that is concerned with understanding the psychological properties of organizations and with the organizational behavior of people. Typical concepts explored in organizational psychology include organizational power, goals, organizational theory, norms and standards, leadership, conflict, structure, productivity, satisfaction, group dynamics, and so on.

Group dynamics is the scientific study of groups and of what occurs in them. Group dynamics is frequently tied to group change efforts. Lewin originated the scientific study and application of group dynamics as a change technology during World War II. He conducted a series of studies for the Food Habits Committee of the National Research Council (Lewin, 1943) to discover if food preferences could be altered more effectively through group discussion and decision or through an attractive lecture. In controlled experiments testing the two basic approaches, he found that the group discussion/decision approach consistently produced significantly positive results in volunteer homemakers using readily available (but unpopular), beefhearts, sweetbreads, and kidneys to feed their families. In another series of experiments (Lewin, 1947), he found group discussion and decision superior to individual presentations in inducing farm women to significantly increase their use of drinking formula, orange juice, and cod liver oil in feeding their babies.

Subsequent research of group discussion and social change by Bennett (1955) showed that group discussion by itself may be relatively unimportant in producing behavioral change or action. Rather, her research showed that the critical element was for a group member to make a positive decision while perceiving that other members also made positive decisions. Such decisions serve to change the group standard and allow for individual change to occur.

Lewin's studies of group dynamics as a change agent stimulated an impressive array of change strategies (Benne, 1976) and of research studies. The latter were conducted primarily in industrial organizations (see Forsyth, 1983). Some of these studies were longitudinal, such as Seashore and Bowers' (1970) study of organizational change in the Banner Company, a large packing manufacturer. Results accumulating from these studies documented the positive effects of group dynamics used for organizational change in industry. Gains were shown in advanced employee satisfaction, reduced turnover, improved organizational productivity, and in participant leadership as a positive organizational force.

Most of the organization change group studies focused on altering people-process aspects of group members. Communication, satisfaction, and participation were often addressed. The organization's task side, comprised of such elements as organizational structure, technical and procedural activity, and its physical arrangements, were usually ignored.

Recent research reviews of contemporary group organization change efforts show these groups to be minimally successful, largely due to an emphasis on human process dimensions to the exclusion of task and context (Porras and Berg, 1978b). These reviews also indicate that this imbalance is being corrected (Porras and Berg, 1978a) by giving increased attention to task and organizational climate elements. This direction is much more consistent with Lewin's own broad conceptualization of ecological psychology.

Faucheux, Amado, and Laurent, in their review of organizational development and change (1982), found that recent publications in the field of psychology are transforming the means for fostering change in the organization (see, for instance, Lippitt, 1982, and his discussion of "total resource utilization" as a model for organization change). This transformation is occurring in two areas, task and context, as illustrated by the two quotations below:

Task

Both intervention approaches — structural and personal — must be seen as complimentary and should operate collaboratively if one is to deal with social change.

Context

In most instances organizational change takes place as a result of changes in the context that organizations create for themselves through their interaction. Planned organizational change can only be a gimmick when it does not fully integrate the contextual dimensions that provide life, meaning, and raison d'etre to organizations (Faucheux, Amado, and Laurent, 1982, p. 366).

Therapeutic group helping approaches represent the third general source for organization change groups. Individual psychotherapy and counseling theories, such as person-centered, behavioral, and analytic, were expanded to apply to group counseling and psychotherapy (Corey, 1981; Gazda, 1982; Sampson and Marthas, 1981; Trotzer, 1977; Yalom, 1975). Basic competencies in individual interviewing and in dyadic communication were broadened to fit the group setting (e.g., Carkhuff, 1969; Clack and Conyne, 1974; Egan, 1977, 1982; Johnson and Johnson, 1982). Recently, Janis (1983) has developed a generic process for change, based on social support and the "dependable enhancement" of client self-esteem, that he suggests can be useful in all helping situations.

These therapeutic group helping approaches, when integrated with knowledge of organizational psychology and of group dynamics, discussed above, form the general theoretical basis for organization change groups. This integration remains for the practitioner to construct because few integrative models currently exist.

The remainder of this chapter will focus on one way in which the three sources for organization change groups is being developed. I label this approach the "social climate group."

SOCIAL CLIMATE GROUPS

Social climate groups are an emerging form of organization change groups. They developed from the field of social ecology (e.g., Moos and Insel, 1974), with origins in the work of Lewin and

Murray. In shorthand, social ecology is concerned with describing the "personality" of an environment, the way in which it is perceived by its members or by others.

Rudolf Moos and his colleagues at Stanford University's Social Ecology Laboratory have created a family of psychometrically sound social climate scales as one method for describing the social ecology of different environments. Irregardless of the organization of reference (e.g., family, residence hall, work group, or correctional facility) these social climate scales all are comprised of three basic opportunity dimensions: Relationship, Personal Growth, and System Maintenance/System Change. These three dimensions each contain subscales that, when taken together, provide for a description of task, personal, and contextual aspects of an assessed environment.

The basic notion is that these dimensions cut across all environments. Once measured accurately through self perceptions, the social climate of an environment can be described. This information allows for an understanding of how a particular environment may affect an individual's, "...attitudes and moods, (his) behavior, (his) health, and overall sense of well being and (his) social, personal, and intellectual developments" (Moos, 1974, p. 3). Further, such information can be used for organizational change. This activity is where social climate groups become important.

Change Techniques Used in Social Climate Groups

Setting aside leader functions until a later section, the change techniques necessary within social climate groups are the following seven, derived from the work of Aulepp and Delworth, 1976; Cochran, 1982; Conyne, 1978; Conyne and Clack, 1981; Dahrer, Corazzini, and McKinnon, 1977; Huebner, 1979; Insel and Moos, 1974; Moos, 1979; Moos and Lemke, 1983; and Schroeder, 1979:

1. Entry into and contracting with the organization by a social climate facilitator (a group leader and consultant).
2. Formation and development of representative *social climate group*.
3. Systematic assessment of the environment (real vs. ideal discrepancies).

4. Data feedback to members.
5. Organizational decision making on how to proceed.
6. Program development and implementation.
7. Reassessment of the social climate.

The representative social climate group is formed in step two of this process. Along with the social climate facilitator, the group becomes responsible for conducting all subsequent steps, numbers three through seven, of the process.

In addition to reflecting the organization members representatively, members of the social climate group need also to possess or acquire a variety of competencies in order for them to function effectively throughout these steps. These competencies include team building and interpersonal skills in step two (Aulepp and Delworth, 1976), environmental assessment skills in steps three and seven (Conyne and Clack, 1981), data feedback skills in step four (Hausser, Pecorella, and Wissler, 1977), obtaining a large group decision in step five (Zander, 1982), and program development and implementation skills in step six (Craig, 1978; Moore and Delworth, 1976).

Acquisition and maintenance of this complex set of competencies by group members requires sufficient training and supervision by the social climate facilitator. The investment of time and effort, however, is worth the price paid and is, moreover, an ethical imperative. The ethic involved is that of "user participation," where environmental change is planned and conducted, not by some expert external to a system, but by representative members of the system itself. Besides satisfying the ethical constraint mentioned, following this practice increases the chances for a successful change effort.

Leader Functions

The leader of social climate groups has been referred to previously as either a "social systems change facilitator" (Insel and Moos, 1974, p. 187) or an "environmental educator" (Moos, 1979, p. 245). I use the term, "social climate facilitator" in this chapter. The facilitator functions to assist the social climate group in promoting greater environmental competency (Steele, 1973), or perceived personal control, throughout the organization.

The facilitator of a social climate group needs to hold an ecological perspective to change. Among other points, this means that the facilitator keeps informed of the group and organizational context, and of the balance between task (e.g., organizational structure, policies and procedures, physical arrangements) and the more familiar personal dimensions. Because the assessed social climate of an organization is premised on an ecological orientation, the fit between assessment data and facilitator perspective is a close one.

Initially with the social change group the facilitator performs interpersonal and procedural training functions through team building experiences and discussion. The goal is to help members to develop a free-flowing working relationship that is characterized by mutual trust and clear procedural guidelines.

Later, but still in the team building stage, the facilitator trains members in the task skills of test administration, data feedback procedures, decision making, and program development and implementation. These task skills are then used by the group as it works with the entire organization in steps three through seven of the social climate change project. Throughout the group's life, the facilitator provides supervision and support to assist members with the handling of issues and problems that arise.

The general purpose of a social climate group is to assist an organization in correcting its task functioning. The modal leader function required for this purpose is that of *executive function* (Lieberman, Yalom, and Miles, 1973). The facilitator guides and mediates group formation, awareness, interaction, and action (Gill and Barry, 1982; Trotzer, 1979) by engaging in such behaviors as:

> ...limit setting, suggesting or setting rules, limits, norms, setting goals or directions of movements, managing time, sequencing, pacing, stopping, blocking, interacting, as well as such behaviors as inviting, eliciting, questioning, suggesting procedures for the group or a person, and dealing with decision-making (Lieberman, Yalom and Miles, 1973, p. 239).

In addition, to continue the Lieberman, et al. (1973) group leader function terminology, social climate facilitators place great importance on the function of *group-oriented meaning attribution,* that is, he or she demonstrates consistent interest in helping group members

to understand and relate more effectively to the social system of the organization. These facilitators exhibit a moderate amount of the *caring* function, through providing relatively high levels of support and affection. Last, again in terms of the Lieberman, et al. group leader function model, social climate facilitators exercise relatively little of the group leader function, called *emotional stimulation*. They are low in charisma but high in peer orientation.

This pattern of group leader functions (high executive function, high group-oriented meaning attribution, moderate caring, and low emotional stimulation) is called a "social engineer" leader type. The social engineer is one of six empirically-derived types identified in the group research of Lieberman, et al. (1973). This label of "social engineer" fits the social climate facilitator very well, as demonstrated by the following examples of specific behaviors a facilitator might be called upon to provide during a social climate group:

- Coordinate and direct team (group) activities.
- Conduct facilitative procedures such as brainstorming, field force (sic) analysis, and consensus making.
- Give systematic, positive feedback and reinforcement to team members.
- Confront team members who are not doing their contracted work.
- Deal openly with conflicts and disagreements as these occur.
- Lead resolution of conflict between team members or team factions.
- Prepare meeting agendas if necessary.

(Aulepp and Delworth, 1976, p. 16).

Leader Training

The facilitator of a social climate group must draw from a complex competency base that extends beyond group facilitation. The other important areas include competencies in a social ecological perspective, communication, applied research, consultation, training and supervision, and action research. Space disallows a discussion of these areas and of appropriate training, but competency in each area is necessary to allow social climate group facilitation to successfully occur. Readers may wish to

examine these areas in greater depth (Conyne, 1983; Conyne and Clack, 1981).

As we have seen in the previous section on group leader function, the social climate group facilitator can be considered a "social engineer of task correction groups," one who actively guides and mediates group behavior, relates this behavior to the larger social system, and supports members. The *group leader* training necessary to prepare an individual to competently perform the role of social climate group facilitator includes both generic group leader knowledge and skill competencies (Kottler, 1981) and specific competencies appropriate to task groups (Schindler-Rainman, 1981).

The critical generic knowledge and skill competencies, as well as a suggested supervised experience training program, have been officially approved by the Association for Specialists in Group Work (ASGW) as "...providing a minimum structure for standardizing the knowledge and skill competencies unique to the practice of group work" (Kottler, 1981, p. 129). Included among the 26 competency areas are knowledge of the major theoretical approaches to group work, of basic group dynamics, and of specific ethical problems. The qualified group leader also would demonstrate skills in such areas as making use of major strategies, techniques, and procedures, facilitating potent group therapeutic forces, and using basic group leader interventions. The reader may wish to refer to the most recent issuance of these ASGW standards (ASGW, 1983) for elaboration.

Schindler-Rainman (1981) has studied task group leaders specifically. She has identified seven areas that she considers as being significant for the training of task-group leaders. These areas for training, which have direct relevance for social climate group facilitators, include: helping the group make decisions; dealing with and using differences among members; giving feedback and guidance to improve the work of the group; mobilizing and using the resources that are needed to do tasks; formulating and clarifying goals; implementing goals; individualizing members' abilities, needs, and skills to fit the tasks at hand; and sharing leadership appropriately with members.

Trainees learning to facilitate social climate groups need to develop knowledge and skills in both therapeutic and task group approaches. Further, trainees need to learn how to form and manage the social climate group as well as how to connect it to the larger social system of the organization itself.

Didactic and practical experience would need to be interdisciplinary to accomplish these training needs. A typical counseling group course or series of courses, for instance, would represent a partial approach. Course work in groups drawn from social work, management, and social psychology also could contribute effectively to the breadth of knowledge and skills necessary.

Illustrative Intervention/Case Example

Several case examples of social climate change projects now exist in the literature. For instance, Moos (1979) has summarized a number of educationally-based efforts that have occurred in university student living groups and classroom settings. A number of these, and other, projects have used the social climate (often called, restrictively, "planning") group as a central change vehicle. Typically, however, the associated group phenomena are left largely unarticulated.

Some especially good treatments of the social climate group process have been provided by Cochran (1982), Dahrer, et al. (1977), and Schroeder (1979). Of these projects, Cochran's case study of the planning group approach in a student affairs organizational consultation provides the most concrete information about group phenomena.

Cochran and his facilitator formed a social climate (planning) group representative of the organization. It was comprised of four administrative staff, two line staff, one support staff, and the two facilitators. The group used a 10-step social climate group technology, a variation of the seven-step model presented earlier. Progression through these steps covered 18 group meetings over a six month period, prompting the group members to begin facetiously referring to the steps as, "ten steps to heaven." These steps were: Form a representative planning group (four sessions), discuss issues to assess (three sessions), select assessment methodology (four sessions), gather data, interpret and disseminate results (four sessions), design

change (three sessions), implement, evaluate, and recycle. Due to space considerations, I will limit this analysis to step two of this project, "Discussing issues to assess." In the author's words:

> As the agency's "morale issues" were discussed, it became apparent that the group was prone to focus on solutions to problems rather than clarifying issues underlying the problems...The group became frustrated and confused about its basic purpose...At this point, the consultants made a shift to a more directive, structured leadership style given that the heuristic, facilitative style was apparently not functioning (Cochran, 1982, p. 315).

This extract suggests useful information about the functioning of this group during its early evolution. One observation readily occurs. General facilitation of task groups, such as this one, frequently fails to provide needed guidance and clarity. Thus, the task-side of these groups can remain characteristically undeveloped. As can be seen in this group, members became unclear of purpose and process except at a general level, and they grew upset. The facilitators then recognized a need for increased direction, structure, and specific guidance, and provided it. Such action is necessary if the group is to function well internally and to effectively work with the larger organization as social climate change is undertaken. To do so, however, demands that facilitators become competent in the task skills discussed earlier in this chapter.

Evaluation

As I mentioned earlier, the literature now contains reports describing social climate change projects conducted within organizations. Social climate (planning) groups have been central to some of these efforts. However, evaluations have not attempted to identify independent effects of the social climate group on the entire change process. Existing information in this area is primarily descriptive and reflective (e.g., Cochran, 1982; Dahrer, et al., 1977). Further development of the social climate group itself may remedy this evaluation deficit.

The existing research is incomplete in another way, also.

Although a reassessment step is included in the social climate change models, the results of reassessment are uncommonly reported in the literature. One suspects that reassessment is not being conducted. Results that are reported tend to be mid-range in scope. These results may indicate a different way of doing something organizationally but an evaluation of the effectiveness of the innovation is usually absent.

An outcome of Cochran's project, described earlier, is illustrative. Here, a major reorganization of staff was accomplished that combined staff from all three staff levels (administrative, line, and support) into new, mixed staff work teams. While this was a large structural change that appeared to have made sense within the context of the organization, its subsequent effects on social climate are unknown. Yet, in all fairness, this failure to reassess following change is a deficiency present in all change techniques, and is not peculiar to this one.

The larger perspective of group organizational change, with which we began this chapter, offers a clouded picture in terms of effects. On the optimistic end, Kelman and Wolff (1976), for instance, found that a combined approach of data feedback and group discussion resulted in a school staff development team making several organizational changes centered on a radical revision of its procedure to use the time of teachers and special services staff more efficiently. The authors conclude that the success of this project was due to the view held by the group that existing problems were organizational and systematic rather than personal and interpersonal. Interestingly, this conclusion further supports the need for organization change groups to respond to task elements, a point that is obvious throughout recent literature on the subject.

On the pessimistic end, reviews of the literature have led some to conclude that the small group is limited (Goodstein and Dovico, 1979) or even unsuccessful (Ouchi and Price, 1978) as a vehicle for organizational change. Goodstein and Dovico (1979) explain that most of the learning obtained through the small group is personal rather than organizational and, further, that the promotion of "love and trust" as a model for organizational change is passe. Ouchi and Price (1978) suggest that the small group change approach insufficiently addresses the intransigence of hierarchical structures and conflicting value orientations dominant in most contemporary American organizations.

Application and Employment

Organizational problems are plentiful — in residence halls, manufacturing concerns, and hospitals, among other settings. The organization change group, derived from a solid tradition in organizational psychology, group dynamics, and the therapeutic group helping field, offers a general methodology for organizational modification.

Recent research tends to suggest that this methodology is restricted in its utility for producing lasting organizational change unless it sharply elevates its attention to task (technical and structural), as well as personal, dimensions of group and organizational life. A continued reliance on personal elements only may help individuals, but seems to miss the broader organizational mark.

The social climate group approach to organizational change is a recent innovation with origins in social ecology, as well as in organizational change groups. It attempts to include all organizational ecological dimensions, certainly including task, thus addressing a comprehensive context of organizational functioning.

As Moos (1979) points out in his discussion of "environmental educators," we need such people who could, "...teach people about their environment, including how to conceptualize its component parts and their interrelationships and, most important, how to understand and control its potential impact on their everyday lives" (p. 245). These people, the group work prototype being the social climate group facilitator, can help organizations to become more productive and humane, both of which are keenly needed in contemporary society.

Therefore, I anticipate that a need will develop for group workers who can facilitate social climate projects in organizations. The related success of quality circles (see chapter 1) and of quality of work life (QWL) groups in a variety of organizations (Faucheux, et al., 1982; Taylor, 1977, 1978) lends support to this expectation.

The challenge is for our academic programs to create the sorts of group work training curricula that will prepare students to move competently into this future employment area. And, for our students to take advantage of the opportunity.

REFERENCES

Association for Specialists in Group Work: *Professional Standards for Training of Group Counselors.* Author, 1983.

Aulepp, L., and Delworth, U.: *Training Manual for an Ecosystem Model.* Boulder, Western Interstate Commission for Higher Education, 1976.

Benne, K.: The current state of planned changing in persons, groups, communities, and societies. In W. Bennis, K. Benne, R. Chin, and K. Corey (Eds.), *The Planning of Change* (3rd ed.). New York: Holt, 68-83, 1976.

Bennett, E.: Discussion, decision, commitment, and consensus in group decision. *Human Relations, 8*:251-274, 1955.

Carkhuff, R.: *Helping and Human Relations: A Primer for Lay and Professional Helpers.* Volume I, II. New York: Holt, 1969.

Cartwright, D., and Zander, A. (Eds.): *Group Dynamics.* New York: Harper and Row, 1968.

Clack, R., and Conyne, R.: *Basic Skills of Small Group Discussion Leadership.* Unpublished manuscript, 1974.

Cochran, D.: Organizational consultation: A planning group approach. *Personnel and Guidance Journal, 60*:314-317, 1982.

Conyne, R.: *Planning Group for Campus Environmental Design.* Normal, Unpublished manuscript, 1978.

Conyne, R.: Campus environmental design for counseling centers. *Journal of College Student Personnel, 24 (5)*:433-437, 1983.

Conyne, R., and Clack, R.: *Environmental Assessment and Design: A New Tool for the Applied Behavioral Scientist.* New York: Praeger, 1981.

Corey, G.: *Theory and Practice of Group Counseling.* Monterey: Brooks/Cole, 1981.

Craig, D.: *HIP Pocket Guide to Planning and Evaluation.* Austin: Learning Concepts, 1978.

Dahrer, D., Corazzini, J., and McKinnon, R.: An environmental redesign program for residence halls. *Journal of College Student Personnel, 18*:11-15, 1977.

Egan, G.: *You and Me: The Skills of Communicating and Relating to Others.* Monterey: Brooks/Cole, 1977.

Egan, G.: *The Skilled Helper: Model, Skills, and Methods for Effective Helping* (2nd ed.). Monterey: Brooks/Cole, 1982.

Faucheux, C., Amado, G., and Laurent, A.: Organizational Development and Change. *Annual Review of Psychology, 33*:343-370, 1982.

Forsyth, D.: *An Introduction to Group Dynamics.* Monterey: Brooks/Cole, 1983.

Gazda, G. (Ed.): *Basic Approaches to Group Psychotherapy and Group Counseling,* (3rd ed.) Springfield, Il.: Thomas, 1982.

Gibb, J.: *Trust: A New View of Personal and Organization Development.* Los Angeles, Guild of Tutors Press, 1978.

Gill, S., and Barry, R.: Group-focused counseling: Classifying the essential skills. *Personnel and Guidance Journal, 60*:302-305, 1982.

Goodstein, L., and Dovico, M.: The decline and fall of the small group. *Journal of Applied Behavioral Science, 15*:320-328, 1979.

Hausser, D., Pecorella, P., and Wissler, A.: *Survey-Guided Development II: A Data-Based Manual for Consultants.* La Jolla: University Associates, 1977.

Holahan, C.: Consultation in environmental psychology: A case study of a new counseling role. *Journal of Counseling Psychology, 24*:251-254, 1977.

Huebner, L.: Redesigning Campus Environments. In G. Hanson and U. Delworth (Eds.-in-chief), *New Directions for Student Service,* 1-22, 1979.

Insel, P., and Moos, R.: Psychological Environments: Expanding the scope of human ecology. *American Psychologist, 29*:179-188, 1974.

Janis, I.: The role of social support in adherence to stressful decisions. *American Psychologist, 38*:143-160, 1983.

Johnson, D. and Johnson, F.: *Joining Together: Group Theory and Group Skills,* 2nd ed. Englewood Cliffs: Prentice-Hall, 1982.

Kelman, E., and Wolff, G.: Data feedback and group problem-solving: An approach to organizational development in schools. *Psychology in the Schools, 13*:421-427, 1976.

Kottler, J.: The development of guidelines for training group leaders: A synergistic model. *Journal for Specialists in Group Work* (Special issue: Issues in the Training of Group Workers), *6*:125-129, 1981.

Lewin, K.: Forces behind food habits and methods of change. *Bulletin of the National Research Council, 108*:35-65, 1943.

Lewin, K.: Frontiers in group dynamics. *Human Relations, 1*:5-41, 1947.

Lewin, K.: *Field Theory in Social Science.* New York: Harper, 1951.

Lieberman, M., Yalom, I., and Miles, M.: *Encounter Groups: First Facts.* New York: Basic Books, 1973.

Likert, R.: *New Patterns of Management.* New York: McGraw-Hill, 1961.

Likert, R.: *The Human Organization.* New York: McGraw-Hill, 1967.

Lippitt, R.: Perspective on development: From PG to GD to OD to HRD to TRU. *Journal for Specialists in Group Work* (Special Issue: Group Work and Organization Development), *7*:8-11, 1982.

Moore, M., and Delworth, U.: *Training Manual for Student Services Program Development.* Boulder, Western Interstate Commission for Higher Education, 1976.

Moos, R.: *The Social Climate Scales: An Overview.* Palo Alto: Consulting Psychologists Press, 1974.

Moos, R.: *Evaluating Educational Environments.* San Francisco: Jossey-Bass, 1979.

Moos, R., and Insel, P. (Eds.): *Issues in Social Ecology: Human Milieus.* Palo Alto: National Press Books, 1974.

Moos, R., and Lemke, S.: Assessing and improving social-ecological settings. In Seidman, E. (Ed.): *Handbook of Social Intervention.* Beverly Hills: Sage, 143-162, 1983.

Ouchi, W., and Price, R.: Hierarchies, clans, and Theory Z: A new perspective on organizational development. *Organizational Dynamics, 7*:25-44, 1978.

Porras, J., and Berg, P.: Evaluation methodology in organization development: An analysis and critique. *Journal of Applied Behavioral Science, 14*:151-173, 1978a.

Porras, J., and Berg, P.: The impact of organizational development. *Academy of Management Review.* April: 249-266, 1978b.

Rogers, C.: *Carl Rogers on Encounter Groups.* New York: Harper and Row, 1970.

Sampson, E., and Marthas, M.: *Group Process for the Health Professions,* 2nd ed. New York: Wiley, 1981.

Schein, E.: *Process Consultation: Its Role in Organization Development.* Reading: Addison-Wesley, 1969.

Schindler-Rainman, E.: Training task-group leaders. *Journal for Specialists in Group Work* (Special issue: Issues in the Training of Group Workers). *6*:171-174, 1981.

Schroeder, C.: Designing ideal staff environments through milieu management. *Journal of College Student Personnel, 20*:129-135, 1979.

Seashore, S. and Bowers, D.: The durability of organizational change. *American Psychologist, 25*:227-233, 1970.

Steele, F.: *Physical Settings and Organization Development.* Reading: Addison-Wesley, 1973.

Taylor, J.: Experiments in work system design: Economic and human results. *Personnel Review,* Part I, *6*:21-34; Part II, *6*:21-42,1977.

Taylor, J.: An empirical examination of the dimensions of QWL. *OMEGA, 6*:153-160, 1978.

Trotzer, J.: *The Counselor and the Group.* Monterey: Brooks/Cole, 1977.

White, R., and Lippitt, R.: *Autocracy and Democracy.* New York: Harper, 1960.

Yalom, I.: *The Theory and Practice of Group Psychotherapy.* (2nd ed.). New York: Basic Books, 1975.

Zander, A.: *Making Groups Effective.* San Francisco: Jossey-Bass, 1982.

MANAGEMENT DEVELOPMENT

Although a chapter on management development groups is not contained in this book, due to production problems, these groups are important organization innovations. A few comments are in order.

As the label implies, management development groups are provided to develop the functioning of selected organizational managers. The thought is that, as these managers enhance their personal and professional competencies through group participation, organization effectiveness will be increased.

Team development represents one popular management development group approach (e.g., Dyer, 1977; Mahoney, 1981) that can be used either to improve the functioning of managers themselves, or that managers can employ to improve the productivity of subordinates. Whichever direction is chosen, the principle of "teamwork" is fundamental in team development. Teamwork produces the coordinated, integrated expenditure of energy among members, leading to both improved production and to employee satisfaction. A team development strategy may be appropriate to use within an organization when such issues as the following ones are present: people feel unrewarded for their good work, staff meetings are ineffective, goals are unclear, production is falling, workers are apathetic, people communicate poorly, trust is shaken, and leadership is ambiguous.

Team development, and many other management development strategies, are based on group research, such as that which led McGregor (1960) to develop his Theory Y system of management (see chapter 11 in this book on organization development groups), and on the effective use of group work skills. Creating a facilitative climate, making and using group process observations, resolving inter-member conflict, and fostering interdependent relations are pertinent examples of such skills.

Doing team development is considered to be an essential part of many managers' jobs today. Participating in management development activities is a common aspect of nearly every managers' role. Obtaining knowledge and skills in group work is a wise investment for contemporary and future organizational managers.

REFERENCES

Dyer, W.G.: *Team Building: Issues and Alternatives*. Reading, Ma.: Addison-Wesley, 1977.

Mahoney, F.X.: Team development, Part I: What is TD? Why use it? *Personnel, 58(5)*:13-24, 1981.

McGregor, D.: *The Human Side of Enterprise.* New York: McGraw Hill, 1960.

CHAPTER 11

ORGANIZATION DEVELOPMENT
Quality Circle Groups

LYNN S. RAPIN

O NE of the most currently popular forms of group work in business and industry, the quality circle (QC), has enjoyed little
formal attention in group work publications and training programs.
In contrast, a wide array of business and industry publications
(Jenkins and Shimada, 1981; Justis, 1981; Rendall, 1981) regularly
include articles exploring group-based approaches for organization
improvements, among them the QC.

While group work goals, methods and principles apply to formal
work organizations, their application to the organization-as-client is
relatively recent. Since the late 1960's increasing interest has developed in formally assisting organizations in responding to change.
The applied behavioral science of organization development has
emerged to help organizations manage planned change efforts more
effectively. One common organization development approach is to
institute structured group methodologies for problem solving in the
workplace. The quality circle is a representative of this type of organization development intervention.

INTERVENTION LEVEL

Quality circles are small groups (from 3-10) of employees who
voluntarily meet regularly on company time to identify and analyze

work-related problems in their work area and to make recommendations to management for the resolution of these problems. Most groups meet for 1-1½ hours per week. The structure of the QC makes it a task group and its presence generally opens and improves information flow between workers and management.

Emphasis is not on the unique characteristics and needs of individual employees, but on the resolution of work related problems and the enhancement of a more supportive work environment. The concentrated focus is on the benefits which the organization will reap in improved work task problem solving and improved organization communication. The employee members of the group are involved because of the work they share, either because they work in the same area or because they have similar responsibilities. Benefits are also often evident at other intervention levels, for example, at the personal level in the speaking and writing skills of group members.

The quality circle is instituted by management and given formal organization support to carry out the problem solving process. The organization thus formally lends credibility to the first line employees' contribution to improving the quality of work. Quality circles attend to the knowledge, skill, and experience of the members of the work force and to the needs of the organization employing them.

INTERVENTION PURPOSE

When considering the purposes of quality circles in relation to the Group Work Grid used throughout this book, it should be observed that QCs do not occupy a "pure cell." That is, they may serve both enhancement and corrective purposes, accomplishing interpersonal skill building and improvements in task performance simultaneously. The primary emphases of the QC group, however, are to enhance the use of employees' expertise in accomplishing their work tasks. While QCs can be used to take corrective action or to recommend to management improvements related to identified work problems, they consistently add to the traditional resources used in problem solving within organizations. Therefore, QCs enhance an organization's capacity to identify problems or improve a service before potential problems become emergencies.

Often a QC may itself be able to correct problems before they become evident to management. In addition, quality circles can also expand the levels of staff willing to share ownership of work related problems and the problem solving process to improve them. Common to these purposes is the development of human resources in the workplace.

Organizations use the quality circle process uniquely, based on their differing and complex purposes. Among these may be the use of the QC as a participative management tool, as a way to build employee morale and motivation, as a means of reducing employee complaints and grievances, as a method for increasing quality and reducing quality errors, as a tool for increasing employee productivity, and as an avenue for personal and leadership development.

Specific needs of the organization and potential benefits to the employees, managers, and organization as a whole must be identified when QCs are being installed. One temptation that arises out of the broad task enhancement purposes of the QC is to view it as an organizational panacea—a cure for a host of organization ills. It is not. The QC is a management tool which, to be effective, is integrated with other management strategies for a smoother functioning organization. In fact, it can assist managers in performing the essence of their role, to accomplish work through managing others. As their responsibilities become more complex, managers must rely on the expertise of others to assist in identifying and resolving work problems. Thus, the effective use of group methods to increase decision making quality can lead to more efficient use of scarce managerial resources.

One common side effect experienced by organizations considering the implementation of quality circles is that management approaches actually used by the organization can become more clearly articulated. If the real managerial approaches are spelled out, then the specific benefits in using QCs can be evaluated before they are taken on in fad-like fashion. Benefits to the organization at all levels can then be identified and nurtured.

This examination of needs and benefits enables key administrators to reexamine the organization's assumptions and beliefs about workers and managers. This type of organization development group, for instance, would not work in an organization which does not value the input and experience of employees at all levels. The specific involvements of various organization levels in QCs are detailed later in this chapter.

SUPPORTIVE THEORY

The quality circles approach to organization development is gaining U.S. popularity based on its tremendous success in Japan (Cole, 1979; Noda, 1980). The theoretical roots of QCs, however, can be traced to advances in the behavioral sciences in the United States over several decades.

The Japanese Influence

While the principles underlying quality circles were developed in the United States (Yager, 1980), QCs were first successfully implemented in Japan in the early 1960's with the guidance of American statistical and production specialists. After World War II, the Japanese were rebuilding their economy, trying to improve the quality and reputation of their products, and to stabilize their work force. Initially, the groups were introduced in 1962 to aid Japanese industry in improving the quality control circles, in which an emphasis was placed on the use of statistical principles by employee groups and their supervisors to identify and reduce production errors.

As well, the Japanese had introduced mechanisms over a period of years to help stabilize and train what had been a high-turnover workforce. Japanese industries created employment patterns in which about one-third of the labor force would be employed by the same firm throughout their career until mandatory retirement age (Fitzgerald and Murphy, 1982). Both employees and companies benefitted. Corporations developed loyal, skilled employees, knowledgeable about their work and involved in inproving product quality. Employees benefitted by the institutional commitment to ongoing training and job security. Because group involvement and loyalty are highly prized in Japanese culture, this kind of group approach to problem solving in business and industry reflected an important cultural value.

Quality control methods were encouraged nationwide with support from the Japanese Union of Scientists and Engineers (Gregerman, 1979). Therefore, they spread rapidly throughout Japanese industry during the 1960's and 1970's to become an integral part of Japanese management. The competitive edge Japan now has attained in world markets has attracted other countries into adopting similar successful managerial techniques (Ouchi, 1982).

American firms first became acquainted with the QC process in the early 1970's, when American aerospace companies toured Japan to learn more about their quality control techniques. As the QC process was introduced in the United States, it was initially adopted by higher technology industries which used both the group problem solving approach and the statistical methods common to the Japanese quality control circles. In more recent years, United States organizations, with both production and service orientations, have implemented QCs and included specific statistical methods appropriate to their workforce and products or services.

Management and Motivation Influences

Management and behavioral sciences theory and practice have greatly contributed to the advent of quality circles. Management theories emphasizing the development of human potential in the workplace have been particularly influential. As well, research on motivation and group processes have contributed to the fundamental group basis of QCs.

While managers have been generally familiar with the theories of leadership and motivation mentioned here, they have not always had practical ways for implementing them. The QC is one organization development group-based option for accomplishing this application.

While a number of need theories are relevant to organization development group work, Maslow's (1954) need hierarchy is one frequently mentioned in regard to QCs. His theory includes five major needs arranged in order from physiological, security, acceptance, self esteem, to self actualization. While progression through the hierarchy is not rigid, people typically respond to unmet needs as motivators when lower needs are met. One significant part of

Maslow's hierarchy is that met needs no longer generally serve as motivators.

When considering rewards available in organizations, physical setting, the environment of the workplace, and basic pay issues serve as lowest order needs. Involvement, self recognition and self esteem, and actualization needs are higher order needs more likely to be addressed by the level of the individual's involvement in the organization.

Another important motivation theory is Herzberg's (1966) two factor Motivation/Hygiene theory. Through interviews, Herzberg identified two different sets of work environment conditions which influence employee dissatisfaction and job satisfaction. He found that several conditions, called the hygiene factor, when absent or inadequate lead to employee dissatisfaction. This factor includes working conditions, wages, company policy and supervision. The presence of these environmental conditions does not guarantee employee satisfaction; it merely eliminates or reduces dissatisfaction and provides basic support.

Herzberg also found a second factor, called a motivation factor, associated with job satisfaction, growth and development. This factor includes recognition, achievement, and the job itself. Its presence leads to employee satisfaction and motivation. In Herzberg's theory, he maintains that motivation can be nurtured only through the development of the motivation factor which, in turn, occurs through a process called job enrichment (in contrast merely to job enlargement).

Frederick Taylor (1911) had early and powerful influence on the way industry treated workers. In an effort to streamline production, Taylor recommended separation of the planning and production functions, so that employees were regarded as those who simply implemented decisions made at higher levels. Many companies still practice "Taylorism."

In contrast, many current managers are struggling to make management more participative. Many of these managers use another of Taylor's contributions, that of taking a scientific and statistical approach to production and other decisions. Members of QCs practice this principle in data gathering and analysis.

Similar to Taylor's model of using workers as a part of the

production process, and not as both planners and producers, is a Theory X approach to managing. McGregor (1960) identified two major views of people, called Theory X and Theory Y, related to how they function in a variety of organizations. Popular applications of this dichotomy have led people to be called Theory X or Theory Y managers.

The Theory X view assumes that people do not enjoy work, will not be productive unless coerced, and prefer to be directed on the job. McGregor proposed that managers holding Theory X beliefs inhibit long term effectiveness rather than increase it (although authoritarian control may lead to greater short term output) and that Theory X managers foster resistance.

In Theory Y, however, the assumptions are that people are willing to work, that people can be creative and responsible, and that they can commit to organization goals. A manager holding Theory Y views would promote a work environment where people are recognized for their ideas and share in responsibility without demanding a great deal of close supervision. McGregor says Theory Y attends to the human side of organizations. Successful implementation and integration of quality circles within an organization require Theory Y assumptions. Nurturing work commitment, creativity and shared responsibility for problem identification and resolution are essential components of good QCs.

Another theorist who has written about leadership and management styles is Rensis Likert. Likert (1967) considered a number of organization factors including leadership, motivation, communication patterns, decision making styles, goal setting, and organization control issues. He identified four different management systems which have generally characteristic ways of responding to the organization factors. These systems are labelled System 1 through System 4.

System 1 management is highly authoritative with control located clearly at the top. System 2 is still authoritative, but in a more benevolent fashion. System 3 management is more consultative—a kind of "check first, then do" system. Increased involvement exists in consultative systems, with information flow occurring more openly both up and down channels. System 4 is the most participative system, and in some ways more of an "ideal" state. A participative system requires firm commitment and involvement from people at all levels of an organization. In Likert's model, QCs fit most naturally with System 4. But because there are probably few true System 4 organizations, QCs would be appropriate in System 3 ones, as well.

Assumptions basic to QCs are evident in all of these theories of motivation and management. All of them accept the "good" existing in employees, which can be developed both for the benefit of the individual and for the organization employing them.

The now famous Hawthorne studies conducted by Mayo in the 1920's demonstrated that attention and social support (the "Hawthorne effect") from a research team and management, not environmental adjustments to lighting, were responsible for production increases (Mayo, 1945). Similar study led to a human relations approach to management, focusing on identifying and responding to workers' social needs in order to increase motivation.

In the late 1950's and 1960's this human relations approach included staff development for higher responsibilities and decentralization of decision making. By the late 1960's organization development became a specialized area, providing planned change and development of the total organization (Beckhard, 1969). Currently there is renewed interest in the application of many of these human relations approaches for more participative organization management.

Group Member Functions

Quality circles have also been influenced by research on effective functioning work groups. Both content and process issues are important in effective QC programs. Group researchers Benne and Sheats (1948) identified major group task and group building and maintenance roles which have influenced group workers for over thirty years.

The task roles deal with the intellectual aspects of the group's work. Some key task roles are (a) initiating and contributing, (b) information and opinion seeking and giving, (c) elaborating, (d) evaluating, (e) orienting, and (f) recording. These task roles are used by members within a general problem solving process described by Likert in 1961. The steps in the process include: (a) defining the problem, (b) identifying the standards (objectives) a solution ought to meet, (c) generating alternate solutions, (d) gathering facts to bear upon the solutions, (e) evaluating potential solutions for best fit, and (f) selecting the most satisfactory solution. This basic problem solving model has been often refined (e.g., Craig, 1978) and is used as the basic structure for quality circles.

By contrast, group building and maintenance roles pertain to emotional needs of the group. These roles involve the members' sense of team, and ability for productive interaction and problem solving. Some examples are (a) encouraging, (b) harmonizing, (c) gate-keeping, (d) expediting, (e) setting standards, (f) observing, and (g) following. Both leader and members are involved in roles in these interrelated functions to produce an effective work group. Sometimes, to their detriment, task focused groups such as QCs neglect these critical team building and maintenance roles.

ORGANIZATION STRATEGIES AND TARGET POPULATION

Successful quality circle efforts are intended to be integrated into the management structure of an organization; they are not meant to be just "programs" to be tried and discarded. Commitments for participation at many levels throughout the organization are required to assure such integration.

First, the major administrator has to be committed to the concept. Quality circles are not credible without real support. Often a steering committee (especially in large organizations with a number of circles) sets policy regarding the work of a number of QCs and coordinates the flow of information about QCs throughout the organization. Steering committee members are often department heads of areas with QCs.

Next, a facilitator serves as the emotional center of the QCs. This person may be selected from within or outside of the organization, but must have a good understanding of the organization's needs and functioning. As well, the facilitator is the key linker among QCs and between each QC and higher administration. The facilitator trains group leaders, may train members, and is in turn trained by a consultant or firm offering packaged QC training. In well established programs with a large number of circles, additional facilitators may be trained in-house. The facilitator secures rooms; gets technical help to the QC group, as needed; and supports the programs throughout the organization.

Department Managers are often most critical to the QC group's success or failure. They need to be informed and included in planning stages so that their valuable role as department manager is not threatened. Where QCs fail, it is often because the middle managers have not been properly included in the program design or training.

First-line supervisors are most often the quality circle group leaders, with the QC serving as an additional avenue for cooperation with the work team. The supervisor is a critical link in day-to-day work accomplishment, and is used in similar fashion in QCs. Some authors (Burton, 1981; Cook, 1982; Ingle, 1982; Metz, 1981) suggest, however, that first-line supervisors may not always possess the most appropriate leader skills, nor have received adequate group leader training prior to being placed in the leader role.

At the heart of Quality circles, members are voluntary participants from a work area or employees who share similar work. While the QC problem solving process follows a general structure and ground rules within that structure, members are *the* problem solvers, with control over problems chosen for investigation. Members are also responsible for recommending solutions for problems investigated. Recommendations for action steps are made through normal organization channels.

Consultants often assist organizations in establishing QCs within the organization structure. They are called on to present management workshops on QCs, tailor materials for the organization, train the facilitator, and sometimes to assist in initial leader training. Organizations may also choose to purchase packaged training materials or send facilitators and leaders to off-site training programs. Organizations large enough for training departments often take on the training responsibilities themselves.

MAIN INTERVENTION CHANGE TECHNIQUES

Quality circles are generally structured groups which employ a number of problem solving tools on a series of work related problems. When the QC completes the process, it begins anew with another problem.

Establishing a cohesive task-focused team is essential to QC success. Even though members come from the same work area, or share similar tasks, they form a "new" group as a QC. All of the elements of sound group work and of team development apply to the QC. Recommended group process techniques include team building, and training in appropriate group member and leader roles. Many QC members have never before been involved in such a group experience on the job, and they naturally need support and assistance in learning effective member roles.

Training activities for members take place in the initial weekly QC meetings. These training sessions occur for a minimum of eight sessions. Members become familiar with the problem solving "tools" and begin to apply them to a team-selected problem. Leaders gain supervised leading experience during this phase and members observe appropriate models for participation. The leader and facilitator guide the QC group through the problem solving steps. Each training step usually involves reading about the skill, hearing a lecturette about how the skill is applied, and discussing examples of application. Manuals, tapes and slides are often prepared for training. Time is taken during each session to discuss how the group is working as a team. Typical components (Beardsley, 1977; Fitzgerald and Murphy, 1982; Gregerman, 1979) of the QC approach are described here.

Brainstorming training is used throughout, and is introduced as the first problem solving skill. Following brainstorming training the formal problem solving process begins by first considering the skill of problem identification. The QC group brainstorms a problem list. From this list may emerge a theme the group wishes to target. The list is then sorted to one problem for the group to work on further. In the first round, the group is encouraged to choose a problem of modest scope, so that chances for successful resolution are maximized. The complete problem list is saved for future use. This step also involves decision making training, compromise and consensus.

Sometimes omitted is the next training step in setting an objective related to the problem. Having clearly identified objectives assists the group in avoiding preset notions for solutions.

The third step involves data gathering about the identified problem. At this point, QCs gain experience in the use of sampling techniques, check lists, Pareto analysis and cause-and-effect analysis to assist in identifying major problem factors.

Fourth, the QC group is trained in generating possible solutions to the problem. Critical is that the QC develop choices of alternate solutions.

Fifth, the strongest solutions are selected from all alternatives. In this step, the QC uses previously introduced skills of brainstorming and Pareto analysis and by using cause-and-effect charting to analyze the strengths and weaknesses of alternate strategies. Force field analyses are appropriate in this step.

Sixth, training is given in data display techniques, including charting, graphing and the like. Members gain experience in determining the most effective display techniques.

Seventh, the QC prepares the strongest solution or a rank-ordered list of recommendations. The QC group is then trained in implementation skills. The recommended solution is considered as a pilot for implementation. With training, the group plans for evaluation of the recommended solution, if it is approved by management.

Eighth, the QC group prepares for its presentation to management. In this step, a written packet is prepared with critical steps outlined. Also assembled are flip charts, graphs, and other media materials. Quality circle participants gain valuable training in written and verbal presentation skills during this phase.

Ninth, the QC group makes its presentation to management, with all appropriate management levels in attendance. Management determines whether they will implement the solution. If so, then a monitoring process occurs and the process repeats with a new problem.

LEADER FUNCTIONS

As implied earlier, the group leader, whether first-line supervisor or elected leader, has a critical role in the QC success (Nosow, 1981). This person is responsible for encouraging participation, developing task focused skills often not before experienced by the group, keeping the QC group on task, modeling appropriate leader and member skills, and serving as trainer. It is clear that this person requires significant support, especially when he or she might not have group skills experience. The leader has the support of the facilitator, and when available, that of consultant or training department, and meets with the facilitator to help plan meeting agendas or handle group process issues.

LEADER TRAINING

Typically, the leader is trained by the facilitator in the problem solving model. The facilitator, as the frequent trainer of the QC leaders, has previously received a minimum of 24 hours training in management styles, group process and problem solving, and QC techniques. Many organizations provide more intensive training for facilitators.

The leader is given training in leadership styles, problem solving, and group process, as well as the specific data gathering and analysis tools. Many organizations focus on the content skills and undertrain on basic group leadership skills, a common problem that serves to detract from overall task accomplishment in the long run. Intensive training in these areas, followed by supervision and support, lead to more able QC group leadership and a more effective group. Many leaders who are first-line supervisors find that the QCs require a different style of leadership than they usually employ. In the QC they are not supposed to serve in a boss role, but rather in a cooperative role with members.

INTERVENTION EFFECTIVENESS

All varieties of organizations, from the aerospace corporations first using QCs to service and nonprofit organizations, have found benefits from QCs (Goldberg, 1982; Zemke, 1980). Gains are sometimes monetary or concrete, with a good product improved, or a deficiency eliminated. Other benefits, just as valuable, relate to reduced absences, improved working relationship with management, more positive employee attitude on the job and clearer communication, both bottom to top and top to bottom. Some of the self esteem gains are evident at management presentations, others in the day to day work.

Failures are often attributable to poor assessment of fit with organization goals, poor implementation planning, poor management preparation, poor training at one or more levels, and lack of followthrough commitment. All of these are critical.

ILLUSTRATIVE INTERVENTION CASE EXAMPLE

This example involves the staff of a Laundry and Linen Department in a university hospital located in a large urban university. The Laundry and Linen Department is one of about seventeen departments in the facilities management support unit of the hospital.

Prior to deciding to implement QCs in facilities management, the key administrator spent time with a consultant over a period of months assessing the benefits of such an approach. After committing to the concept, support was gained from the hospital administrator, managers of departments within the unit, and the employee union. Managers received training in the QC process prior to employee involvement. The managers assisted in defining limits for the QC process, eliminating "hygiene" problems (e.g., personality conflicts, grievance issues, benefits, salary). They also generated ways that they could support each other and the QCs. As implementation progressed, participating managers moved from healthy skepticism and some feelings of threat to participation themselves in their own QC. They have one of five QC groups currently functioning in the unit.

The Laundry and Linen Department was selected as an initial QC site for several reasons. It had experienced turmoil within the workforce and between staff and supervisors and manager. Second, it was a true production unit, similar to industrial QC settings. Additionally, the employees were in the lowest pay grade in the state classification system and generally suffered from low morale. Equipment failures and grievances were both high.

In a February, 1982 staff meeting with the unit administrator, department manager, facilitator, and consultant, Linen and Laundry employees were introduced to the QC program and given the opportunity to volunteer for participation. Twenty-eight of 44 employees signed up. From that pool, ten staff were selected as the first QC, balanced for work station and time in the department. Those who could not be in the first group were encouraged to participate through their representatives. Because of a negative history between employees and supervisors, the consultant and facilitator served in training and leading functions, respectively.

Conducted first were two four-hour training sessions in team building. This was particularly important because the staff had had many conflicts. The members reviewed the unit's goals for the QC and were introduced to their member roles and the general problem solving steps. Program goals included: (a) to recognize that the person actually performing work functions knows more about the job than anyone else; (b) to share in identifying job related problems, assessing their causes, recommending specific solutions to Management and implementing solutions themselves, where possible; (c) to provide an opportunity to improve and enhance working relationships and communication; (d) to promote the awareness and development of quality in all work functions; and (e) to provide means for management to review and recognize QC achievements.

To prepare for working together as a group, structured exercises (for example, a get acquainted exercise) and practice in basic group skills of listener, talker, and observer were conducted (Goodstein and Pfeiffer, 1983; Pfeiffer and Jones, 1972-82). The group members shared what they had learned from the communication exercises, practicing the skill of feedback. They also discussed their individual investments in participating in the QC.

All exercises were chosen to promote comfort and participation. A Johari Window (Luft, 1984) exercise was used to introduce trust and disclosure and to help set group goals for cooperative team work. The trainer introduced the use of listening and participation skills in the problem solving process. Circle members discussed how they might include other staff members in the process.

The last team building activity included an introduction to brainstorming rules and using them to establish a group name. From a brainstormed list of 38 names, the group selected "Quality Century Team," representing their 100 years of combined experience in the department. The team name reflected members' pride in their contributions to the Laundry.

Thereafter, weekly one and one-half hour sessions in QC skills were conducted. Skill development and confidence building were constantly reinforced, both during the instruction phase of each meeting and at the end of each session. Initial low participation levels from several members climbed as their comfort and confidence grew.

An initial problem list was generated using the Nominal Group Technique (Delbecq and Van de Ven, 1971). From this list of 48 problems the QC selected a problem which affected all Laundry employees and had a good chance for success. The selected problem was that too much static and electric shocks were emitted by the laundry machines. The group then converted their problem statement to an objective, using objective setting guidelines. The Quality Century Team's objectives were to minimize the number of shocks from the machines and reduce linen static.

The group used brainstorming and Pareto analysis to identify and narrow for further examination potential factors in the shock problem. A number of factors from lint in the air to moisture in linen and use of insulating gloves and shoes were considered.

The group invited their department director to a group meeting to share with him the selected problem and to arrange for data collection. The group carefully planned and rehearsed for this meeting. With the department head's approval, the group held a meeting with all Laundry staff to update them to gain staff cooperation in identifying the sources of shocks. Members of the QC prepared and made this presentation to the staff.

The QC identified six industrial machines which seemed to give staff the most shocks. The group designed a check sheet for employees to use at the six machines. Gathered were (a) level of shock, (b) weather conditions, (c) fabric being processed, and (d) employee using equipment. These tallies were grouped into four periods during the work day, from 7:00 a.m. to 3:30 p.m. and gathered over five working days.

Based on data analysis, three machines with the greatest number of shocks were targeted for improvement. In this step the QC learned the value of gathering information to check perceptions and to identify the major problem machines.

At this point the QC members realized that they needed assistance in understanding how electrical principles might be involved in the problem. The facilitator arranged for three mechanical and electrical experts at the hospital to join the group temporarily as internal consultants (Director of Maintenance, Assistant Director of the Physical Plant, and the Director of Design and Construction).

The QC and technical experts generated eight potential solutions to the problem. These eight options were consolidated to four and evaluated for effectiveness and cost. The group decided that the simplest and least expensive solution would offer the most potential benefits. The solution was to install formica as insulation on the work table portions of the machines and to attach a discharge bar to each machine. The discharge bar, when touched periodically during the day by an employee, would reduce electricity flow between body and machine, thereby reducing shocks.

The QC then spent several sessions preparing their management presentation and rehearsing individual parts. Key department, unit and hospital administrators were invited to the first management presentation. The QC process was described and specific recommendations were made. The modest funds (approximately $400) to implement the recommendation were approved.

During the critical first six months, the group had both the facilitator and consultant working with them. While the steps in the problem solving process have been described, at each step in the process considerable time was spent on group process issues. Most of the members had never been in any formal training except that related to their specific tasks in the laundry. Few imagined that they could have the skill and confidence to give a management presentation after five months. Careful, consistent reinforcement of appropriate participation was essential to their success.

Since that first presentation in July, 1982, five months after they began, the group has proceeded to other problems. The QC is still intact and using the process successfully. Benefits included increased morale, visibility and recognition within the hospital, markedly reduced employee-management problems, a complete reduction of union grievances, reduced equipment breakdowns and a generally more systematic approach to everyday problems in the laundry.

EMPLOYMENT

Exciting employment opportunities exist for group specialists trained in QCs. They serve as in-house trainers, facilitators, and consultants to organizations in profit and non-profit settings. They may even serve as leaders of QCs in their own organizations. Organizations either using or considering QCs do not always initially appreciate the importance of group skills in the training process. Group specialists can assist in educating QC users to this need, thereby contributing to a more potentially successful organization.

REFERENCES

Beardsley, J.: *Facilitator Manual.* San Jose: Beardsley and Associates, 1977.

Beckhard, R.: *Organization Development: Strategies and Models.* Reading: Addison Wesley, 1969.

Benne, K. and Sheats, P.: Functional roles of group members. *Journal of Social Issues, 4(2)*:41-49, 1948.

Burton, G.: The Group Process: Key to more productive management. *Management World, 10(5)*:12-15, 1981.

Cole, R.: Made in Japan — Quality control circles. *Across the Board, 16(11)*:72-78, 1979.

Cook, M.: "Quality Circles — they really work, but...." *Training and Development Journal, 36(1)*:4-5, 1982.

Craig, D.: *Hip Pocket Guide to Planning and Evaluation.* San Diego: Learning Concepts, 1978.

Delbecq, A. and Van de Ven, A.: A group process model for problem identification and program planning. *Journal of Applied Behavioral Science, 7*:466-491, 1971.

Fitzgerald, L. and Murphy, J.: *Installing Quality Circles: A Strategic Approach.* San Diego: University Associates, 1982.

Goldberg, J.: Quality circles enhance workers' attitude. *Bank Systems and Equipment, 19(5)*:120-121, 1982.

Goodstein, L. and Pfeiffer, J.: *The 1983 Annual for Facilitators, Trainers, and Consultants.* San Diego: University Associates, 1983.

Gregerman, I.: Introduction to Quality Circles: An approach to participative problem-solving. *Industrial Management, 21(5)*:21-26, 1979.

Herzberg, F.: *Work and the Nature of Man.* Cleveland: World Publishing, 1966.

Ingle, S.: How to avoid quality circle failure in your company. *Training and Development Journal, 36(6)*:54-59, 1982.

Jenkins, K. and Shimada, J.: Quality circles in the service sector. *Supervisory Management, 26(8)*:2-7, 1981.

Justis, R.: America feasts on Japanese management delicacies — Quality Circles, JIT and kanban. *Data Management, 19(10)*:30-32, 43, 1981.

Likert, R.: *New Patterns of Management.* New York: McGraw-Hill, 1961.

Likert, R.: *The Human Organization: Its Management and Value.* New York: McGraw-Hill, 1967.

Luft, J.: *Group Processes: An Introduction to Group Dynamics,* (3rd ed.). Palo Alto: Mayfield Publ., 1984.

Maslow, A.: *Motivation and Personality.* New York: Harper and Row, 1954.

Mayo, E.: *The Human Problems of an Industrial Civilization.* Boston: Harvard Business School, 1945.

McGregor, D.: *The Human Side of Enterprise.* New York: McGraw-Hill, 1960.

Metz, E.: Caution: Quality Circles Ahead. *Training and Development Journal 35(9)*:71-76, 1981.

Noda, M.: The Japanese way. *Executive, 6(3)*:22-25, 1980.

Nosow, S.: The first-line supervisor, the linchpin in the Japanese quality control circle. *Industrial Management, 23(1)*:19-23, 1981.

Ouchi, W.: Defining the quality control circle. *Modern Office Procedures, 27(4)*:14-20, 1982.

Pfeiffer, J. and Jones, J.: *The Annual Handbook for Group Facilitators.* San Diego: University Associates, 1972-82.

Rendell, E.: Quality circles — A "third wave" intervention. *Training and Development Journal, 35(3)*:28-31, 1981.

Taylor, F.: *The Principles of Scientific Management.* New York: Harper and Row, 1911.

Yager, E.: Quality circle: A tool for the '80's. *Training and Development Journal, 34(8)*:60-62, 1980.

Zemke, R.: Honeywell imports quality circles as long-term management strategy. *Training, 17(8)*:91-94, 1980.

SECTION IV
COMMUNITY-POPULATION LEVEL
OF INTERVENTION

B Y the community-population level of intervention we mean to include group work that is undertaken to produce corrective or enhancement alteration in a community or population of interest. This is a macro level group intervention. That is, the group method is used to induce the broadest of effects. Although alternative intervention levels, such as individuals, interpersonal relationships, and organizations might be affected in such group endeavors, these would represent micro changes necessary for leveraging the macro community or population change intended.

Groups for community or population modification are the most neglected in the professional literature, despite their increasing use. Concerted effort needs to be given to matching the presence of such groups with appropriate conceptual, training, and research efforts, for the community-population level of intervention is the "new frontier" of group work.

The four chapters in this *Handbook* section provide a good reference point for exploring what I have termed the "new frontier." In chapter 12, Silverman discusses the place of mutual help groups in, "...preventing the disabling consequences of (the) illness with attention directed to the quality of life of the afflicted person." Her emphasis is on secondary and tertiary corrective prevention accomplished through groups of people, such as alcoholics in Alcoholics Anonymous, who give each other mutual self help. Extended widely enough, these groups can affect a population of individuals in a community who all experience a similar psychological and/or physical disturbance. The role of the professional group worker in mutual help groups, as well as in the other forms of community-population group intervention, is challenging due to its current relative amorphousness. Silverman, and the other authors in this section, help to clarify some role possibilities for us to be considering.

While mutual help groups focus on personal elements in community-population change, Christensen's description of community change groups demonstrates the task emphasis in correction. Groups for community action, social change, environmental modification, political advocacy, and so on, represent this type of group work. Christensen gives special attention to the importance of a community change group worker stressing functions of guiding, educating, and facilitating the active participation of community members throughout the community change process.

Community-population enhancement through group work is discussed in chapter 14 by Pearson and in chapter 15 by Lippitt. Pearson presents a model for understanding primary prevention interventions and, more specifically, their group application. These groups, offered to individuals who are currently unaffected by a certain disturbance, embrace a health promotion perspective that can be generalized to the community level. Examples might include: freshmen students at a university, couples approaching new parenthood, improving nutrition, and managing stress effectively.

While these issues are primarily of a personal enhancement nature, Lippitt considers those that are more centrally of task enhancement. He presents an extensive case example that illustrates how a community can plan for its future development through a series of structural group activities. This chapter identifies many stimulating ways that basic group skills can be novelly applied to advance community functioning.

Group Work Grid

Intervention Purpose Emphases

Intervention Level Emphases		Correction		Enhancement	
		Personal	Task	Personal	Task
Individual	Type	Personality Change	Rehabilitation	Personal Growth	Skill Development
	Eg.	Psychotherapy	Remedial Social Skills	Personal Development	Human Relations Skills Training
Interpersonal	Type	Interpersonal Problem Solving	Resocialization	Interpersonal Growth	Learning
	Eg.	Counseling	Social Control	T-groups	Systematic Group Discussion
Organization	Type	Employee Change	Organization Change	Management Development	Organization Development
	Eg.	Employee Assistance	Social Climate	Team Development	Quality Circles
Community-Population	Type	Secondary/Tertiary Prevention	Community Change	Health Promotion/Primary Prevention	Community Development
	Eg.	Mutual Help	Action	Life Transition	Futuring

Figure 6. Group Work Grid, Community-Population Level

CHAPTER 12

TERTIARY/SECONDARY PREVENTION
Preventive Intervention: The Case for
Mutual Help Groups

PHYLLIS R. SILVERMAN

THE cost of care for people with various emotional or physical disabilities is rising. In addition, the number of chronic conditions is increasing as medical science discovers treatments that mediate the consequences of various conditions to allow people "new leases on life." These factors lead to an overload of the human service system. This excess stems not only from an economic point of view, but from the point of view of quality of care and the ability of the system to provide services geared to meeting the accompanying emotional problems of living with chronic illnesses or handicapping conditions.

Questions are being raised about the possibility of preventing many of these conditions, in the first place. Where this is not possible, the focus turns to preventing the disabling consequences of the illness with attention directed to the quality of life of the afflicted person. This chapter will explore one strategy for implementing preventive programs, mutual help groups. Since there is not always consensus about what is meant by prevention, the chapter will begin with a discussion of issues involved in arriving at a definition that will guide the subsequent discussion.

A DEFINITION OF PREVENTION

The concept of prevention, as it is generally understood, is taken from a public health model. This model was developed when it became possible to specify particular bacteria or other environmental hazards that were identified as risk factors. Clear and direct associations could be made between such factors and subsequent problems or disabilities. By developing specific vaccines or other interventions, such as sterilizing instruments or prescribing vitamin B complex, a negative outcome could be invariably forestalled, such as beri beri as a mental illness. Intervention at this level was called primary prevention. Efforts to prevent subsequent problems from developing, once an individual became ill, were identified as secondary and tertiary prevention.

At present, we are facing problems that do not lend themselves to simple solutions because they are a result of complex interactions between a multiple of human and environmental influences. Preventive programs cannot follow a simple linear model, especially when often no simple offender can be identified. In addition, as attention is turned to conceptualizing life cycle events as stressors that can cause emotional disabilities or physical illness, these events, such as natural disasters or the death of a loved one, are not always in our power to prevent. Another paradigm has to be developed for where preventive efforts should be focused. It may be more productive to ask if the event itself may not be the offender but, rather, how people react to the event. Does their difficulty result from their inability to develop effective coping strategies? For example, we cannot prevent a woman from becoming a widow. Instead we need to look at what she needs to facilitate coping with her new status, and the changes it has caused in her life.

Bloom (1982), in reviewing current research in prevention, notes that a substantial body of research converges on social competence building as one of the most pervasive preventive strategies for dealing with individual or social issues. We talk, then, not of preventing symptoms or specific illness, but of promoting adaptive capacity (Silverman, 1978). We are less concerned with primary or secondary prevention and more interested in preventive intervention as a general approach.

Once the focus turns to promoting people's capacity to cope we are talking about education, not treatment (Goldston, 1977). For example, people who have had no experience with a particular stressor, such as a job loss, will not necessarily know how to cope with either the anxiety associated with the loss or with the need to be identified as an unemployed person who now needs to look for other work. They need to learn appropriate skills for coping with the emotional and social sequelae they are experiencing. Broad social and economic programs may try to prevent unemployment, but on an individual level the focus is on promoting and enhancing the competency of this person to deal with his or her new situation.

What conditions facilitate such learning? I am suggesting that mutual help groups may be one of the more powerful modalities for facilitating learning subsequent to stress. The remainder of this chapter will be devoted to describing how this takes place.

MUTUAL HELP GROUPS AS EDUCATORS

A mutual help group is an aggregate of people sharing a common problem or predicament who come together for mutual support and constructive action to solve their shared problem. The help offered is based on the participants' experience in coping with their problems and is not a result of any professional training or education group members may possess. Most of the time this type of help takes place in informal exchanges in one's family or among friends and neighbors. Often, however, these informal exchanges evolve into a formal organization with its own governing structure to which people with the same problem are recruited to join as members.

Mutual help organizations can be identified by their helping program, and organizational structure that distinguishes them from other types of helping programs. This section deals with the nature of the mutual helping programs while the next section will focus on mutual help organizational structure.

In a mutual help group, people are helped by receiving information on how to cope, obtaining material help if necessary, and by feeling cared about and supported. These types of help are uniquely effective for several reasons: people find others "just like me;" they learn from the group experience that other people have similar feelings and that these feelings are "normal;" and they obtain the option of becoming a helper, thus not bound to the role of recipient in order to remain in the organization. Help provided emerges from the personal experience of helpers who have coped or are coping with the same problem that is shared by new comers to the group and who are willing to share their experience. People, in turn, are helped by the opportunity to help others.

The assistance offered by mutual help organizations can take many forms. It may include one-to-one exchanges, informal rap sessions, educational seminars, either on an occasional basis or as part of a regular series on a range of topics specifically relevant to the problem of group members, social gatherings, and the sharing of personal experiences by small groups in informal settings. Some organizations have hotlines through which persons in need can reach them to get immediate help with a problem; and others have active outreach programs in which experienced members make unsolicited offers of help to potential members. Many mutual help organizations have formal orientation or training programs for members who will become outreach volunteers, facilitators in small group discussions, or leaders in other efforts. While we may talk about mutual help groups as a focal strategy, actually help in a group setting is only one of the kinds of help offered in most of these organizations.

The help itself is directed at people in stress. Often they are faced with a new status, a need to live with a chronic illness, the addition of a baby in the family, or other changes in their life situation that can occur in the course of development or as a result of unexpected trauma or disruption. They may need to learn how to stop abusing other children (Comstock, 1982). Typically, the stress results not simply from the trauma or deficit, as noted above, but from the individual's need to accommodate to change.

Generally, the kind of stress we are considering leads to a transition state. Transitions are generally associated with some status change or loss of a familiar role in the individual's social network. The integration of such a fundamental change occurs over time (Silverman, 1981). A person's typical coping strategies may be insufficient, not because of any personality deficit, but for lack of experience in this particular situation. Such persons need to develop a new repertoire of adaptive strategies. This development involves learning.

Little is known about what facilitates learning in a time of change. White (1974) suggests that adaptation involves learning and that the adaptive strategies people develop are affected by the learning opportunities available to them. Hamburg and Adams (1967) note that effective coping with transitions, that involve major illness or life cycle role change, was related to the availability of pertinent information. The Community Support Systems Task Force of the President's Commission on Mental Health (1978) found that access to guidance and information is an essential aspect of an individual's helping network, whether it is a matter of coping effectively with problems of daily living or with major transitions.

Much recent interest has been focused on the buffering qualities of support provided by social networks (Gottlieb, 1981). In one predominant view support is seen as a mediator of stress and the availability of support relates positively to people's sense of well being. The provider of support helps the individual mobilize their psychological resources and master both their emotional and physical burdens.

Caplan (1974) differentiates between emotional support, such as providing approbation, and instrumental support, as evidenced in the provision of funds or resources for people. Providers of support share the tasks by not only offering extra supplies of money, materials, and tools, but by teaching new skills and by offering cognitive guidance to improve the handling of the stressful situation.

Other aspects of support include legitimation of feelings, feedback and social participation (Barrera, 1981). Support as just defined, can be used to maintain a system (the status quo), as well as to facilitate change. Gore and Eckenrode (1981) emphasize the importance of the context in which support is offered and its constraints in order to differentiate the purpose for which it is used. Some people are part of dense networks that appear supportive. Instead of facilitating coping with stress the members place more demands on the person in trouble. For example, a young widow was asked for money by her mother now that she is getting a regular social security check from which she was supporting herself and her three young children. The stress in such a situation is compounded and the goal of adequate accommodation to change is not achieved. Learning is not facilitated and it may be necessary for many people to look outside of their existing social networks for assistance.

Havelock and Havelock (1973), in looking at change on a broader level, studied what characteristics of a situation lead to effective change. They describe the role of change agents. People in this role are either formally or informally assigned, and they function as catalysts. Their main function is establishing linkages between people in need and available resources and information. Linking agents can also demonstrate how to use resources and information. They can be instrumental in creating the supportive atmosphere that facilitates adaptive behavior.

What are the characteristics of these linking agents that make them most effective? One body of data emphasizes the special value of helpers who have been through a similar experience. There is evidence that learning in crisis or in emotionally laden situations is enhanced by the presence of a peer (Bandura, 1977). Reporting on a study of affiliative tendencies in college students during periods of anxiety, Schacter (1959) observed that subjects first chose to be with others in the same situation. They chose to be alone under stress rather than with people who did not share their experience. He concluded that whatever the needs aroused by anxiety, it seems that satisfaction demanded the presence of others in a similar situation. In a small sample of members of three mutual help groups—Kidney Transplant and Dialysis Association, the Cured Cancer Club, and the Spina Bifada Association of Massachusetts—Silverman and Smith (1983) found that people who joined these groups did so out of a pressing need to find someone else who had had a similar experience with whom they could share feelings and discover new ways of coping.

From a follow up study of the original Widow-to-Widow Program, data were available on every new widow under the age of 65 in a Boston community in which the program operated over a two and one half year period, and in particular on those women who refused the offer of help. Silverman (1974) found that most of those who had refused had friends or relatives who were widows.

Silver and Wortman (1980) noted that peers—in the sense of having been through the same experience—are unique sources of help for people in stress. They are more understanding and patient, and their expectations are more appropriate. The impact of learning from peers as an important source of information, experience, and assistance with change needs to be appreciated and further examined. As a child grows, we recognize his or her need to learn from peers who serve as role models or with whom they can explore ways of coping with their common needs (Rubin, 1980). Children who have role-model peers do not tend to feel alone, unique or isolated; they feel legitimated. This type of relationship probably pertains to an entire lifetime and not just to adolescence. I would hypothesize that at times of critical transitions in an individual's life where no opportunity for a mutual help experience exists, the individual will try to create one to fill the gap.

Not only may the need to find someone like oneself be central to learning to cope with change, but the opportunity to change roles and become a helper may be as important, as well (Riessman, 1965). A survey was conducted of the members of a group called Mended Hearts, and of heart surgery patients not affiliated with the organization, to determine how participation in the group affected adjustment to their illness (Lieberman and Borman, 1979). It was found that significant differences appeared between the two groups only among retired men who were active in the organization. Those who became helpers made the best adjustment to open heart surgery. The role of helper tends to foster competency in the helper. In addition, receiving help from a peer tends to minimize a sense of weakness or incompetence in the person needing help (Silverman, 1980). I am suggesting that during periods of change when people must obtain new information in order to cope, their ability to use this information is affected by the availability of someone who has gone through the experience and with whom the individual can identify. In addition, the opportunity to change roles from recipient to helper further enhances accommodation. The context in which help occurs is critical in terms of the personal experience of the helper and the opportunities within the helping framework for mutuality and role mobility.

Mutual help organizations are one of the few places in contemporary society where expertise in coping with transitions can be found (Silverman, 1982). In mutual help organizations members obtain pertinent information from others who have had similar experiences; they find role models, legitimization for their feelings, and a direction for change and accommodation. Helpers in mutual help organizations also fulfill linking functions of change agents. They amass bodies of necessary information and know where and how resources are available.

To the extent that people's competency is enhanced, and their capacity to cope is facilitated, these are programs doing the work of prevention. Note that they have not prevented an illness or a disease. In contrast, an environment is created that promotes people's learning what to do with the consequences of their disabling situation.

INTERFACE BETWEEN THE HELP OFFERED AND THE ORGANIZATIONAL STRUCTURE

The organizational setting in which the work is carried out and the helpers' relationship to that organization may be critical to the success of the help offered. In contrast to the formal organizational structure of bureaucratic or professional organizations, mutual help groups are fluid organizations. In formal human service organizations, people typically relate in a hierarchical order, with each position regulated by specific rights and duties. Unlike the professional organization, mutual help organizations have a structure which allows for mobility in the system—from recipient to helper—and which enables the consumers or members to control resources and policies.

Members develop ways of governing themselves to maintain control of the organization. This process becomes essential as organizations grow from an informal association. Members must formalize the way they work. Many groups, such as Parents Without Partners, take the form of a club or voluntary association depending on their members' prior experience. They follow parliamentary procedures with established committees and regular election of officers. Some, such as the Gray Panthers and the Mental Patient Liberation Movement, develop a consensus, anti-hierarchical way of governing themselves. The latter groups often come into being as alternate systems, with a strong anti-establishment bias, because they feel they have been poorly served by established mental health agencies. They spend a good deal of energy maintaining their differences and, therefore, they avoid any type of hierarchical organizational structure. Efficiency is sacrificed to ensure maximum participation of all their members in the life of the organization.

Some groups, such as the LaLeche League, are organized as service delivery systems with authority coming from the national office down. Although leadership is appointed through an elaborate state-national ascending hierarchy, it is always recruited from among people who attend meetings and who have been helped by the group. However, even when a hierarchy exists in these groups, leaders lack a formal reward and sanction system to enforce their power. Members leave when a group stops meeting their needs. Most often an informal consensus determines group policy and usually organizational viability is maintained through the application of new rules, which can be invented as needed.

Most mutual help organizations are small with limited memberships, ranging in size from 10 to 20 people. They seem constantly struggling to maintain themselves, and most seem to have similar problems. They need help in developing and maintaining leadership and in creating procedures for involving more members in the work of the organization. They usually experience difficulty in defining their goals, in developing helping programs that meet all their members' needs, and in implementing their goals and program ideas. They tend to let one or two people carry the burden of the organization in order to get things done. Some groups are only partly aware of the value of the help that group members provide each other. Such groups feel self conscious when interacting with professionals, feeling that what the group is doing is not adequate. Sometimes they place a greater value on professional help than on what they are doing. These groups need approbation and support about the appropriateness of their own activity.

One way in which they find stability and enhance their organizational effectiveness is to turn to community agencies and ask for help from their staff. Some groups, for example, form alliances with established and prestigious organizations, such as the American Cancer Society. The price of such affiliation often involves some loss of autonomy (Tracy and Gussow, 1976). In such cases, members feel constrained by controls imposed by the board of directors of the parent organization. These boards are often dominated by medical and organizational professionals.

Organizations have found ways of sustaining themselves by joining with each other. They form local federations or coalitions of organizations with similar agendas. Such coalitions exist, for instance, for battered women's groups and for parent groups for children with various special needs.

The most effective way for groups to sustain themselves in the long run is to be affiliated with their own national organization from which they can receive direction and advice on programmatic and organizational issues. Several types of national organizations exist. The simplest form is a loose network of autonomous groups. However, the most common arrangement is a formally organized national association that authorizes the establishment of local branches or chapters that use its name. Dues from these affiliated chapters often support a national office with a paid staff who develop program materials for the local groups. Some associations also provide consultants from regional offices to help promote strong chapters. Well known examples of this model are Alcoholics Anonymous, Parents Without Partners, LaLache League, and Compassionate Friends.

There is a growing proliferation of mutual support groups sponsored by professional agencies. It is essential to distinguish between these groups and the type of organizations described in this chapter. In these groups, professionals choose the participants and are generally responsible for convening the meetings, facilitating them, and for any continuity that may be required. Since all the participants in these groups share a problem, they meet some of the criteria for being a mutual help group. However, since members do not control the resources or direct the flow of the meeting, these are technically not mutual help groups.

It is not clear how much the helping process in a mutual help group depends on the members controlling the resources, and using their own experience as the basis of help, while also being able to move from the role of beneficiary to that of helper (without acquiring a professional education). The difference in status between member and client cannot be ignored. A client is a person in a deficit situation who seeks help from an expert. This expert, using his/her professional knowledge can help alleviate the problem. In a mutual help organization an individual may come for assistance, but instead of being assigned the role of client, is recruited as a member. Members control the group's resources and use their personal experience as the basis for the helping program. This is not to demean professionally led groups, but simply to distinguish between them and other kinds of help, and to recognize that they may function differently. The context in which the help is offered and the helper's relationship to that system may make a critical difference in the effectiveness of the help offered.

IMPLICATIONS FOR PROFESSIONAL PRACTICE

Most of the interaction between formal human service agencies and mutual help groups has been characterized by tension and even competition. Members of mutual help organizations have often had poor experiences with formal helping systems. At times, they may denigrate the services that these systems have to offer, encouraging members to rely on each other for any and all assistance required. This posture occurs, in part, because historically professionals have often attempted to co-opt mutual help organizations or to impose the authority of professional knowledge alone, so that now many mutual help organizations consider professionals to be intruders (Collins and Pancoast, 1976; Katz, 1961).

As noted above, sometimes groups turn to agencies for assistance and, instead of developing a collaborative relationship, a struggle for control results. Mutual help organizations also see their identity endangered when agencies emulate mutual help group activities by providing their own mutual support groups. Agencies have observed the special value of help being offered by a peer. Instead of encouraging the development of peer run groups, they have promoted the role of the professional as convener and leader. This phenomenon is inevitable in some ways, since few professional agencies can justify sponsoring organizations with officers and rules for services not subject to review by the agency (Silverman, 1980). On the other hand, it may deprive clients of a very positive opportunity to take charge of their own problem solving efforts.

Baker (1977) noted that the two systems, professional and mutual help, compete for clients, political sanctions, financing, volunteers, and information. Huey (1977) identified a source of tension resulting from the professional's need to maintain a superordinate position as "expert." Differences in perspective about the value of the help offered is another cause of tension. Professionals sometimes judge mutual help to be superficial because it does not involve restructuring or rebuilding the participant's personality. In addition, professionals often see continuous participation in the mutual help group as an indication of dependency rather than as a demonstration of new-found strength to help others (Silverman, 1978). Further, professionals traditionally value objectivity and detachment and are uncomfortable with the level of personal involvement exhibited by members of mutual help groups. Finally, professionals feel that credentials are required to work with people who are experiencing serious personal difficulties. As long as professionals continue to hold these positions tension between the two systems will grow.

In contrast, where there is mutual respect and understanding, interesting and valuable collaborations have developed between these two systems. Most mutual help organizations are not anti-professional. For example, LaLeche League, the Ostomy Societies, and Recovery, Inc. are actively involved with the professional helping system. They have professional advisory committees that provide the organization with the latest medical information that would affect their members. However, it is up to the organization to decide how to use this information for the benefit of the membership. The concern in these organizations is with effective collaboration and with helping their members become competent consumers of needed services.

Professionals usually relate to mutual help organizations in one of four ways. They can make referrals. This is a straight forward activity, that involves learning about the groups and telling clients about one that seems appropriate to their situation. To this end, many professionals have facilitated the development of self help clearing houses that specialize in providing this type of referral information (Gartner and Reissman, 1980). A second way to relate to groups is to serve on professional advisory boards, as noted above. A third way is to provide consultation to groups that may ask for assistance with particular problems. A fourth way is to initiate efforts that would lead to the establishment of new mutual help organizations to meet particular client population's needs. Several books have been written on how to proceed with this type of activity (Silverman, 1980). If it is accepted that a mutual help experience may be particularly effective in promoting competent coping strategies in response to stress and situations of change and transition (Silverman, 1982), then professionals should consider promoting such programs in communities where none exist.

Another way to enhance preventive programs in a community is to strengthen existing groups. In such activities professionals need to first clarify their own attitudes so that they are clear that they come to consult and facilitate rather than to bring "enlightenment." In addition, they need to look at the skills they may need to be effective. Most clinicians trained as therapists, either in individual work or with groups, do not possess these skills. In a clinical setting, the group is a therapeutic tool and the leader is the therapist. In a mutual help organization, there are many types of activities that take place in a group setting. The group can be an educational and organizational tool. The leader in this instance is usually chair or president of the organization. The organization may provide member run small discussion groups where more personal helping and sharing among members takes place. The leader is first among equals rather than a personally disinterested superior. As informal groups grow they will need to know about developing an organizational structure, delegating responsibility, designing an effective helping program that could include small discussion/sharing opportunities. They may ask professionals for help in developing skills to accomplish these tasks. These are not the same skills that the typical clinician has developed.

Whether the professional initiates a new group or comes as a consultant to an existing group, the parameters that define the role of consultant would apply in both situations. Essentially, the consultant arrives as an outside expert to share what he/she knows with the consultee. A consultant does not have any responsibility for implementing the advice given, and is present by invitation. Therefore, the relationship can be terminated any time by the consultee. It may be easier to terminate a relationship of this sort when the group invited the consultant to help. It may be harder for both the group and the professional to end or change their relationship to each other if the professional was the initiator of the group.

However, for a group to be an effective mutual help organization that promotes competency of its membership, a professional helper has to know when to walk away. In addition, the professional needs to be very flexible in defining his or her role. The informality of most mutual help groups makes it impossible to clearly delineate roles. The consultant has to match his or her activity with the uneven rhythm of the organization. For instance, he/she can be asked to serve coffee, share in a pot luck supper, react to events that are taking place at the moment, talk about his/her personal situation as it may relate to a topic the group is currently discussing, or meet with an ad hoc committee working on a special problem. Since membership is changing, the same consultees may not be available over time. In fact we may be talking about a collaboration with dimensions that evolve as the relationships develop. There is a need to develop a model for working together that will enhance this collaboration, while clearly acknowledging that expert knowledge may reside in the consultee as well as the professional. As observers have become aware of the problems potential consultants face in working with mutual help groups, many have suggested that they not work with them or that they should do so only after additional training.

I have proposed an alternate model (Silverman, 1982), in which the professional's role is that of linking agent. This model uses other aspects of the professional role, such as the ability to facilitate group process and mobilize community resources, while capitalizing on the existing knowledge and experience generated by mutual help organizations themselves. A mutual help group literature has evolved, dealing with organizational problems, leadership development, training of helpers, fund raising, as well as substantive material on the groups themselves. Few groups have any awareness of the material generated by others, and each group tends to struggle anew with the same problems (Silverman, 1980). They need to be put in touch with each other. Thus opportunities to learn from each other need to be created. The professional can become this linking agent, the "middle man" between groups in need and available resources (people, ideas, and materials) which would solve their problems. This linkage could be accomplished with one group or by bringing groups together.

Several steps have been identified in the linking process:

- There is a need to develop mutual trust, understanding and respect.
- The group is better able to identify its problems and to reveal difficulties it could not deal with alone.
- The consultant is able to point out that other groups experienced the same problems — the group is not unique — thus legitimating the group and its concerns.
- Ideas, experiences, and written materials from other groups are presented to indicate how they approached similar problems.
- There is a review on how to use the new data.

Havelock most accurately describes this activity. Generally, linkers stand between two parties, and the way they are seen may have considerable effect on their ability to introduce users to information or services (Havelock, Guskin, Frohman, Havelock, Hill and Huber, 1971). A linking agent has the task of building awareness and understanding of a body of information in the consultee. In my model the consultant's primary task is to link groups directly with each other or to provide them with relevant information gathered from other groups when they cannot meet directly.

From the consultee's point of view three stages can be identified in the linkage process:

a) Discovering that the groups' common problems are not unique and that there are commonalities across divergent organizations;
b) Sharing respective experiences of successful and unsuccessful solutions, members engage in a mutual learning exchange, identify with each other, and provide models for how to implement new knowledge.
c) Searching for additional answers, solutions and techniques together, mutual helpers help each other.

The reader will recognize that this process is a replica of the mutual help experience that occurs for individual members in their organizations. In an atmosphere in which people can identify with each other, they find their dilemma typical rather than unusual and learning is enhanced. As noted above, people seem to be able to integrate and use new knowledge when it is presented by peers with whom they can identify and who have had similar experience. Some of the institutional barriers that exist between the two systems are minimized in duplicating the mutual help experience. The role of the professional is a) to facilitate contact between the two systems; b) to legitimate the systems learning from each other, using experiential knowledge rather than professional knowledge; c) to help mobilize resources; and d) to share skills in group process. Above all, the professional has to know when to step back as groups take over this process for themselves and each other without additional help. To exemplify this process, a closer look at how professionals share skills in group process follows.

SHARING SKILLS IN GROUP PROCESS

As noted above, most groups complain about responsibility falling on a limited number of people to keep their organization and program going. They need to learn to share responsibility, to make room in the organization for others to develop organizational skills, and to be invested in the life of the organization. The skills needed to do this work include knowing how to conduct a meeting, how to chair a committee, perhaps how to do publicity or put out a newsletter. The opportunity to learn these skills should be available to all members in order to encourage them to assume, in time, other roles than that of recipient (Silverman, 1980).

Most organizations are also concerned with their helping program. These programs, for example, may take the form of informal rap groups, one-on-one outreach, or a time limited educational series for new members. Usually people who aspire to helping roles in such programs are chosen from among the membership because of their interest in becoming a helper and, typically, only if they meet certain prerequisites.

When groups ask for help from professionals, these helpers may not always recognize that the members have two separate problems that should be responded to differently. For instance, the organization leadership may simply complain about being overworked. Only after discussing with the leaders what activities they are involved with may it become apparent to the professionals that these leaders are doing both the helping and the organizational work — a very complex assignment.

The consultant's first job, then, is to help organizational members identify the problem. Members need to look at the organizational structure of their group to see if there are mechanisms for sharing responsibility and for involving others. They need to look at what stands in the way of implementing these guidelines, if adequate ones exist. The consultant should point out to them that these problems are not unusual, that other groups have similar difficulties. Together they may identify other mutual help organizations in the community that seem to be doing well. The consultant should encourage the leadership to visit these groups and to talk about how they deal with these problems. Members may want to ask how these groups elect officers, how they delegate responsibility, and how they prepare their membership for assuming some leadership roles.

Some organizations, such as Parents Without Partners or La-Leche League, have annual training programs for people who want to become leaders. The group may discover that it may be necessary to rewrite the by-laws, to develop a better committee structure, or to actually teach people how to chair a committee. It may be necessary for the consultant to help the very competent charismatic leadership that initiated a group to be patient with those who have less experience and less innate knowledge about how to make an organization run.

Sometimes leaders need to be supported (which could come from a trusted outsider) in letting go and finding other ways of being involved. Generally speaking most people who initially come because they need help subsequently need training and a good deal of encouragement to assume leadership roles in an organization. The professional may want to encourage the group to develop an orientation for members to develop these needed skills. Sometimes a voluntary agency has an orientation for new board members to teach them how to lead a meeting and this model could be copied. In communities where there are self help clearing houses or coalitions of organizations, groups may come together to pool their resources in developing a leadership training program for their membership. Teachers in such settings are often experienced members whose organizations have solved some of these problems.

Groups can use the same general approach to get assistance with their helping programs. They can learn from each other. A typical reaction of most new helpers is their self consciousness about not being a professional. Often people are socialized to think that special training in a professional school is needed before an individual can provide assistance with personal problems; that only professionals should be helpers (Friedson, 1970). New Groups, or new members, need to see what others like themselves can do and to learn from the outset to appreciate their own experiential knowledge and the power of the assistance that can emerge from it. The professional can be very helpful within these constraints.

As an outsider, the professional also can help the members clarify what kind of helping program they want, how it should relate to other aspects of the organization's program, and what criteria should be established for recruiting helpers. For example, A.A. requires that someone who is interested in becoming a sponsor of new members has to be dry for a fixed period of time. Some widow programs will not accept a volunteer for their outreach who has not been widowed for two years. Volunteers have to be able to talk about their situation with some perspective and to be willing to share both their successes and failures with new members. In addition, they must have the ability to listen (Silverman, 1980). Groups often need to put these criteria on paper for future helpers to see.

Once they have stated who is eligible to help, groups may want to plan an orientation program for helpers in addition to the one described above for managing the organization as described by Silverman (1980, p. 111). They may ask the professional to help organize and teach in such an orientation. Once a group develops experience, experienced members may do the teaching themselves for the next group of helpers. Sometimes professionals are asked to maintain an on-going relationship with what is sometimes called the outreach or helping committee. Consultants may be asked for assistance with unusual personal problems that may emerge and to identify appropriate community agencies that the group may need to use.

During an orientation program, skills that helpers should acquire or deepen include: a) sensitivity to others, b) ability to show they care, c) the ability to listen, d) knowing when and how to ask questions, e) sharing information, giving advice, and f) using group skills (Silverman, 1980). Brief definitions of each skill follow:

a) Sensitivity to others: Helpers must be sensitive to the state people are in when they come to a mutual help group. They need to know to what extent people accept their personal situation; if they are holding themselves together with a slim cord; are they ready to talk, or do they just want to listen. The helper also needs to know when sharing his/her own story will help.

b) Caring: Volunteers often need assurance that it is all right for them to follow their instincts to reach out, touch, share, even to cry or be angry when helping someone. Making sure that people feel welcome when they come to a meeting for the first time is one small, but important, way of showing concern. In getting involved, volunteer helpers leave themselves vulnerable to hurt if the person they reach out to is rejecting. Volunteers don't and should not have the detached view of the professionals. They need to recognize that, although their helping efforts may not be successful, their own value as people is not being tested.

c) Listening: Helpers need to learn the value of simply listening and giving people the opportunity to talk freely.

d) Asking questions: Volunteers can often help by asking leading questions; for example: "what steps do you need to take to change things?" They must then learn to give the other person ample time to ponder the question rather than jumping in with an answer.

e) Information sharing: The helper should be prepared to provide a variety of types of information, such as what is the normal course that the problem takes, what variations in timing may occur, what problems need to be anticipated, what kind of solutions different people have found, and what resources are available for solving these problems. To some extent people see this type of information giving as advice and they think that advice-giving is bad. However, the distinction can be made between telling people what they *should* do and providing them with guidance about what choices they may have.

f) **Group skills:** The layperson may find helping in a group setting more intimidating than in one-to-one conversation. If an organization decides to provide both kinds of help, volunteers can have a choice of what they want to do. To gain experience and confidence, inexperienced volunteers can serve as co-leaders initially. Volunteers need to learn not only how to create a warm and friendly atmosphere but how to facilitate the group discussion. They need to learn ways of starting things off such as, for example, going around the room and asking everyone to give a brief description of why they are there, or how things had gone during the week. They also need to learn about the responsibilities of a leader, such as giving people time to talk, encouraging both positive and negative comments, noticing silent people and encouraging them to contribute, making sure the group notices a call for help, seeing that participants stick to the subject, pulling things together, helping people deal with negative feelings. The leader has to start the meeting on time and try to end on time and to recognize that his or her job is not to run the group, but to help members help each other. The reader will recognize that these are skills that any good leader should possess, whether in a helping group or in an organizational meeting.

The professional, in sharing what he/she knows, is preparing the current leadership to train the next generation themselves.

CONCLUSION

In this chapter I have noted that prevention involves promoting the competency of people to cope with stress or adversity. Learning from a peer in a mutual help group context may be the most effective way of accomplishing this goal. Not only is it often easier to learn from a peer but, by assisting others, both the helper's sense of self and of effectiveness can be enhanced. In this context, the professional role is changed from hands-on-helper to that of consultant, linking agent and collaborator. Out of these new alliances between professional and consumer systems creative solutions can be found to some of the difficult human dilemmas facing us in the latter quarter of the twentieth century.

REFERENCES

Baker, F.: The interface between professional and natural support systems. *Clinical Social Work Journal, 5(2)*:139-148, 1977.

Bandura, A.: *Social Learning Theory.* Englewood Cliffs, N.J.: Prentice-Hall, 1977.

Barrera, M.: Social Support in the Adjustment of Pregnant Adolescents. In Gottlieb (Ed.), *Social Networks and Social Support.* Beverly Hills: Sage, 1981.

Bloom, B.: Advances and obstacles in prevention of mental disorders. In H.C. Schulberg and M. Killilea (Eds.), *The Modern Practice of Community Mental Health.* San Francisco: Jossey-Bass, 1982.

Caplan, G.: Support systems. In G. Caplan (Ed.), *Support Systems and Community Mental Health.* New York: Basic Books, 1974.

Collins, A. and Pancoast, D.: *Natural Helping Networks: A Strategy for Prevention.* Washington, D.C.: National Association of Social Workers, 1976.

Comstock, C.: Preventive processes in self-help groups: Parents Anonymous. In L.D. Borman, et al. (Eds.), *Helping People to Help Themselves: Self-help and prevention.* New York: The Haworth Press, 1982.

Friedson, E.: Dominant professions, bureaucracy, and client service. In W. Rosengren, and M. Lefton (Eds.), *Organizations and Clients.* Columbus, Ohio: Merrill, 1970.

Gartner, A. and Reissman, F.: *Help: A Working Guide to Self Help Groups,* New York: New Viewpoints, 1980.

Goldston, S.E.: An overview of primary prevention programming. In D. Klein and S. Goldston (Eds.), *Primary Prevention: An Idea Whose Time Has Come.* DHEW Pub. No. (ADM) 77-447. Washington, D.C.: Superintendent of Documents, U.S. Government Printing Office, 1977.

Gore, S. and Eckenrode, J.: Stressful events and social supports: The significance of context. In B. Gottlieb (Ed.), *Social Networks and Social Support.* Beverly Hills: Sage, 1981.

Gottlieb, B.: Social networks and social support in community mental health. In B. Gottlieb (Ed.), *Social Networks and Social Support,* Beverly Hills, Ca.: Sage, 1981.

Hamburg, D.A. and Adams, J.E.: A perspective on coping: Seeking and utilizing information in major transitions. *Archives of General Psychiatry, 17*:277-284, 1967.

Havelock, R. in collaboration with A. Guskin and others: *Planning for Innovation Through the Dissemination and Utilization of Knowledge.* Ann Arbor: Institute for Social Research, University of Michigan, 1969.

Havelock, R.G. and Havelock, M.C.: *Training for Change Agents.* Ann Arbor: University of Michigan, 1973.

Huey, K.: Developing effective links between human service producers and the self help system. *Hospital and Community Psychiatry, 28(10)*:767-770, 1977.

Katz, A.H.: *Parents of the Handicapped.* Springfield, Il.: Thomas, 1961.

Lieberman, M. and Borman, L. (Eds.): *Self Help Groups for Coping with Crisis*. San Francisco: Jossey Bass, 1979.

President's Commission on Mental Health. *Task Force Panel Report*. (Vol. II-IV). Washington, D.C.: U.S. Government Printing Office, 1978.

Riessman, F.: The helper therapy principle, *Social Work, 10*:27-32, April, 1965.

Rubin, Z.: *Children's Friendships*. Cambridge: Harvard University Press, 1980.

Schacter, S. (Ed.): *The Psychology of Affiliation*. Stanford, Ca.: Stanford University Press, 1959.

Silver, R. and Wortman, C.: Coping with undesirable life events. In J. Garber and M. Seligman (Eds.): *Human Helplessness*. New York: Academic Press, 1980.

Silverman, P.: Anticipatory grief from the perspective of widowhood. In B. Schonberg, et al. (Eds.): *Anticipatory Grief*. New York: Columbia University Press, 1974.

Silverman, P.: *Mutual Help Groups and the Role of the Mental Health Professional*. Washington, D.C.: U.S. Government Printing Office, NIMH, DHEW Publication No. (ADM) 78-646, 1978.

Silverman, P.: *Mutual Help: Organization and Development*. Beverly Hills: Sage, 1980.

Silverman, P.: The mental health consultant as a linking agent. In Atarasak and Biegel (Eds.), *Community Support Systems*. Baltimore: Springer, 1981.

Silverman, P.: Transitions and models of intervention. *Annals of the Academy of Political and Social Science,* Nov. 1982, Special Issue on Transitions, F. Berado (Ed.).

Silverman, P. and Smith, D.: Helping in mutual help groups for the physically disabled. In Gartner and Reissman (Eds.), *Mental Health and the Self Help Revolution*. New York: Human Science Press, 1983.

Tracy, G. and Gussow, Z.: Self help groups: A grassroots response to a need for service. *Journal of Applied Behavioral Science, 12*:381-396, 1976.

White, R.: Strategies of adaptation: An attempt at systematic description. In Coelho, Hamburg and Adams (Eds.), *Coping and Adaptation*. New York: Basic Books, 1974.

CHAPTER 13

COMMUNITY CHANGE
Community Change Groups — Helping Groups Help the Community

E.W. CHRISTENSEN

COMMUNITY change groups represent an extremely variable kind of activity. Groups of this kind may be called "social planning," "social action," "political action," "advocacy," "protest," "citizen participation," "community action," or "neighborhood action," to cite the most common titles.

Community change in some form or other is as old as human society, and the group has been a critical medium of this activity. Klein (1972) points out that the commune as a form precedes the Christian era. This country's history has been characterized by citizen participation.

A central theme of this chapter is the variability among the targets of interventions, the interventions themselves and, therefore, in leader functioning and training. The kinds of interventions, leader activities, evidence of effectiveness, etc. are all affected by the differential nature and complexity of a "community," as will become clear in the following pages.

A community is like any interdependent system, where change in one part causes change in the entire system. Intervention in a "community" is not clear cut, given the varying types of communities. In addition, the *level* of intervention interacts closely with the *purpose* of the activity.

Community change may focus on a unit as small as a few people dedicated to working with a specific group of citizens (e.g., gays or the protection of a unique ecological site), or as large as an entire country. The literature on this level of intervention reveals cases ranging up through neighborhoods, political subdivisions including entire towns or cities, to regional, national and even international "communities."

The level of intervention is closely related to the purpose of the intervention. If the objective of the intervention is to affect national legislation, for example, the characteristics of the "community" are linked to that purpose. Attempts to halt construction of a shopping center in an area felt to be ecologically unique, on the other hand, will usually involve a very circumscribed "community." In each case, the specific characteristics of the community modify the intervention and its purpose.

The motivation of the interveners also interacts with level of intervention. All attempts to intervene at the community level involve complex motivations. What seems to be intervention to aid the community may in reality be a manifestation of the efforts of an organization to survive. The motive, on the other hand, may be individual; the level of intervention is not really the community, but the personal investments of specific leaders in the "community."

Despite these ambiguities, however, community change is an accepted part of the social and political activity of this country. Intervention at this level has been legitimized in many ways, perhaps none more dramatic than the legislation associated with the Great Society (Rich and Rosenbaum, 1981; Wohlford, 1974; Zurcher, 1969).

Other levels of community change, not always as broad and sweeping as Great Society legislation, may relate to environmental concerns. Examples range from a small locality through state, regional, national, and even international levels, as in the recent Greenpeace activities near Siberia. Political advocacy at various levels provides another instance of community intervention, spanning local, national and international levels.

The broad range of communities provides evidence of the variability and ambiguity of the concept. There are many manifestations, and an examination of the yellow pages of the local telephone directory confirms the existence of a wide variety of communities (mine lists a potential community under "Dial an Atheist Association"!).

The real purposes of community change are complex, interrelated, and often at least partially unknown to either members of the community or external observers. Typically, however, the purposes can be categorized as those relating to *deprivation*, improving community *functioning*, *evolving* from other groups, and legislative *requirement*.

Securing benefits previously denied is a common purpose behind community interventions. A typical example of deprivation is that of power, and the resulting intervention is aimed at securing power for those who are powerless (Gilbert and Eaton, 1976; Rivera, 1972).

Another example typical of social action aimed at erasing community deficits revolves around securing equal opportunity (Saltman, 1975). In this case the objective is to ensure equality, as typified by the aims of affirmative action, civil rights, and similar efforts.

Compensatory action, however, is not as clear cut and noble as the rhetoric professes. There are those, like Orum (1974), who contend that a deprived community is characterized by apathy and lack of skill and knowledge. Deprivation, therefore, may actually be a disincentive to creating change. In a similar vein, Gilbert and Eaton (1976) found that community members voiced less dissatisfaction than was anticipated, suggesting that the purpose for change may come from outside the people themselves.

A related question is the degree to which the community recognizes the alleged deprivation. Systems theory suggests that a community, like a family, may view itself as functioning well even when it is not. Scapegoating provides an important role for the scapegoat and the total effect allows the system to conclude that it is functioning adequately. Dynamics such as this underline the complex nature of compensatory activity as a purpose for intervening.

In improving the *functioning* of the community, the objective is more like that of organization development: a more effective community (McClelland, Rhinesmith and Kristensen, 1975). The purpose here is pragmatic rather than political; for whatever purposes the community exists it must be efficient in meeting its needs. The intervention is to improve functioning, not remediate.

Over time an organization may *evolve* from its original purposes and intervene on behalf of itself or some selected community for different reasons. Groups, for example, may originally emerge for the purpose of enhancing or correcting individuals or organizations, and subsequently become involved in community action on a different basis. A group founded for pleasure may later become involved in community action in response to laws, regulations, etc., or to ensure its survival. In the same way a group of learners, or even a group of clients in a mental health agency, may organize to influence the larger community (Christensen, 1983; Culbert, 1976; Jaffe, 1973; Zeitlin, 1972).

Finally, one purpose for community action is that it is *required* by the nature of the community's existence. The total community is ultimately formed by a series of coalitions and interlocking groups (Lewis and Lewis, 1977; Zeitlin, 1972). The larger system (i.e., federal government) may enact legislation mandating citizen participation "for their own good." This contextual objective in community change was specified by Great Society legislation (Rich and Rosenbaum, 1981; Zurcher, 1969) and subsequent social legislation at the national level. Further, it is characteristic of grants, financial aid, etc., at all levels in our society.

What are the theoretical constructs which undergird the activity of groups working to help the community correct itself? The answer is modified in part because there are really two groups associated with social action activity: the first is the community itself, however it may be defined; the other is the group which is the *working* unit of the community. While on some occasions these may be the same, often the unit of change is too large and ungainly, and therefore the primary functions are carried out by a smaller group of leaders, which acts for the community. Communities come in many sizes, viewed in this way.

The theoretical basis of community change relates to the variable nature and purpose of each "community." Therefore, one cannot a priori discuss theory supporting a specific intervention. Needs will differ, obstacles and support systems will be diverse, and therefore intervention must vary as well.

Despite these cautions, it is possible to consider general theoretical underpinnings for working with the community. Most of the theory is valid whether the group under consideration is the community itself or the working body of individuals who act for the community.

Social action is generally accepted as aimed at assisting community members cope with their environment; for many authorities it also means changing conditions where feasible and appropriate (Klein, 1972). In this construct we acknowledge the close relationship between the individual and the community. The very process of helping individuals may also lead to a force brought to bear on the larger society. One theoretical construct behind community change activity, therefore, is that *individual and social goals are not incompatible* (Cowen, 1982; Culbert, 1976; Lifton, 1972; Zeitlin, 1972).

Another theoretical concept which is generally applicable is that of *participation* and *involvement* (Berry, 1981; Buck and Stone, 1981; McClelland et al., 1975; Menlo, 1981; Rich and Rosenbaum, 1981; Schindler-Rainman, 1981). In a democratic society involvement and participation are accepted as central to social legislation and change.

Sharing power and decision making is a central concept undergirding social change, as well as task groups, in general. It is advocated as a principle for leaders and change agents, whether the community change is political or otherwise (Lewis and Lewis, 1977; Rosener, 1981; Rothman, 1974).

Other theoretical concepts typical of community change literature are: interdependence; credibility; process and outcome goals; organizational efficiency; advocacy; and representativeness. From the literature of small groups one would add such concepts as cohesion, leadership, communication, and influence as prime factors in groups helping communities to change.

Corey (1976) uses most of these concepts in his theory of structues of community change. He advocates taking into consideration one's personal constructs as well as the structures inherent in knowledge and action. His approach is that of organization development community planning, involving the implementation of community change by change agents. These change agents should be personally aware, understand organizational structure and the change process, and work in an interactive way with the various elements of the community (clients, support groups, agencies, etc.).

Corey's assumption is that one can have a potential impact on the community only in degrees, that the most amenable part of the community is oneself and, therefore, action will begin with the change agent. If we assume that members of the community are potential change agents, we return to the basic concept that the individual and the community are closely related, each influencing the other. Changing the community is to change the organization and the individual, and this *interactive* concept is a keystone to the theoretical understanding of social action groups.

Basic to community action theory are the seminal concepts of Lewin (1936) regarding unfreezing, change, and refreezing of a social system. The idea is to enable the community to destabilize, incorporate a change, and then restabilize once this occurs. Alinsky's (1970) work was an example of this concept in the civil rights arena.

The person who works with community change is unable to depend heavily on proven established techniques. This situation is partly due to the fact that community change involves both a large, often politicized community as well as the councils, committees, task forces, etc., which form the nucleus of any such endeavor. Therefore, many of the techniques must be created more through educated guesswork than established techniques. As Rothman (1974) emphasizes, leader function and other group dynamics will differ according to the type of group and its purpose.

The literature regarding social action interventions often omits attention to group dynamics and group processes; in some cases it fails to overtly acknowledge the group format of such activities (Jaccard, 1981; Rivera, 1972; Saltman, 1975). Primary consideration in the literature seems to center on political pressure and power issues, and less on the group techniques used to help the community accomplish those ends.

Techniques vary according to which members of the community are involved. For example the age of the participants influences the kind of intervention. Rothman (1974) asserts that voluntary associations, which may render service as well as attempt to influence the community, are most often associated with middle aged people. Social movements, on the other hand, will have a predominance of young adults in its ranks, while political movements have the lowest level of participation of young people and the highest for middle aged persons. Who the members of a community are, in addition to other key factors, demands a different set of intervention techniques.

Intervention may vary also because a skewdness exists with regard to those actively involved in the community action and/or in leadership positions. Milbrath (1981) and Rosener (1981) assert that traditional selection methods for citizen participation result in selectivity and a lack of representativeness. Buck and Stone (1981), in describing citizen participation in a development program for Yosemite National Park, reported a bias on the high side of the socioeconomic scale. The leaders of many change programs are not typical of the community, and control could center on an elite group of activists (Gilbert and Eaton, 1976).

Despite these concerns, there are suggestions from the literature with regard to specific techniques, although relatively little empirical data have been compiled to guide us in their use. Gilbert and Eaton (1976) and Lifton (1972) warn us about power issues and the potential divisiveness in the use of power. Rich and Rosenbaum (1981), Menlo (1981), Wohlford (1974), and Gricar and Baratta (1983) are among those who emphasize the centrality of involving community residents in the activities of a community change program. Much of the literature underlines the need to have members of the community learn to share in the power and decision making as attempts are made to influence the public or other agencies in favor of the community (Berry, 1981; Lewis and Lewis, 1977; McClelland, et al., 1975; Rosener, 1981; Rothman, 1974; Schindler-Rainman, 1981).

In more specific ways the literature reports a variety of techniques which have been used to effect change in a community. The following samples underline both the universality and uniqueness of community change techniques.

Most techniques are a mix of activities focusing on the individual or on small groups initially, working up to or simultaneously involving the community on a broader, more sweeping scale. Berry (1981) reported an example of a community intervention where citizen groups worked with administrative agencies in order to increase advocacy efforts. In this case power was the key, as both citizens and the agencies wanted it. In addition to the central involvement of citizen groups, Berry found that preparation and communication about the particulars of an issue were critical.

In a similar case, Milbrath (1981) found that the typical techniques of involving community members, through citizen committees and public hearings, was not sufficient because of lack of representativeness of the participants. Milbrath advocated the use of citizen surveys to increase the representative nature of any community member participation, and to augment the more traditional methods.

Other techniques, while initiated to change the community, are more individual and group oriented. Jaffe (1973), for example, advocated the use of support groups as well as moving into the social network of the community. His interventions were essentially an overlap of individual and group *treatment*, with a wider goal of changing the community. McClelland, et al. (1975) reported on an intervention which began with a similar premise. They tried to increase individual efficacy in order to subsequently increase organizational efficacy in the community. They began with training groups, not only to help the individuals acquire skills needed to influence the community, but with the assumption that training was needed in the agencies which the participants represented from the community.

Schindler-Rainman (1981) also advocated training in human relations skills as an intervention. The rationale is that community members who participate in committees or other deliberative bodies need skills commensurate with that responsibility. The use of intergenerational groups in the community in order to move from conformity to a greater appreciation of differences was also advocated.

Wohlford (1974) used community member participation itself as an intervention. In this case, the involvement was of Head Start parents in groups, with the objective of creating interdependence among family, children, the neighborhood and the school.

Zurcher (1969) reported a typical intervention: the use of neighborhood action committees. The rationale for the use of neighborhood groups was to secure grassroots participation, encourage and aid local leadership, and develop bridges into the community. Zurcher reported an analogy between the stages of development of these neighborhood groups and those generally found for more growth-oriented groups (orientation, catharsis, focus, action, limbo, testing and purposive).

Rosener (1981) reported the use of task-oriented workshops, featuring sharing of decisions and power between participants from the community and engineers from the Army Corps of Engineers. In this case the vested interests were concerned about the *process* of the workshops, as their goal was to ensure citizen participation. However, community members viewed the mode of participation primarily as a means to an end, and focused more on *outcome*. This suggests that community intervention must ultimately fulfill the needs of more than just one faction of the community.

Culbert (1976) advocated the use of consciousness raising as one way to affect the community. Like Jaffe (1973) and McClelland, et al. (1975), he begins with both the individual and the community, viewing the community member as a change agent who ultimately will have an effect on the community. Culbert also shares with Jaffe the advocacy of support groups in this process.

The preceding examples of techniques used for community change are wide ranging, but participation, power, decision making and the interaction of individual, group and community are all central to them. Since communities and their particular circumstances come in an almost limitless range, it follows that intervention techniques are equally difficult to categorize.

The target populations of community change efforts are logically related to the nature of the community as a level of intervention. We must view a given target population against both *geographic* and *demographic* dimensions, which are in turn related to the *issue* under consideration.

Target populations will be at a geographic location, involving a specific issue or concern, and characterized by a certain demographic cross section of that community. The dimensions may interact, in that some issues (e.g., environmental concerns and consumerism) do not necessarily indicate more or less concern by any stratum in the society. At the same time, some issues may be directed toward more than one demographic or geographic group. Target populations, therefore, are variably defined.

In reality the target may simultaneously be the individual, the organization or system, and the community. Attaining goals for an individual or for the organization in which the individual is located is to also affect the community, and vice versa (Jaffe, 1973; Klein,

1972; Lifton, 1972). The actual work with the community may begin at any point. Accordingly, we can consider a target population as the community, however defined, plus the various units of which the community is composed, in the same way that a therapeutic group is conceived of as a number of unique individuals who in a collective fashion form a unique unitary grouping as well. Efforts to aid one are considered to benefit the other.

Leader functions will usually depend on a variety of factors characteristic of the community. One critical factor is which group one is leading. Is the "group" the entire organization (community) or at least a significant part of it, or is the group a smaller part of the community (e.g., council, committee, task force, executive board)? Size, location, cohesiveness and presence of conflicts are other community factors which affect leader functioning.

Other determinants relate to the nature of the leader. Often leaders in community action programs are not prepared, either by training or psychologically (Klein, 1972). While this may be problematic in terms of actual leader functioning, therein lies a dilemma: the ideal that leaders be trained and experienced and that they also be a part of the community served is too often an impossibility.

Professionally trained leaders may eventually be the more appropriate ones to work with the community, as the helping professions come more and more to recognize the need to deal with a client's environment (Blocher and Biggs, 1983; Cowen, 1982; O'Neill, 1981). These *trained* leaders will tend to take on wider functions, some of which reflect their own professional identity and background. However, they tend to be viewed as alien to the community, and thus issues of credibility and trust may supersede more pragmatic concerns. Some writers advocate a training or consultative role for the professional leader, a difficult and frustrating role, but one which avoids the possibility that those who ultimately are the most responsible for action taken on behalf of the community are those least invested in that community.

Leader functions commonly mentioned in the literature are similar to those common to other manifestations of group work. One of the general functions, which Rothman and others (McClelland, et al., 1975; Lewis and Lewis, 1977; Schindler-Rainman, 1981) stress is that of helping the group members in decision making and

problem solving functions, thus setting up a stance which emphasizes the ability and responsibility of members to contribute ideas
aimed at creating solutions for community problems.

Klein (1972) views the group worker involved with the community as a guide, educator and facilitator, a role which requires a high
level of patience and sensitivity on the part of the leader. Central to
this role of the leader is the advocacy of participation by community
members. Most of the literature about leader function, stated or implied, emphasizes that participation in their own solutions by community members is critical. It follows, then, that efforts to facilitate
this involvement is a primary function of social action leaders, professional or lay (Culbert, 1976; McClelland, et al., 1975; Menlo,
1981; Rosener, 1981; Schindler-Rainman, 1981).

Goals of effective groups include building trust, resolving conflict, facilitating cooperation, planning, dealing with differences, using resources, goal setting and implementation, and shared
leadership, to enumerate some of the most prominent (McClelland,
et al., 1975; Schindler-Rainman, 1981). Leader functions will
usually be most effective if they focus on these general goals.
Leaders in a given social action program, however, may need to focus more intently on one or two functions because of the unique circumstances of the community group or a special crisis prevailing at
the time. Leaders may want to concentrate on training community
members about a specific dynamic (decision making, conflict resolution, etc.) on a temporary basis due to existing crises, but in the final
analysis all of the goals listed above will be part of the leader's function in a social action program.

As indicated, many lay leaders have not been provided training,
and professionally trained groupworkers are less apt to be involved
with the community. Moreover, much of the literature about working with social action programs highlights dimensions other than
specific leader functions, and the training of those leaders is even
less noted.

Typical of the literature is a suggested need to train the *community*
leaders. This training frequently is viewed as the intervention itself,
or at least a major element in the intervention. In this concept leader
training is to be provided to community members, leaders, or potential leaders, usually by more professionally trained helpers. An

unstated assumption seems to be that where the professionals themselves are directly involved as leaders such training is unnecessary, which is questionable.

A number of writers in the field of community action have established models for preparing community leaders. Schindler-Rainman's (1981) model, while designed for all task group leaders regardless of setting, focuses on several issues which are especially significant for community leaders. One is a more flexible pattern of leadership, wherein coleadership, temporary leadership and shared leadership are stressed. These functions would seem more relevant to the community leader than the more traditional leadership, which is likely to be part of the assumptions of most lay people. In this model individual differences, resistance and lack of resources are viewed as opportunities to intervene and facilitate change, also quite relevant concepts for community change group work.

Menlo's (1981) theory of participation is of interest to the training of community leaders. It states that in almost all adult groups the non-participation by members, or simply the threat of non-participation, is a central issue. Menlo's model for training details a theory of participation and the steps used to facilitate participation in a group. As espoused throughout this chapter, active participation of community members, both in groups and in the community itself, is critical.

Readers who would like to delve more deeply into the issue of training of leaders of groups might consult these sources more directly. The basic concepts are discussed in any good text on group dynamics, but specific cases of attempts to train community leaders are detailed by McClelland, et al., (1975) and Zurcher (1969). As for the dilemma of trained external group leaders versus untrained internal group leaders, it is worth noting that many helpers may possess a high level of leadership skills without special training (Cowen, 1982).

Evidence of the effectiveness of interventions in community and social action programs tends to be limited, and often not empirical in nature. Common to naturalistic research, there are many obstacles in obtaining empirical evidence. Variables are difficult to define or control, the measurement of outcome is often subjective, procedures are not evenly carried out, and the impact of other influences in the environment cannot be controlled or, at times, even detected.

It often is impossible to contrast one intervention with another since so many dimensions of the community in which it is implemented are unique. Much of the research suffers from studying only outcome, and less on the process of the intervention. All in all, the empirical evidence of effectiveness of community action programs is sparse and beset by problems. Speaking of citizen participation in public policy, a typical manifestation of community change, Rich and Rosenbaum (1981) put it this way: "Not nearly so much is known about citizen participation in public policy as the voluminous literature might suggest. Much of that literature is polemical; little of it is based on empirical evaluation" (p. 440). They do, however, go on to state that there have been some accomplishments, although evidence is inconclusive.

Space does not permit a survey of research findings about this widely based approach. However, some typical kinds of studies are presented with the caveat that empirical data are too limited to draw hard conclusions.

Gricar and Baratta (1983) reported that public involvement in monitoring radiation at Three Mile Island added credibility to data, sensitized authorities to the public's fears and doubts, and involved the community in being responsible. They felt that this public involvement raised significant questions about the issue of radiation.

Wohlford (1974) reported mixed results in his attempt to create an interdependent atmosphere among Head Start participants. He also stated that such an attempt was infrequently reported in the literature.

Berry (1981) found that state and local citizen groups were less successful than national ones in working with governmental agencies, and that citizen participation was largely ritualistic. Gormley (1981) joins with Berry in the belief that advocacy through lobbying efforts may be more fruitful.

Milbrath (1981), viewed direct community access to government as problematic, listing evidence to support his position, and suggested the use of citizen surveys to gain more valid and reliable data.

Research regarding the use of training as an intervention is perhaps more common. McClelland, et al. (1975) provided training for community members of a Poverty Program agency, and found it to be beneficial. Training was group oriented, and they recommended that future training groups be kept small, from 8-18 members. Saltman (1975) reported effectiveness in the form of increased awareness and potential for open housing, through the use of "audits" to make public subtle forms of discrimination which, in turn, brought Federal pressure to remedy the situation.

Zurcher (1969) studied the developmental stages of neighborhood action committees and found that they related to similar stages found in other small groups. In addition, he studied those interventions which affected the sequence of the stages. He also reported that the training procedure strengthened group cohesion and member self-confidence.

Rosener's (1981) study involved community cooperation with a governmental agency. A relevant conclusion for potential community group leaders was that participants were concerned about change as an outcome, while the agency focused more on the process. This is one example of the difficulty of research in community action: determining "success" based on dual expectations.

Despite the problems of obtaining consistent empirical data about the effectiveness of social action programs, the record has not been a negative one. The history of this country is replete with examples where communities, large and small, were able to alter their conditions, and the leaders and their ways of influencing others are well known. These efforts continue today, with some degree of "success."

However, there is no list of tried and proven techniques. The more dramatic successes in social change cannot be solidly attributed to specific techniques or interventions, because of a variety of factors beyond our control. The individual success cases are important reinforcers, even though we add to our empirical knowledge slowly and painfully.

As discussed previously, social action groups generally emerge either to cope with societal *deficits*, to aid the community to *function* adequately, through *evolution* from groups established for other purposes, or due to legislative *requirement*. This section will briefly describe three illustrative examples. One case alone is not representative of the breadth of practice; perhaps three more briefly traced cases will demonstrate the variable nature of communities, intervention, and outcomes.

The first example is from a report by Rivera (1972), a response to perceived deficiencies, in this case the lack of political power of Mexican Americans. The case study took place in a small agricultural town in southern Texas, where Chicanos were numerically dominant but politically and economically submerged. Through efforts by Chicano leadership, Spanish speaking organizations, in coalition with the Teamster's Union, were able to take political power. However, within four years Chicano leaders were displaced, and failure of this effort was followed by the introduction of La Raza Unida in Texas, in a new effort to gain power.

With the organization of young Chicanos, later subsumed as part of a larger political group, an active campaign to gain seats on the school board was undertaken. It was partially successful, and various programs beneficial to the Mexican American population were instituted. As Rivera reports it, the first "victories" were premature, and the populace was not able to consolidate gains until later, as they learned from the experience.

Significant in this case was the emergence of a few key leaders who were able to galvanize and organize the people. The report recognized that the Chicano position was still fragile, despite some gains. Rivera suggested that the difference between the first and second interventions, in addition to having learned and organized better, was the efforts to increase Chicano consciousness, a technique also suggested by Culbert (1976) in another context.

The other two illustrations are similar, yet with different implications about purpose and intervention. The first is an example of a family treatment intervention being transformed into a social action intervention as well. The setting is a child care agency in my community. The parents of the children in most cases have some legally imposed compulsion with regard to having their children in this popular center (e.g., child abuse, spouse abuse, parent in jail). Part of the treatment required parents to attend group sessions.

One result of the group sessions and the motivation to keep their children in the center was a high degree of cohesion and loyalty. When state funding for the agency was threatened, some of the parents made appointments with the funding officials and with legislators, and were successful in securing funds. In this case social change originated for reasons which were less related to broader, idealistic conceptions of a "better world" than to a concern for each other and for their children.

The final example is that of study circles (Christensen, 1983) or at least a potential use of some study circles. Study circles are primarily educational interventions, originating in Scandinavia and now introduced into this country as a non-formal adult education format.

The study circle format has been involved as a community change intervention, based on the small group learning format. In Scandinavia, study circles which were sponsored by the government aided Swedes in deciding about the future of nuclear energy and helped the Danes decide about the feasibility of entering the Common Market. In this country they have been used to help adolescents learn about sexuality, with the idea that these young people will also act as change agents in the local community. Study circles could similarly be used to help community members cope with concerns about consumerism and environmental issues.

From the three examples it should be apparent that community change interventions are not uniform in their applications or the reason for their occurrence. Social change efforts may become activities which fulfill personal needs, while educational or treatment intervention, on either a group or individual basis, may give birth to social change. In the latter case, such involvement not only perpetuates the social nature of the organization within which treament occurs, but serves to protect it politically and financially (Jaffe, 1973).

The very nature of community change is such that it is extremely unlikely that one will be a full time leader of social change groups, although there are many people who spend a good portion of their lives in it. As this occurs, the "job" is usually avocational or related to the survival of the organization within which one's vocation exists.

To say that one is "employed" as a leader of social action groups is therefore misleading. Berry (1981), in referring to the need for citizen leaders said, "Developing a realistic strategy for staff recruitment is a difficult task. People do not plan careers as citizen lobbyists" (p. 475).

It is true, however, that many people will spend a significant portion of their personal and professional lives in community change activity. Many helping professionals, for example, will find themselves, willingly or unwillingly, participating in some kind of social change or community involvement, for a variety of reasons.

Lay leaders need to be trained, and professional helpers must know how to do this as well as how to intervene directly with the society within which they work. Private citizens, regardless of occupation, will probably find some kind of social change activity increasingly touching their lives. Thus, while one is not likely to interview for a job of this nature, it will be part of the work of many of us.

REFERENCES

Alinsky, S.: The professional radical, 1970. *Harpers*, CCXL, 1436, 35-42, January 1970.

Berry, J.: Beyond citizen participation: Effective advocacy before administrative agencies. *Journal of Applied Behavioral Science, 17*:463-477, 1981.

Blocher, D., and Biggs, D.: *Counseling Psychology in Community Settings.* New York: Springer, 1983.

Buck, J., and Stone, B.: Citizen involvement in federal planning: Myth and reality. *Journal of Applied Behavioral Science, 17*:550-565, 1981.

Christensen, E.: Study circles: Learning in small groups. *Journal for Specialists in Group Work, 8*:211-217, 1983.

Corey, K.: Structures in the planning of community change: A personal construct. In W. Bennis, K. Benne, R. Chin and K. Corey (Eds.), *The Planning of Change.* New York: Holt, 1976.

Cowen, E.: Help is where you find it: Four informal helping groups. *American Psychologist, 37*:385-395, 1982.

Culbert, S.: Consciousness-raising: A five stage model for social and organization change. In W. Bennis, K. Benne, R. Chin and K. Corey (Eds.), *The Planning of Change.* New York: Holt, 1976.

Gilbert, N., and Eaton, J.: Who speaks for the poor? In W. Bennis, K. Benne, R. Chin and K. Corey (Eds.), *The Planning of Change.* New York: Holt, 1976.

Gormley, W.: Public advocacy in public utility commission proceedings. *Journal of Applied Behavior Science, 17*:446-462, 1981.

Gricar, B. and Baratta, A.: Bridging the information gap at Three Mile Island: Radiation monitoring by citizens. *Journal of Applied Behavioral Science, 19*:35-49, 1983.

Jaccard, J.: A comparison of three theories of social behavior implications for social action programs. *Journal of Applied Behavioral Science, 17*:212-245, 1981.

Jaffe, D.: A counseling institution in an oppressive environment. *Journal of Humanistic Psychology, 13*:25-46, 1973.

Klein, A.: *Effective Groupwork: An Introduction to Principle and Method.* New York: Association Press, 1972.

Lewin, K.: *Principles of Topological Psychology.* New York: McGraw Hill, 1936.

Lewis, M. and Lewis, J.: The counselor's impact on community environments. *Personnel and Guidance Journal, 55*:356-358, 1977.

Lifton, W.: *Groups: Facilitating Individual Growth and Societal Change.* New York: Wiley, 1972.

McClelland, D., Rhinesmith, S., and Kristensen, R.: The effects of power training on community action agencies. *Journal of Applied Behavioral Science, 11*:92-115, 1975.

Menlo, A.: Training leaders to facilitate participation in adult groups. *Journal for Specialists in Group Work, 6*:175-182, 1981.

Milbrath, L.: Citizen surveys as citizen participation mechanisms. *Journal of Applied Behavioral Science, 17*:478-496, 1981.

O'Neill, P.: Cognitive community psychology. *American Psychologist, 36*:457-469, 1981.

Orum, A.: On participation in political protest movements. *Journal of Applied Behavioral Science, 10*:181-207, 1974.

Rich, R., and Rosenbaum W.: Introduction to Special Issue: Citizen participation in public policy. *Journal of Applied Behavioral Science, 17*:439-445, 1981.

Rivera, G.: Nosotros venceremos: Chicano consciousness and change strategies. *Journal of Applied Behavioral Science, 8*:56-71, 1972.

Rosener, J.: User-oriented evaluation: A new way to view citizen participation. *Journal of Applied Behavioral Science, 17*:583-596, 1981.

Rothman, J.: *Planning and Organizing for Social Change: Action Principles from Social Science Research.* New York: Columbia University, 1974.

Saltman, J.: Implementing open housing laws through social action. *Journal of Applied Behavioral Science, 11*:39-61, 1975.

Schindler-Rainman, E.: Training task-group leaders. *Journal for Specialists in Group Work, 6*:171-174, 1981.

Wohlford, P.: Head Start parents in participant groups. *Journal of Applied Behavioral Science, 10*:222-249, 1974.

Zeitlin, S.: The effect of individual psychological needs on the group process of the Beacon community action group. *Dissertation Abstracts International, 34*:1361, 3-A, 1972.

Zurcher, L.: Stages of development in poverty program neighborhood action committees. *Journal of Applied Behavioral Science, 5*:223-258, 1969.

CHAPTER 14

HEALTH PROMOTION/PRIMARY PREVENTION
Primary Prevention-Oriented Groups

RICHARD E. PEARSON

IN the literature of the mental health field, primary prevention
has variously been described as "an idea whose time has come"
(Klein and Goldston, 1977), and "a mental health revolution" (Albee, 1978; Hobbs, 1964). Its central perspective, namely, that in
terms of resources and human suffering it is less costly to prevent the
onset of psychological impairment than to try to stem the tide and
undo its harmful effects once it has occurred, is forceful and convincing.

Whatever the logic of the primary prevention perspective and
however impressive its influence (e.g., the development of community psychology and psychiatry specialties; its endorsement by a
presidential commission on mental health in 1978; an impressive array of books, journals and articles in which primary prevention is
highlighted), the theme that there are many barriers to be overcome
is a prominent one in the primary prevention-oriented literature.

This chapter focuses upon the issue of using small group formats
to promote primary prevention in the mental health field. Examples
relating to group settings will be emphasized and issues, if not
unique, at least particularly relevant to, small group work will be
isolated. However, it will be recognized that much of the discussion
has implications for interventions other than those using small group
formats. Indeed, one of the agendas of this discussion is to consider

277

the general application of primary prevention-focused activities in such a way that the nature of some of the barriers to its acceptance will be clarified.

PRIMARY PREVENTION

Though the old adage would have us believe that "an ounce of prevention is worth a pound of cure," such is not immediately apparent from an examination of the historical and contemporary couse of the mental health field in the United States. As Cowen (1973) has noted, the overwhelming emphasis of the "parent" (i.e., the medical field) is reflected in the characteristics of the "child" (i.e., the mental health field). Clinical practice, programmatic objectives, and institutional orientation have tended to focus upon the remediation of pathology.

Of late, however, there have been stirrings of change. An increased amount of attention paid to issues of, and approaches to, primary prevention acknowledges the obvious reality that a disease is not eliminated by just treating its victims (Bloom, 1979).

Defining Primary Prevention

Recently, Conyne (1982) has offered a definition that comprehensively pulls together the major points that have provided the conceptual footing of primary prevention in the mental health field.

> *Primary prevention* is proactive and population-based. It includes anticipating potential disorder for a population at risk and introducing before-the-fact interventions that are delivered directly or indirectly. These interventions are intended to reduce the incidence of the disorder by counteracting harmful circumstances that contribute to it by promoting the emotional robustness in the population at risk so that population members are both protected and become more fully competent (p. 332).

This definition continues the emphasis, found in the positions of Caplan (1974), Cowen (1978), and Plaut (1982), upon interventions occurring before the onset of impairment. It also reflects Caplan's (1964) view that the risk faced by primary prevention beneficiaries can range from the likelihood of major mental disorder, through to the possibility of a lowered, though still adequate, level of effectiveness caused by failure to resolve a developmental task or life transition effectively as might have been true with a helping intervention.

However, by definition Conyne's position continues the practice of excluding those one-to-one and small group activities which focus upon individuals *as* individuals from inclusion in primary prevention. I believe it is important to note that one of the consequences of the requirement that primary prevention interventions be focused upon populations seems to be that many group workers conclude that the sort of individually-focused activities from which they derive their identity, satisfaction and sustenance is not only outside the pale of primary prevention, but perhaps even antagonistic to it. Unfortunately, this impression tends to be reinforced by a literature which more often stresses differences and discontinuities between primary prevention and traditional approaches than explores overlap in goals and methodologies. That notwithstanding, individually-focused group workers, accustomed to reactive intervention, should not be discouraged from exploring the manner in which their skills and experience can be put in service of primary-prevention objectives. For group workers who usually work with individuals who are not heavily impaired to begin with, a knowledge of at risk populations can provide sensitivity to possible difficulties facing their clients of which they, as helpers, might usually not be aware. Other group workers whose clientele are already experiencing psychological difficulties may find that awareness of primary prevention issues can lead to a focus upon the risk which the clients themselves may pose for their significant others. For example, knowing that the parents, spouses and children of persons who attempt suicide often experience debilitating psychological reactions can lead the worker who conducts groups serving suicidal individuals to focus, as well, upon the needs of those significant others.

A FRAMEWORK FOR CONCEPTUALIZING PRIMARY PREVENTION-ORIENTED GROUPS

To say that a small group focuses upon primary prevention

provides some information about its goals and, in a general sense, its participants. Members would be expected to be free of marked dysfunction (at least with reference to the focus of the group) and, typically, the group would have the goal of reducing the likelihood of their developing future pathology. While this information does allow one to generate some predictions about the group's format, structure, activities and content, the level of specificity at which this can be done is very general.

One approach to developing a fuller description of a primary prevention-focused group is to examine it in light of the following questions.

In promoting primary prevention:

- Upon what aspects of individuals and/or their situations does the group focus?
- Does the group deal directly with "at risk" persons and/or their significant others?
- What intervention modality is used?

Figure 7 presents a matrix whose axes (i.e., the focus, the target, the format) focus upon the data generated by these questions. The constituent categories of each axis represent ways of organizing the resulting data. For example, the three categories which make up the format axis (education, consultation, self-exploration) provide a schema which permits the description of a primary prevention-focused intervention's format in terms of forms commonly used in primary prevention activities.

While the questions themselves and the axes which describe them are quite basic, it is apparent that the particular categories used are the result of arbitrary choice. For example, the categories which make up the individual axis (i.e., transition, individual, context) are based on a model developed by Nancy Schlossberg (1981) for analyzing life transitions. For this and the other axes, however, an attempt was made to draw upon conceptualizations either directly from the primary prevention literature or from those which are closely related conceptually.

The overall character and constituent parts of each axis will be described as a background to a consideration of its subsequent discussion of theoretical and practical issues in preventive group work.

A Framework for Analysing
Primary Prevention-focused Groups

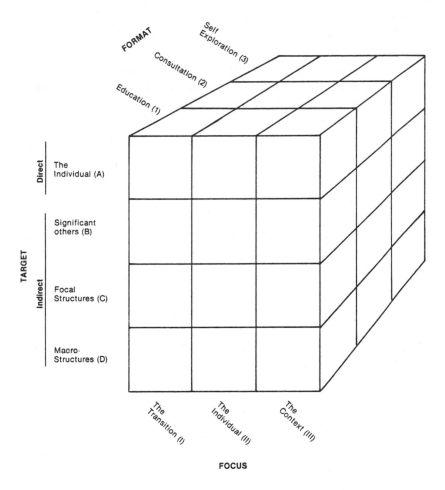

Figure 7.

First Axis: The Focus, Life Transitions

As has been mentioned, Nancy Schlossberg's (1981) work on life transitions is used as a base for consideration of the aspects of individuals and their situations which are important to the pursuit of primary prevention for group members or their significant others. The conceptual literature related to life transitions seems particularly relevant to a consideration of primary prevention-focused groups because transitions are a regular, often unavoidable part of life. As such, many of the issues and concerns which people bring to small group situations can be tied directly or tangentially to life transitions which they or their significant others are facing.

Schlossberg's model identifies the factors which affect the process of coping with life transitions. She specifies that the quality of an individual's resolution of life transitions is a function of three factors:

1. the characteristics of the transition with particular attention paid to the manner in which it is perceived by the individuals (e.g., welcomed/unwelcomed; expected/unexpected);
2. the characteristics of the individual's environments (e.g., physical, social) before, during, and after the transition;
3. the characteristics (e.g., physical, psychological, experiential, demographic) of the person in transition.

These three perspectives, the transition, the context, and the individual, make up the elements of the "focus" axis in Figure 7. In the case of transitions which can be anticipated, these factors can be used as a basis for assessing the intra- and extra-personal resources of individuals. This permits the initiation of interventions designed to support positive factors and reduce, or eliminate, those which are negative.

The impact of these focii can be seen in the operation of three hypothetical groups, each of which variously centers upon one or another aspect of the needs of prospective, first-time parents. The first group seeks to forestall the development of difficulties by helping participants examine the nature of the transition to parenthood itself. The accuracy of their expectations of the nature and scope of the changes parenthood is apt to involve is a central concern of the group. Emphasis is also placed upon identifying and correcting inaccurate or fragmentary expectations as a means of helping the participants enter parenthood equipped with as thorough and realistic a notion as possible of what they will encounter.

The second group focuses upon the physical and social contexts within which the transition occurs. By helping group members recognize existing sources of personal and institutional support (e.g., child rearing assistance, financial assistance, comfort, encouragement, medical facilities) it is hoped that the participants will be helped to encounter the transition with expanded resources of environmental assistance.

The final group centers upon a consideration of the personal resources (experience, skills, knowledge) of the group members and considers the impact of these resources, for good or ill, upon their parenting effectiveness. Existing resources can be mobilized by examining the degree to which past experience can be extrapolated to the upcoming transition, or new resources developed by activities (e.g., skill training) aimed at ameliorating deficits. Also, attention might be focused upon the extent to which such personal variables as age, socio-economic status or minority group membership might exert an important influence in making the transition.

Second Axis: Targets of Intervention

Primary prevention-oriented intervention can focus directly upon at risk persons, or they may attempt to reduce their risk by altering pathogenic factors not based in the individuals themselves. Cowen (1980) refers to this as *direct* and *indirect* targeting of interventions.

The decision as to whether a group intervention will focus directly or indirectly upon the identified clients, or combine both strategies, usually depends upon: the ideology of the worker, the preferences of the people involved, and the practical demands of the particular situation. In some instances one might prefer to work directly with the person at risk but be forced, for various reasons, to work with their significant others. For example, sometimes individuals with a high likelihood of developing psychological problems refuse to recognize their situation and thus reject direct preventive interventions as irrelevant. In such a situation one might set up a group in which their significant others (e.g., family, friends, co-workers) could deal with their reactions to individuals' self-destructive actions. The group could also serve as an opportunity for them to learn approaches which might increase at-risk person's willingness to acknowledge their conditions.

Beyond the recognition that indirect targeting can have significant preventive benefits to persons at risk, it is important to recognize that the targets upon which these interventions focus can vary tremendously in character. For example, an indirect target can be as immediate to the individual as his or her spouse. In contrast, an indirect primary prevention intervention might be targeted at distant administrators or bureaucrats who make and implement policy with important implications for the individual.

Impressed with the power of social, economic and political factors to affect the psychological well-being of people, some theoreticians and practitioners consider it more effective to focus primary prevention activities upon those institutions which, through their policies and actions, exert tremendous influence upon the daily lives of people. These institutions may be what Cowen (1980, p. 264) calls *focal-structures*, which are close to the individual (e.g., school, the work place, church), or they may be more distant *macro-structures* (e.g., governmental agencies, industries, national unions).

Third Axis: The Format

The term "group" has been applied to such a wide range of interventions that if something is called a group about the only thing of which one could be sure is that the procedure would involve two or more persons. The distinction which Gibb (1954) makes between aggregates and groups can be used as a basis for differentiating among interventions which involve more than one participant. Gibb has taken the position that while aggregates are comprised of two or more persons, the association of the participants is based solely on such external factors as continuity, homogeneity or contact. In contrast, group interaction reflects more than simple contact, the association among persons serving as a vehicle for mutual need satisfaction.

Against the broad background of the differences between groups and aggregates, there are several processes which are often put forth in the community mental health and clinical literature as particularly suited to the promotion of primary prevention. These modalities can be used to specify the main forms which primary prevention-focused groups can take. They are: educational formats, consultation activities, self exploration.

Education

In the primary prevention-oriented literature it is often asserted that the most impactful strategies in promoting primary prevention are those which have the effect of modifying the outlook and behavior of large numbers of people (Vayda and Perlmutter, 1977). For that reason, education is often put forth as one of the most important intervention modalities of the community mental health movement. In this sense education is defined quite broadly and includes such interventions as media campaigns, skill training, psychoeducation and staff development.

Consultation

Consultation is another vehicle for fostering primary prevention objectives through population-focused intervention. It is usually an indirectly-targeted intervention aimed at persons who, because of their status and responsibilities, are in a position to exert important influence on the policy and/or practice of primary prevention-relevant organizations. Through such methodologies as needs assessment, goal setting, analysis of communication and decision-making structures (Kurpius, 1978), the consultation process can be used to foster changes at the organizational and community level that will make such settings more conducive to the development and maintenance of positive mental health.

Self-exploration

Turning from the perspectives of the Community Mental Health movement to those of clinical practice, the individual and small group processes through which persons pursue enhanced understanding of themselves, their relations to others, and the impact of their social and physical environments, can be identified as basic modalities for personal change. Though it is true that under the name "psychotherapy" these processes have largely been used to remediate psychopathology, small group practitioners often use these same modalities to pursue primary prevention objectives with normal, but at risk, persons.

Such therapeutically-oriented constructs as "relationship," "insight," and "responsibility" can be considered to have important significance in helping persons become receptive to the manner in which they can promote their own well-being and that of others. Perhaps "relationship" (Rogers, 1962) warrants special mention in a discussion of primary prevention-focused groups, since one of the common themes that runs through discussions of the factors which contribute to the development of psycholopathology is the detrimental impact of social isolation and the feeling that one is cut off from the recognition and caring of others. Given this, one of the most valuable resources which the clinical tradition can provide to the quest of preventing psychological impairment are methods of conceptualizing and fostering close relationships in which persons feel confirmed and recognized as individuals. This does not imply that the preventive benefits of "relationship" can only be gained within traditional individual and small group methodologies. Rather, it is to suggest that with reference to such new approaches as mutual help groups, peer counseling, or the enhancement of natural support systems, in which the role of "relationship" seems to have important primary prevention import, traditional clinical insights represent a rich conceptual and practical resource.

Using the Framework

It is possible to use the matrix presented in Figure 7 to locate many of the mass and group modalities that have been used to provide assistance to persons approaching and coping with life transitions. For example, career development courses as found in many high schools occupy cells I-III, A, 1 and/or 1-III, A, 2 depending upon the degree to which an educational or self-exploration approach is stressed.

By contrast, we can consider a program to reduce first semester attrition by sensitizing (through presentation of information and first-person accounts) college staff to students' perceptions of the task of adjusting to college and the students' view of the attitudes and expectations of faculty and staff. This intervention would occupy cells

I and II, B, 1 or I and III, C, 1 depending upon the extent to which these staff, in their jobs, actually come to be significant others to students.

From a Community Mental Health perspective, the cells of the matrix presented in Figure 7 which have the most promise for fostering primary prevention are those bounded by dimensions I-III, B-D and 1 and 2. Thus excluded are the cells which are targeted at individuals and use a modality which stresses intra- and interpersonal exploration. In contrast, practitioners who gravitate toward small group procedures bounded by dimensions I-III, A B and 2 and 3 are apt to be those who prefer to pursue primary prevention through small group formats which have been associated with clinical practice (i.e., counseling and psychotherapy).

GENERAL ISSUES IN PRIMARY PREVENTION-FOCUSED GROUP WORK

Of the many issues which confront group workers considering the use of primary prevention-oriented groups, there are three which will be highlighted for particular attention: recruiting group members; use of cultural specialists; and, interfacing with natural support systems.

Recruitment of Group Members

A point which has been touched upon several times in this discussion is that factors (e.g., perceptual defense, lack of experience) exist which can serve to reduce the likelihood that many potential beneficiaries of primary prevention-focused groups will see these groups as being relevant to their needs. Pathology forces itself upon one's awareness. Though it can be ignored, to do so is a much more difficult task than turning one's back on the likelihood of pathology developing at some time in the future. Even more subtle, and thus more apt to be overlooked, is the possibility that, though pathology may not be an immediate threat, there is a chance that factors might make it impossible for one to develop as high a level of effectiveness as might otherwise be possible. A major hurdle encountered in the establishment of primary prevention-oriented activities is convincing potential clients that it is relevant to them before the opportunity for primary prevention has passed.

Often the attempt to convince people that a primary prevention activity is relevant to them simply consists of offering facts which support the contention that they are really at risk. Such vehicles as speeches, films, or pamphlets can be used to communicate that message. The presentation may be personal and face-to-face, or media-based and mass-oriented. Beyond the straight-forward presentation of information, which assumes that if people are given relevant facts they will act in their own best interests, sometimes an attempt is made to heighten the impact of information by presenting it in an affect-laden manner. Survivor's accounts and horror stories which emphasize the very real danger which may lurk just around the corner are the stock in trade of this approach.

In addition to making potential risk real to persons by the reasoned or the highly emotionalized presentation of information, awareness can also be raised by arranging to have them experience the possible danger in a lessened form or through simulation. Role-playing activities (e.g., caring for an egg as if it were one's child for a week) can have a tremendously powerful impact in making the need for preparation real to individuals approaching a situation about which they would otherwise be quite complacent.

Interfacing with Professional and Indigenous Resources

A recurring point in the literature of primary prevention in the mental health field is that new perspectives and methodologies are required if there is to be success in breaking out of the limitations imposed by traditional, pathology-focused orientations (Reiff, 1967).

Use of Cultural Specialists

If, as Cowen (1980) suggests, a major concern of primary prevention in the mental health field is to extend prevention services to segments of society whose needs have been largely ignored, a likely consequence is that group workers are increasingly apt to be focusing upon persons whose characteristics and experience differ from those who have traditionally been the recipients of mental health services (Lorion, 1974; President's Commission Report, 1978). Consultation from professional (e.g., anthropologists, linguists) and non-professional (e.g., indigenous "experts") persons who are knowledgeable concerning the outlook, customs, expectations and preferences of these populations can contribute to the design and implementation of preventive interventions which will be seen as relevant by their participants. Guttman (1982), for example, has asserted that different ethnic groups (in this case, elderly from different Euro-American backgrounds) present different patterns with reference to the type of concerns they will and will not seek assistance for, and that they react differently to various outreach approaches. To possess such information is to have a point of reference which may make the difference between offering a prevention which is viewed as helpful by the persons for whom it is intended, and one which is rejected as irrelevant, inappropriate or noxious.

Interfacing with Natural Support Systems

Concerning the use of natural support systems a number of writers (e.g., Golan, 1981) have pointed out that when self-help efforts prove ineffective, the first source of assistance to which people typically turn is their natural support system, composed of friends, family, neighbors, co-workers and other persons whose relationship to the person is natural and unplanned. These support systems, as House (1981) has noted, serve to reduce the likelihood of physical and psychological impairment by: contributing to the individual's health; ameliorating pathogenic influences; and, serving to buffer persons from the negative consequences of harmful conditions which are already operating. As a context in which they are known as unique individuals and where symbol systems and outlook on life arc familiar to them, natural support systems are often the most readily available source of assistance for persons facing ordinary and extraordinary issues of development. Also, the systems are often the most preferred source of help.

Noting their role as the first line of assistance, Caplan (1974) has stressed the importance of recognizing the tremendous preventive and curative influences exerted by natural support systems and the necessity of interfacing with them in constructive ways. There are several facilitative roles which the group worker can take toward natural support systems, all of which rest upon the ability to transcend the tendency, common among treatment-oriented persons, to view families and peer groups as pathogenic rather than health-enhancing influences (Heller, 1979).

These approaches include:

- a respectful, hands-off approach to NSS that seem to be functioning well;
- a collaborative approach in which the resources of the NSS and those of formal helping services are meshed;
- strengthening or expanding the resources of essentially-positive NSS through such interventions as provision of information, resolution of long-standing barriers to communication, and fostering mutual problem-solving among members of the system.

This is apt to be familiar ground for the small group practitioner since many of the common educational and self-exploration formats, procedures and materials can be used. In passing, it may be noted that such natural support system interventions by the group worker are examples of indirectly targeted activities as specified in Figure 7.

CONCLUSION

A major thrust of this chapter has been to suggest that group workers need not be "put off" by the tendency of its advocates to place great emphasis upon what is and what is not primary prevention. Not that parameters are unimportant, they are. However, it is possible for some, who have not been extensively involved with primary prevention activities, to come away from such boundary-defining with the impression that somehow primary prevention exists on a plane of its own with little possibility of its ever rubbing shoulders with secondary or tertiary prevention. In this discussion, examples have been given of the manner in which adjunctive groups for their clients' unimpaired, though at risk, significant others can serve as a natural entry to primary prevention-oriented group work for those whose usual practice is to deal with individuals as individuals and with clients manifesting psychopathology. Moreover, even more classically "correct" primary prevention-focused interventions which begin with the identification of at risk populations or disability-producing situations (Conyne, 1982), can stand side-by-side with the usual clinical activities of a group worker. Indeed, primary prevention group forms offer potent alternatives to the "compleat" group worker in the quest to preserve and foster the development of positive mental health in others.

A final point needs to be made. In the midst of all of this focusing upon primary prevention activities as a "new" direction for group workers, perhaps it is important to point out that a case can be made that group practitioners have long been at the forefront of whatever prevention-oriented thrust there has been in the mental health field. As the prime vehicle for that variegated phenomenon called the "human potential movement" and, as the *sine qua non* of recent mutual help activities as stress management, preparing for transitions, relationship enhancement, and social skills training, have flourished. In the main, participants of these activities seek out assistance on a voluntary, self-initiated basis, usually within the context of settings (e.g., schools, religious institutions, industrial firms) which center upon the ordinary activities of people.

From one perspective, the flourishing of these preventive, voluntary activities stands as an example of what the mental health field might have become if it had actuated a health-oriented "future" (Rappaport, 1977) rather than the pathology-focused one that it did.

REFERENCES

Albee, G.W.: Primary prevention: A fourth mental health revolution. Philip J. Zlatchin Memorial Award Address delivered at New York University, April, 1978.

Bloom, B.L.: Prevention of mental disorders: Recent advances in theory and practice. *Community Mental Health Journal, 15*:179-191, 1979.

Caplan, G.: *Principles of Preventive Psychiatry.* New York: Basic Books, 1964.

Caplan, G.: *Support Systems and Mental Health: Lectures on Concept Development.* New York: Behavioral Publications, 1974.

Conyne, R.: Two critical issues in primary prevention. What it is and how to do it. *Personnel and Guidance Journal, 61*:331-333, 1982.

Cowen, E.L.: Social and community interventions. *Annual Review of Psychology, 24*:423-472, 1973.

Cowen, E.L.: Some problems in community evaluation research. *Journal of Consulting and Community Psychology, 47*:792-805, 1978.

Cowen, E.L.: The wooing of primary prevention. *American Journal of Community Psychology, 8*:258-284, 1980.

Gibb, C.A.: Leadership. In G. Lindzey (Ed.) *Handbook of Social Psychology*, vol. 2. Reading: Addison-Wesley, 1954.

Golan, N.: *Passing through Transitions: A Guide for Practitioners.* New York: The Free Press, 1981.

Guttman, D.: Neighborhood as a support system for Euro-American elderly. In D.E. Biegel and A.J. Naparstek (Eds.) *Community Support Systems and Mental Health: Practice Policy and Research.* New York: Springer, 1982.

Heller, K.: The effects of social support: Prevention and treatment implications. In Goldstein, A., and Kanfer, F. *Maximizing Treatment Gains: Treatment Enhancement in Psychotherapy.* New York: Academic Press, 1979.

Hobbs, N.: Mental health's third revolution. *American Journal of Orthopsychiatry, 34*:822-833, 1964.

House, J.S.: *Work Stress and Social Support.* Reading, Ma.:Addison-Wesley, 1981.

Klein, D.C., and Goldston, S.E. (Eds.): *Primary Prevention - An Idea Whose Time Has Come.* U.S. Government Printing Office, DHEW Publication No. (ADM) 77-477, Washington, D.C., 1977.

Kurpius, D.: Consultation theory and process: An integrated model. *The Personnel and Guidance Journal, 56*:335-339, 1978.

Lorion, R.P.: Patient and therapist variables in the treatment of income patients. *Psychological Bulletin, 81*:344-354, 1974.

Plaut, T.: Primary prevention in the 80's: The interface with community support systems. In D.E. Biegel and A.J. Naparstek (Eds.) *Community Support Systems: Practice, Policy and Research.* New York: Springer, 1982.

President's Commission on Mental Health: *Report to the President* (Vol. 1). Washington, D.C., U.S. Government Printing Office, Stock No. 040-000-00390-8, 1978.

Rappaport, J.C.: *Community Psychology: Values, Research and Action.* New York: Holt, 1977.

Reiff, R.M.: Manpower and Institutional Change. In E.L. Cowen, E.A. Gardner, and M. Zax (Eds.), *Emergent Approaches to Mental Health Problems.* New York: Appleton-Century-Crofts, 1967.

Rogers, C.R.: The interpersonal relationship: The core of guidance. *Harvard Educational Review, 32*:416-429, 1962.

Schlossberg, N.K.: A model for analyzing human adaptation to transition. *The Counseling Psychologist. 9(2)*:2-18, 1981.

Vayda, A.M., and Perlmutter, F.D.: Primary prevention in community mental health centers: A survey of current activity. *Community Mental Health Journal, 13*:343-351, 1977.

CHAPTER 15

COMMUNITY CHANGE
Community Futuring and Planning Groups

RONALD LIPPITT

T HIS case example describes a process of community-wide collaboration to project future goals for enriching quality of life of the community and to design for the implementation of action toward those goals.

Developing a Community-Wide Client System

We discovered quite early in our work with communities that it was a serious trap to attempt to start a community project under the sponsorship of one or another of the major vested interests, such as the Chamber of Commerce, or the United Way, or the Junior League, or the School Board. As soon as such sponsorship became visible, it turned off the potential involvement and cooperation of several other vested interests who would feel left out or who would feel committed to an adversarial posture in relation to those particular sponsoring groups. But we found it quite possible to work with any interested *trigger group* to identify a cross-community panel of key nominators from the different sectors of community life, e.g., political, economic, religious, educational, health, recreational, social welfare, security and protection, etc. This nominating panel had the responsibility of nominating a half a dozen key figures (shakers and movers) in each of the sectors. We used a criterion of agreement of several nominators on the figures who would emerge as top nominees in each of the areas. Of course many nominees cut across more than one area of community function.

293

These nominees received a memorandum of invitation to a start-up event. The memorandum indicated their basis for invitation as having been the nominations they received in regard to their community leadership role. Typically the invitation was to attend a three-hour startup micro-conference to explore a possible approach to community goal setting and to providing collaborative leadership for this activity. This startup session might be held from 7 to 10 p.m. at the local community college (a good neutral setting) with dessert being served by students who are majoring in food services. Rather typically there might have been 47 key persons nominated and 45 would be on hand for the exploratory session. In our work in over 80 cities, never less than 90 percent of the invitees appeared at this opening session.

The Entry Intervention

As the participants entered, they were invited to identify themselves by checking on wall charts their participation in the various community sectors, types of leadership roles, the places in the community where they lived and worked (on a wall map), and also where they fit into the total population of male, female, young, middle aged, elders, ethnic and racial populations, newcomers and old-timers, etc. They received name tags pregrouping them hetergeneously at tables of six.

Several of the participants who had arrived had been asked, when they finished their wall chart entries, to take responsibility for analyzing the data on one of the sheets as they were entered. They were asked to be prepared in a few minutes to provide us with a summary of "Who we are and where we're coming from." So the meeting started with brief summaries with data from the wall sheets and a very brief statement of the purpose of this single session which would determine whether or not the group found a valid basis for continuing to work together in providing leadership for a community goal-setting activity. A brief statement was made of the successful experience of leaders in other communities with this as a basis for a community-wide participation process.

It was stated that during the course of the evening several activities would be explored and assessed to determine whether or not they seemed to provide a basis for expanding the procedures to the wider community. It was going to be up to this group to decide whether or not the approach seemed to be significant and worthwhile. We then moved ahead to the following flow of activities:

Sharing perspectives on our past, "Where we are coming from." The participants were quickly taught the rules of brainstorming and each table was asked to brainstorm a list of all the significant events and memories of the past which they felt were important as determiners of the characteristics and life style of their community today. The participants then milled, reading the lists on each table and individually voted for two or three significant items on each table. When they resumed their places, each table identified the two or three most significant images of the past by tabulating the number of votes the items had received. These items were called out and reported up front on newsprint as "Our Key Images of Our Past" or "Where We are Coming from as We Move into Our Future."

"Proud and Sorries" about today. This activity was introduced by indicating that we are leaving the past and are now moving to the present, to the here and now of a week in the life of the community. With a large sheet of newsprint on the table, each table brainstormed two columns of items: 1) "All the things we are proud about in the quality of life in our community," and 2) "All the things we are sorry about concerning the quality of life of our community."

Again, after the seven or eight minute brainstorm, everyone had a chance to move around and vote for the two "proudest prouds" and the two "sorriest sorries" on each table list. These again were summarized by a call out from each table and documented on a master sheet in the front of the room.

Scanning the environment for EDTs. Futurists put great emphasis on the importance of scanning our environment for the events, developments and trends (EDTs) which are indicators of the cutting edges into the future. In the particular situation we are reporting, the leaders began a call out with examples of national and community trends and developments. Everyone in the room called out additional items. In ten minutes, some thirty-five items had been called out, which were seen by the participants as samples of "where things are going in the areas of technology, state-community relationships, environmental quality, community government, utilization of volunteers, family life, population, occupational trends, and other relevant dimensions of current social, economic, and technological change."

A trip into preferred futuring. With the products on past, present, and cutting edge trends up on the wall, the table groups were invited to take a trip into the future. Each table became a helpcopter, going ahead five years in time, and hovering over their community making observations of "What you see going on that pleases you very much with the improvement of the quality of life of the community since back in 1983." These observations were strictly a right brain brainstorming activity without discussion and with a table documentor jotting down the images which were reported. Emphasis was placed on the images being concrete, so that anybody not on their future trip could read them and see what they thought. In fifteen minutes the tables had generated some 120 images of preferred future which were then posted on the wall. Everyone had an opportunity to read and to mark the fifteen items they felt were the most important and desirable images of the future. As the votes piled up into priority clusters, three members of the convening team kept notes on the items with the high votes and noted similar items on different lists. So that by the time the voting was completed, it was possible to write up on the overhead projector the twelve preferred scenarios of the future which had been selected as top priorities by the participants.

The Emergence of a Community Futuring Plan

It was now explained to the group that the process they had just completed was a small sample of what could be a community-wide process participated in by many different groups and segments of the community under their leadership. If they wished to sponsor such a community-wide future planning activity, which included identification of top priority images of preferred future, there would be opportunities to form task forces or interest groups, with goals of putting energy into developing steps of action toward the preferred future images. There would be leadership training and support for the successful functioning of the task forces. It was noted that this had been a very successful process in other communities. The important question now was whether this group wanted to make a decision to provide leadership for the development of such a process of community futuring and planning.

There was enthusiastic endorsement of the project, a steering committee of eight persons was elected, and almost everyone signed up to participate in the startup task forces which were identified by signup sheets on the wall. These included: a media committee to work with newspapers and other sources of information to the community about the project; a futuring kit committee to put together the necessary materials to use in conducting futuring sessions with a wide variety of organizations, boards, neighborhood groups, etc., a committee to recruit and train volunteers to lead the one to one and one-half hour sessions of community groups, a team to explore sources of funding for the activity, an analysis team to receive and analyze the preferred futures data from the variety of community groups, and an EDT scanning committee to begin collecting trend and development data relevant to the community and its future.

Community Involvement in Futuring

During the next three months, there were many newspaper items about the futuring sessions of various groups in the community, with special interest in some of their "Prouds and Sorries," some special feature on the memories of old-timers about key events and decisions in the past of the community, and some interviews with community leaders about their perceptions of the significance for the future of the community of major trends going on in the society and in the state. One interesting development was the sponsoring of futuring sessions by high school student groups stimulated by the student council. It was necessary to recruit and train more pairs of futuring session leaders because of the increasing varieties of groups in the community that wanted an opportunity to hold a session and provide their data as part of the total project. The research and analysis team added membership from the staff and students of the community college to cope with the flow of data from the futuring sessions. The research team also generated another subgroup to begin collecting basic resource data which would be important as task forces began to work on some of the priority scenarios of preferred futures which were beginning to be identified. By the end of three months, over two hundred sessions (attended by over 3,000 persons) had been held and provided data on preferred future images for the community. The research team was having a busy time integrating the data and writing up one or two-page scenarios of preferred futures from the items which were emerging as priorities.

The Community Assembly

The ballroom of the local college was made available for the Saturday Community Assembly on Future Planning. All those who had participated in futuring sessions had been invited. Also the local newspaper printed a coupon on the front page which readers were invited to clip out and bring as a ticket to their participation in their assembly, no matter whether they had been involved in previous activities or not. The assembly committee did a great job of arranging table seating in groups of eight for the several hundred participants. The historical society made an exciting wall exhibit on the past of the community, and a group of young high school musicians provided entrance music, "Music for the Future." At each table, the participants found a set of the future scenarios prepared by the research committee from the priorities emerging from the community futuring sessions. Each table had a leader who could help the participants review the scenarios and ask questions of clarification. The procedure for the work of the assembly was then presented and the process began.

Around the wall were newsprint sheets, each one had a heading labelled with one of the scenarios of the preferred future, e.g., waterfront development, transportation for the elderly, bicycle paths, integration of city and township government, etc.

After reviewing the scenarios at their table, everyone was invited to walk over and sign up for the task force they would most like to do startup thinking on during the course of the day, i.e., where they would like to put their energy in making something happen. The rule was that a task force would be formed if three or four people signed up. As soon as a task force formed, they were assigned a table as their work space for the rest of the day. A member of the resource committee took over to their table the materials which had been collected relevant to their topic area.

Now the process began of supporting high quality task force work. The task forces were helped to go through a period of converting their future images into a meaningful and concrete goal statement. This statement was checked out by one of the members of the floating consultant team. Then the task forces were helped to do a "Forcefield Analysis" of the factors they could identify which were inhibitors and which were supporters of movement toward their particular goal. They then were helped to conduct brainstorms of all the possible actions they could think of that would facilitate first steps of action and would cope with key blocks to action. The teams continued to work during their catered lunch period, and by two o'clock each task force had formulated a one-page statement of their goal and the key first steps of action which they perceived as important to get movement toward their goal. This included ideas about who would need to be involved, what kind of sponsoring resources would be needed, and who of the table group was ready to continue as part of an ongoing task force, who had agreed to be convenor, and where they were proposing to hold a next meeting. These one-page sheets were taken over to the duplicating team, working with a borrowed high speed duplicator. Each task force distributed several copies of their one-page newsletter to each of the other task forces for review, questions of clarification, offers of assistance, and also to provide an opportunity for some persons to shift to other priority task forces if it now appeared to them that their interests were elsewhere.

Each table was provided with a brief group discussion guide to evaluate the procedures of the day and to project their feelings and commitments about the future of the effort. Each table called out some of the findings of these discussions. This callout period became a contagious sharing of learnings and plans, a celebration of the day and a revelation of commitment to future efforts. There was an announcement that the temporary convenors of the next meetings of task forces would have a ten minute "linger longer" meeting to set plans for a future meeting.

Training and Support Functions for Quality Follow-Through

Our research on the follow-through significance of community futuring efforts indicates that the most crucial determiners of follow-through success are the commitment of the planners to continuing their leadership and steering committee functions through a follow-up period, the plan for the training of task force leaders, and the design for visible support and celebration of first steps of progress of task force work. In our particular situation, the task force convenors had about an hour and a half brown bag lunch session before their first task force meetings to help them with designing and planning significant sessions. They also set a time for a monthly meeting to report progress to each other and to have "Clinic Discussions" about problems that were emerging in task force work. The media committee took on a special responsibility for getting news notes from task forces to report through a continuing newspaper column about the project. It was proven again that co-chairmanship of task forces was a much more effective way of guaranteeing high quality leadership of the continuing citizen groups.

An Application of Group Work Methods: The Task Force Process

In addition to the training session with the task force convenors, we developed a task force guide sheet for the leaders to distribute to their members, and to use as a basis of discussion. Here is a copy of that guide sheet which our evaluations indicated was a major support for the quality of task force work:

A GUIDE SHEET FOR TASK FORCE LEADERS AND MEMBERS

Your energy and your teamwork as task forces in planning, in acting, and in activating others is the heart of the action effort. The successes from our collective efforts can be many, and the most important cause of each success will be the creativity and energy of a task force.

That's why the success of your task force — of each task force — is so important.

So becoming, and being, a productive and successful task force is a great challenge — and not an easy one.

Teaming up and getting things done that nobody can do by themselves is difficult — demanding and personally rewarding.

The appreciation of your efforts will grow with time and with visible successes.

So the purpose of this brief memo to you is to report on the things each and all of us can do to create and maintain vital productive task forces.

Please use these notes as an agenda for building your group, a tool for improving your productivity, a checklist of "do's" and "don'ts." The notes are based on the successful and unsuccessful experiences of many task forces.

Some Very Important "Do's"

1. Narrow your "mission" down to a very doable first goal. Next goals will follow as a solid first goal is accomplished.

2. Be sure someone is responsible for *planning* your meeting, so your collective time together will be well used. (See later notes below on designing a turned-on meeting.)

3. Always be thinking about what additional persons you need to add as resources for your action — and decide on who should recruit with what strategy of approach.

4. Always be thinking about division of labor in getting the work done — who can best do what?

5. Keep giving yourselves deadlines, and help each other keep them.

6. Clarify your needs for help — the kinds of support you need — and ask your leadership team for the help you need. That is a sign of strength — to know what you need — when — who to ask for it — and how.

7. Consider whether co-leadership might not make things go better — and how you might rotate leadership over time.

8. **Keep good records of your meetings, your decisions, your actions, your contacts, your accomplishments.** This is very important for keeping everyone informed, for orienting new members, for clarifying and celebrating progress as a basis for maintaining energy and support.

9. Project your calendar of meetings *well ahead*. Don't set dates from meeting to meeting.

10. Pick a comfortable place to meet, with good work space and facilities.

A Few Important "Don'ts"

1. The most important "don't" is: Don't start by tackling too big a goal! Define some concrete short term goals or steps that will lead in the direction of your bigger purpose.

2. Don't try to do it all yourselves if there are only two or three active members. Put your energy and creativity into recruiting the involvement of others, and then get a division of labor on making things happen.

3. Don't get together for a meeting without having a plan for the meeting and what you want to come out with as results of the meeting.

4. Don't assume important people will say "no" to your requests, and so avoid approaching them. Just concentrate on the best strategy of getting them interested.

5. Don't assume it's better if you "do it all by yourselves." One of the greatest strengths is asking for help, at the right time, from the right persons.

Some Characteristics of a Good Meeting

1. The furniture is arranged so everyone is looking at each other.

2. There is a place to record ideas up front, preferably on a newsprint pad, so it can be saved. (Blackboards have to be erased.)

3. An agenda is presented, added to, agreed on.

4. There are time estimates of how long each agenda item should take.

5. Someone has agreed to be the recorder of the thinking and decisions of the meeting—and is ready to write the notes up and get them to everyone.

6. In the notes, it is indicated who has agreed to what before the next meeting—and the names are underlined in the notes as a reminder.

7. Dates of future meetings are set well ahead (not just for the next meeting) so everyone can get it on their calendar.

8. At least once or twice every meeting the leaders, or someone else, asks, "How are we doing on our way of working together today? Any ideas about how we can improve to be more productive?"

9. Usually the question will be considered, "Who else do we want

to involve?"

10. Usually the last item of a good meeting is a summarizing of who will be doing what between now and the next meeting.

Planning the Good Meeting — and the Next One

One advantage of having a co-leader is that the two of you can do a better job than one of sitting down and planning the purpose, agenda, and flow of activity of the next meeting.

If you don't have co-leaders, then the leader should develop a practice of asking one or two members to be an informal planning team to think together ahead of time about the meeting.

A good meeting cannot just happen!! You need to have some creative think time and agenda preparations. The items to cover at this pre-think session are:

1. The best flow of the agenda.

2. What can people get started on as they walk in the door and everyone isn't there yet? There are often things to read, some starting thinking to do, etc.

3. How to get the reports of what's happened since the last meeting.

4. How to start the discussion on each item.

5. Which items call for decisions, which ones just need information, which ones need brainstorming, but no decisions, etc.

6. Guesses as to how long each item might take, as a working plan to present to the group.

7. Who will be asked to lead off on each item.

8. Who will bring what needed supplies, take care of the coffee, etc.

And After the Meeting

While things are still fresh — that night or the next day — it is the time for the very crucial "de-briefing review" with your co-leader or informal planning team — over coffee, or even over the phone if it isn't easy to get together.

The best chance of improving each meeting, and keeping things going strong is to have this brief post-mortem session, which should include the following items:

1. How did the meeting go?
2. How could we have improved it?
3. What shall we try next time to make it better?
4. What kind of follow-up on commitments do we need to plan on?

That's enough of an agenda for a post-mortem. But it's **very important!**

Using These Ideas

The best chance of incorporating these ideas and to make your task force stronger is to give a copy of this document to each member, and put discussion of this memo on the agenda. If the group agrees with the ideas, or adds to them, you will be building mutual expectations and support to make these expectations happen — and that's what counts.

SUMMARY

Several Important Principles of Community Development and Preferred Futuring

Here are a few of the guiding principles we have found important in the facilitation of community-wide involvement in future planning and action-implementation:

1. It is crucial to identify and invite key figures from all sectors of community life, including generation levels, minority populations, male and female representation, and leaders from the various community functions which we've identified above.
2. It is very important to have a significant startup experience with these key figures demonstrating what this process is all about and to give them an opportunity to buy in with adequate understanding and motivation.
3. It is important to provide continuing technical consultation on the design and implementation of this total futuring, planning, and implementation process.
4. It is very important to have the cooperation of community-

wide communication media and networks.

5. One of the important ingredients of the process is the recruiting and training of volunteer leadership pairs to do a high quality job of data collection of futuring discussions by a wide range of community groups.

6. It is important for everyone to understand the difference between preferred futuring and efforts at prediction of the future, and to be involved in the necessary value explorations underlying preferred futuring.

7. One of the important responsibilities of the consultants is to recruit and train a cadre of skilled group leaders who will provide continuing leadership of group activities and will continue to exchange learning and innovative practices.

8. One of the crucial strategies of community organization is to provide for linkage between all the volunteer ad hoc energy of the temporary task forces and the ongoing establishments of the professionals and paid workers of the community structure.

9. One of the great gains for basic democracy is the discovery of the great resources of operating in heterogeneous groups and utilizing the great resources of pluralism of the community.

10. The basic skills of group work practice are a major resource of this activity, combined with an understanding of the dynamics of total community systems and the strategies of effective change agentry.

AUTHOR INDEX

SUBJECT INDEX